A RELIGIOUS OUTLOOK
FOR MODERN MAN

A RELIGIOUS OUTLOOK
FOR MODERN MAN

by

RAYNOR C. JOHNSON

M.A. (Oxon), Ph.D., D.Sc. (Lond.)
Master of Queen's College, University of Melbourne

With a Foreword by

The Reverend

LESLIE D. WEATHERHEAD

C.B.E., M.A., Ph.D., D.D.,
Minister Emeritus, The City Temple, London

HODDER AND STOUGHTON
LONDON SYDNEY AUCKLAND TORONTO

BX 9998
J58
1964

Copyright © 1963 Raynor C. Johnson. First published 1963. Third impression 1972. ISBN 0 340 01653 1. Printed in Great Britain for Hodder and Stoughton Ltd., St. Paul's House, Warwick Square, London, EC4P 4AH by Lowe & Brydone (Printers) Ltd., London

To my friend
C. IRVING BENSON, C.B.E., D.D.
Minister of Wesley Church
Melbourne
in appreciation of his great work
for Australia

FOREWORD

IN 1951 I spent three months in the Australian home of the author of this book, who even then had been a close friend for a quarter of a century. In the last ten years, though separated in space, we have remained close in spirit and corresponded regularly.

Being acutely dissatisfied by the seeming inability of conventional religion to present Christianity in a way which commended itself to the thoughtful modern, we planned to write a book together which might offer a sane and sound religious outlook for the modern man, but my own commitments of writing, preaching, and interviewing made it clear that the book would be long delayed if we waited until we could collaborate, decide which of us should write the various parts, and discuss those points at which we were almost bound to differ.

I am proud, however, of the privilege of writing this Foreword. Having read what follows, I am delighted to find how closely our minds are in agreement. Dr. Johnson will not mind my saying that I did not feel too happy after reading his chapter on "How am I to regard Jesus Christ?" The chapter is deeply reverent, but who among all the sons of men can do more than confess that this theme is utterly beyond him. The mystery of Christ puts Him beyond all words. For me He fills the word "God" with more meaning than any other before or since, but I am as slow to dogmatise, as is the author of this book. The word "human" is certainly true of Him. Yet it is not nearly big enough adequately to account for Him. We use the word "divine" and include the meaning that He is man to the nth degree, but we do not ourselves know what we mean by "divine". Words fill with meanings which we load upon them until, like frail vessels weighted to the water-line, they sink, unable to carry the cargo of meaning we ask them to bear, and we are left on our knees in adoration which has passed into silence and "thoughts that lie too deep for tears".

Another point I should want to discuss with the author is his attitude to public prayer. I think more highly of it than he does. Much of what passes as public prayer is frequently simply wasted time. "God bless India, China, Africa and the islands of the sea" was a sentence in a prayer I heard recently! But when I conduct a service and open with the prayer, "O God, let the hush of Thy presence fall upon us," it does seem to me as if a fellowship of people are opening their minds and hearts to the influences of the unseen world, with an immense return in terms of power, serenity and joy. And when I ask the people to let their minds go out in loving intercession to this individual or that, be it the Prime Minister or the local postman who perchance lies ill, it does not seem to me impossible that God can use the machinery of telepathy for a spiritual purpose of His own, just as we use the postman's ministry, including a material thing like his bicycle, to receive a letter of cheer from a dear one. But this latter point I think our author would concede.

Further, I think more highly of the Christian Church than does our author. In spite of much which he rightly condemns, the Church can be the healing fellowship of loving persons through which the individual both receives and gives. God can say things to the individual *through the fellowship* of the Church which He cannot say to the isolated individual, and the individual can give *through the fellowship* what he could not otherwise give. Dr. Johnson asks the question, "Can I worship better alone?", but the question and implied answer do not go deep enough. Jesus could certainly worship better alone, but He went "as His custom was to the synagogue on the sabbath day", and when He entered the whole spiritual temperature rose. If I were a minister in Dr. Johnson's area I should be sad indeed if he worshipped alone, because I know how much he can give to a fellowship just by being there, and he could help to make a fellowship an instrument to sustain the individual.

I expect, like myself, the reader will find his mind almost startled by some of the daring thought of this book, but the truth cannot be undermined, and by relentlessly testing suggestive ideas by the touchstone, "Is this true or have I been content hitherto with conventional orthodoxy and what others have said?", the truth, with all its convincing and self-authenticating power, will emerge.

The older I get, the more I feel that the essential ideas of Christianity are exceedingly few in number. Of these essentials I grow more and more certain. But their number grows less and less. Around that area of the certain there is for me a vast hinterland concerning which the assertion of certainty seems childish and silly. I feel like a man who lands on a vast continent and makes his home near the shore, but realises that behind his frail and homely dwelling are impenetrable forests and unscalable mountains, of which he can as yet know nothing. Scholars may make a few inroads and saints climb a few foothills. But what lies in the depths of the silent forest, and what could those unstained heights reveal?

"Dangerous it were," says Hooker, "for the feeble brain of man to wade far into the doings of the Most High, whom, although to know be life, and joy to make mention of His name, yet our soundest knowledge is to know that we know Him not as indeed He is, neither can know Him. Our safest eloquence concerning Him is our silence when we confess without confession that His glory is inexplicable, His greatness above our capacity and reach. He is above, and we upon earth. Therefore it behoveth our words to be wary and few."*

A teacup of water taken from the sea can tell me the chemical composition of the vast Atlantic. But what can that teacupful tell me of the majesty of an Atlantic storm? Actually, there is no such thing as a storm in a teacup! The life and teaching and death and resurrection of Jesus can tell me the *nature* of God; what His essential character is like, but it cannot tell me the whole truth of His doings, the million activities in which He may be engaged. As that teacup reveals nothing of the silent depths of the ocean to which no one has yet penetrated, or the terrific storms that sweep across it, so an earthly life — however perfect — reveals only hints of the doings of the Most High, the Infinite, the Ineffable God.

With the universe opening before us as it is now doing, it would be as narrow-minded and self-important as the old astronomy, which thought the earth the centre of the universe, to suppose that no beings exist but ourselves in the innumerable galaxies. Are we to suppose that to us *alone* God revealed His nature by becoming one of us? May He not have become one of them? God may have become incarnate (if, indeed, that is the word), on a million planets. If so, what becomes of the dogma of the Trinity? God may be not three in one but three million in one. How can we presume to run a creedal tape of human words around the mysterious Being who created the universe that makes our minds reel already, though we are only beginning to see an infinitesimal corner of it?

What we *can* do, and what this book helps us enormously to do,

* Hooker, *Ecclesiastical Polity*, Book 1. Chapter 2, Section 3, p. 201 (seventh edition).

is to be ashamed of our intolerances, to see the childish weaknesses
in our dogmatic creeds, to open our minds to new ideas, to recognise
that many find the way to God along paths quite strange to us,
and to test the value of a religion not by its theological pronouncements but by its power to make men loving, the insights with which
it provides them so that they re-assess their scale of values and sit
more loosely to temporal trivialities and anchor their souls in eternal
realities. Religion's test is its power to help them make such decisions
and such reactions to crises and demands that will spell progress
along that road which ends only in unity with God.

I have been thrilled, comforted, and mentally stimulated by this
brave and splendid book, and I commend it to all who are trying to
keep what Christ called the first and greatest commandment: "Thou
shalt love the Lord thy God with all thy mind."

LESLIE D. WEATHERHEAD

October 1962

AUTHOR'S PREFACE

IF you are an ordinary person of a religious turn of mind, but puzzled and disappointed by what passes for religion today, this book is written for you. It assumes no specialised knowledge or higher education on the part of the reader. It has been written as an attempt to offer reasonable answers to the questions which men and women ask in their thoughtful moods.

Although by training a physicist, I have for the last twenty years been questing for the meaning of life in different fields. The fruits of this search are in three published books for those who wish to delve more deeply into them. Here I am attempting the task — far from easy — of simplification. Many people who talk to me about the problems of life say they can find no satisfying answers in the contemporary presentations of religion, and they often do not know where to look for help. My purpose here is to offer my own thoughts and intuitions to fellow-seekers. I am not concerned whether my answers and thoughts are orthodox or not. I have certainly no wish to add to the multitude of books which seem designed to repeat and defend traditional ideas, rather than look afresh for truth. I shall try to express some facets of truth which I think I can see. None of us can see very far: we should be very humble in the face of our abysmal ignorance as we look out at the starry universe or inward at our own selves. Questing for Truth is necessarily endless, but we can share in the spirit of Socrates when he said, "The adventure is noble and our hope is high."

R. C. JOHNSON

ACKNOWLEDGMENTS

I DESIRE to thank the following publishers, authors, and owners of copyright for permission to use passages from their books:

Messrs. Edward Arnold Ltd. for a passage from *The Human Situation* by W. Macneile Dixon; the Syndics of the University Press, Cambridge, for a passage from *The Mysterious Universe* by Sir James Jeans; Miss Geraldine Cummins for a passage from her book *The Road to Immortality*; Messrs. Constable & Co. Ltd. for a poem by Sir Owen Seaman from *War-Time Verses*; Messrs. Faber & Faber Ltd. for quotations from *This World and That* by Payne and Bendit, and also from *The Geeta* as translated by Shree Purohit Swami; Messrs. George Allen & Unwin Ltd. for three quotations from *Letters to a Friend* by Tagore; Messrs. Victor Gollancz Ltd. for three quotations from *Commentaries on Living* (Third Series) by Krishnamurti; Messrs. A. M. Heath & Co. Ltd. for two verses of the poem *The Man to the Angel* from *Collected Poems* of A. E.; Messrs. Longmans Green & Co. Ltd. for a quotation from *Grey of Fallodon* by G. M. Trevelyan; Messrs. Macmillan & Co. Ltd. for extracts from *Creative Unity* and from *Sadhana* by Tagore, also from *Tess of the D'Urbervilles* by Thomas Hardy; Messrs. Methuen & Co. Ltd. for a quotation from *Supernormal Faculties in Man* by Eugene Osty; Sir Francis Meynell for the last verse of the poem *Christ in the Universe* from *The Poems of Alice Meynell*; Oxford University Press for a quotation from *Eastern Religions and Western Thought* by Sir S. Radhakrishnan; Miss Jane Sherwood for quotations from her book *The Country Beyond*; the Student Christian Movement Press Ltd. for a quotation from *The Significance of Jesus* by W. R. Maltby; Lady Salmond for a verse from her brother Julian Grenfell's poem *Into Battle*; and Mr. Cyril Upton for several verses from his book of poems *Musings in Provence* (Les Editions de L'Imprimerie Nationale de Monaco).

I wish to thank three friends, Mr. Kenneth Henderson, C.M.G., of Oxford, Mr. Graeme de Graaff of Melbourne, and Mrs. Gwyn Long of Sydney, all of whom have read the typescript critically and have made valuable suggestions which have improved the book. I need hardly say, however, that it should not be assumed that they agree wholly with its contents.

R. C. J.

CONTENTS

INTRODUCTION

TIMES of rapid change in the world are always times of great insecurity for the ordinary person.

In the international scene we are all aware that Western technological civilisation has created a world-wide ferment. It is not that our Western culture is always greatly admired or thought to be superior by awakening nations, but that certain aspects of it are felt to be fundamental rights of human nature. These are chiefly two: economically, the right to live without being hungry, and politically, the right to self-government.

In the fields of science and technology change is so rapid that if our grandfathers could return to view the world they once knew, they would feel like children with almost everything to learn afresh. In the early days of Queen Victoria the fastest way for a man to travel was on horseback, and this had been the case since man first inhabited the planet. Now he can fly a plane at three times the speed of sound. Specialists in one field can scarcely understand the language of specialists in another. In many directions we are being swept along by the excitement of new discoveries and inventions, and we seldom stop to ask ourselves, "To what goal is this leading us?" The counterpart of this excitement is menace, for everything which puts more power into the hands of a few men can be used for either constructive or destructive ends. If it is used for the latter then the ordinary man is the chief sufferer.

In the field of world-politics changes of enormous significance are proceeding. China, now a nation of over six hundred million people, may well be over one thousand million by the end of the century. If China achieves in industrialisation in the next forty years what Russia has done in the last forty, it may attempt to dominate the world unless it is wise and fortunate in its leadership. The world's greatest problem today is fear-insecurity. To attempt to alleviate its apprehensions each nation is seeking to acquire more power and wealth and technological ascendancy, so that no other nation dare challenge or attack it. Of course all nations feel more menaced and try to do the same thing, so that we have a vicious circle.

The individual's problem is also fear-insecurity. Added to those

B
15

inner fears which have always been part of the human lot are these menaces arising from world-tension. Never before, perhaps, has the ordinary man felt so threatened, so helpless in the face of fate, so lonely in the universe. Naturally enough he seeks to escape from his fear-insecurity in many forms of sport, in the euphoria of alcohol, in the excitement of gambling, in sex, in entertainment, and in tinkering with the manifold machines which our technological age has provided for him. Can we blame him? To live with the menaces of our nuclear age is well-nigh intolerable.

I want to affirm that in so far as these are forms of escape they will not prove satisfying: they will yield but temporary forgetfulness. The only satisfactory solution of man's dilemma is to be found in his discovery of the enormous resources of his inner self. This is no easy quest or achievement, but it is a possible one, and the only satisfying one. In this way he may ride out the storms of this modern age with inner serenity, in the assurance that come what may, there is nothing really to fear.

Some men follow the national trend and seek to alleviate fear-insecurity through a constant pursuit of power and possessions. There is no peace to be found in this. The crises of life come upon a man unexpectedly: it may be a serious accident, a severe illness, the death of someone dearly loved, the loss of possessions, or the frustration of plans. A man is thrown back upon himself, and he may then long with all his heart for some answer to the riddles of life, some assurance that life does have meaning in it and that it is not just "a tale told by an idiot, full of sound and fury, signifying nothing".

At such times religion should have something very important and relevant to say to man. But does he find it so? Has he not the impression that religion is something remote from everyday life, since apparently it cannot easily be expressed in plain language? Most important, how much truth is there in religion? What can a man believe when he finds that different races have different religions all proclaiming the general superiority of their viewpoint, and when within any nation the religious minority is split into scores of sects and denominations, all in varying degrees of disagreement? More fundamental still is the question: is *belief* important?

I hope in this book to help the honest seeker. I have formed the conviction that certain basic things in religion are true, important, and relevant to life. It is equally clear to me that all religions have gathered accretions in the form of theories and ideas, dogmas and doctrines which are unessential, which are sometimes false, and which generally obscure the simple and sublime truth. This Truth is such that words distort, obscure and limit it, for the essence of religion is something to be experienced in living rather than something to be believed. In a book we are inevitably trying to capture something of this spirit in language, and probably easily understood parables are the best way to do this. It was done superbly in such parables as those of the Prodigal Son and the Good Samaritan, which tell us how God loves man and how man should love his neighbour.

In this book I am attempting the hazardous task of trying to answer some of the plain man's questions. These are related to a religious outlook, but they are not religion. I have been more concerned to present a sound attitude to the experience of human life than to offer a framework of belief. There are enough of these already and they are all restrictive so far as Truth is concerned.

Chapter

I

DO SCIENCE AND RELIGION CONFLICT?

That which exists is One: men call it by different Names.

WE must first be clear what we mean by science and by religion.

WHAT IS RELIGION?

Religion seems to me to exist on four different levels. At its centre or core are certain profound experiences of the soul, which we describe as mystical. We shall say something about these in Chapter 3. Whoever has had such an experience knows with complete certainty the reality of a spiritual world and perhaps a little of its nature. The majority of religious-minded people are seeking for this experience and this certainty, but until it is granted to them they must needs accept the testimony of the few who can speak with first-hand experience.

The second level of religion is one of belief or intellectual acceptance. Men have asked themselves questions about the spiritual experiences of the few. What do these insights imply? The minds of clever men have consequently busied themselves all down the centuries constructing frameworks of thought and belief, and building systems of teaching which can be handed on. It is on this level that sects and denominations arise, and theologians find themselves disputing with each other.

On the third level religion involves our feelings, sometimes indeed, very deep feelings and emotions. It would be strange if so important an element in man's life did not do so.

On the fourth and outermost level, religion relates itself to social customs and ends, and guides action in the world. It becomes expressed and embodied in communities and churches. Within them people find mutual support, encouragement, and inspiration, through sharing a common worship and fellowship: they also enjoy a constant stimulus towards good works. On this level many people are religious. Of these, a certain proportion participate in the third level and feel deeply devotional. A smaller proportion participate intelligently in

19

the second level. Of only a small minority is it probably true to say that they have touched the first and innermost level. These can say, not "I believe", but "I know".

WHAT IS SCIENCE?

The literal meaning of the word is knowledge. The facts about the world around us which have been learned and studied by careful observation and countless experiments, once they are classified, constitute science. But there is more to it than this. Scientists discover certain recurrences and relationships, and they endeavour to distinguish cause and effect in these. Happenings are correlated with each other and explanations are attempted. Hypotheses usually suggest further observations which can be made, or further experiments which can be carried out to test them. This important sequence of observation, theory, deduction, more observation, and improved theory, is the basis of what is called scientific method. Gradually hypotheses or theories are rejected, modified, or confirmed, and they lead in the end to what we call Natural Law. These are reliable statements of the way which Nature works.

It is because of detailed knowledge of Nature's methods of working that science can direct and apply its energies to the service of man. All invention and technological achievement has been made possible by the scientific knowledge which men have gained and preserved. The motive behind much scientific work in the past has been love of knowledge for its own sake based upon a deep instinctive curiosity about the world. Commercial and military pressures have introduced other motives in these modern days, but the distinction between science and technology is still valid. Broadly we may say that science is pursued for the satisfaction of our understanding of Nature and adding to the sum of truth. Technology is the application of such knowledge to practical ends in the service of man.

If in broad terms these descriptions of religion and science are correct, it is difficult to find any fundamental grounds upon which they could find themselves in conflict. Science is concerned with the outside world which the senses disclose to us. Religion is concerned with the inner world of man's relationship to a spiritual order, although this must inevitably influence thought, feeling, and action. I propose first to examine some of the grounds upon which scientists criticise religious thinkers, and then to consider the criticisms of scientists by religious thinkers. We shall find that most conflict has arisen because of lack of understanding of the true nature of these fields of man's concern.

WHERE SCIENCE IS CRITICAL OF RELIGION

Science is suspicious of "revealed truth" for the obvious reason that it cannot usually be tested or challenged by the objective methods which science uses. Revealed truth can only be accepted on the basis of faith. Whether it seems plausible or implausible to the reasoning mind is regarded by theologians as quite irrelevant. With revealed truth regarded as axiomatic, deductions can be made and frameworks of belief can be built which have just the same validity, or lack of validity, as the basic revelation. Such systems of dogma become an integral part of institutionalised religion, in spite of the fact that there may be conflicting evidence in other fields of man's enquiry. Those who cannot accept them lack "the eye of faith". Personal and intimate religion is not exposed to this dilemma but organised religion is inextricably tied to this situation with the result that its history has been full of intolerance.

G. M. Trevelyan* describes an episode which sounds fantastic to the ear of modern man. In 1457 a Bishop Pecock was tried and imprisoned "because in arguing against the Lollards he had appealed partly to human reason instead of wholly to the authority of the church".

This attitude of authority over men's minds, requiring the faithful to accept certain things and not to question them on pain of penalty, persecution, or excommunication, is one of the blackest aspects of the history of religion. "To *think*, my son, is an infirmity from which God hath mercifully delivered His saints, and those whom He hath ordained to His special felicity." Thus an Abbé speaks for his church, in one of the novels of Anatole France. Now the repression of freedom to challenge accepted belief is one of the serious grounds of mistrust of religion by scientists. In its own serious beginnings in the sixteenth century, science had immense opposition to overcome from those who held the traditional views of Aristotle which the medieval church had endorsed. Let us take one example of Aristotle's ideas.

He affirmed that rest was "natural" for all bodies. It was admitted

* *A Shortened History of England*, p. 209 (Pelican Books).

that heavy bodies fell "naturally" to the centre of the earth, supposed to be the centre of the universe, but it was dogmatically affirmed that all other sorts of motion required a mover. It was said, moreover, that the movements of all such bodies could only continue while the mover was actually in contact with the moving object. None of these statements would be accepted by a modern schoolboy, but as long as such assumptions were sacrosanct everything that conflicted with them had to be explained away. Everyone could observe that once a stone left the hand of the thrower it did not immediately fall to the ground. A reason had therefore to be found for this anomaly. It was suggested that air rushing into the vacuum behind the stone must propel it forward!

Although Copernicus published his great book in 1543 stating that the Earth and other planets moved around the sun, it was the greater part of a hundred and fifty years before this viewpoint was generally accepted. The reason for this was that all the weight of ancient tradition supported by a powerful Church was opposed to it. On the view of Copernicus, the Earth was being displaced from its central position in the Cosmos, and this, by implication, raised serious questions, of the relation of God to man (who was His special creation).

Once the mind of man has been anchored to fixed pre-conceptions, it will proceed to inordinate lengths of credulity before its system of fantasy starts to break down under the weight of contrary observations. Only when some individual's mind is sufficiently detached from current orthodoxy to be able to look at facts without prejudice, is a new and more fruitful start made possible. This was what in fact happened in the seventeenth century, and the new attitude was so important in its implications (for it gave rise to modern science), that Professor Herbert Butterfield has impressively said "it outshines everything since the rise of Christianity".* Expressed in simple terms, the new attitude amounted to this. One cannot sit in an armchair and decide how Nature works. The only way is to observe the facts of Nature's working carefully, then we may legitimately start to formulate hypotheses and theories. But again and again these hypotheses must be tested by observation and experiment, and if necessary they must be modified or discarded in favour of new ones to include all the facts. It is difficult for us today to realise how much this emancipation of thought from tradition really meant. It is called by historians the "scientific revolution".

* *The Origins of Modern Science*, 1300–1800 (G. Bell & Sons, Ltd., 1951).

Do Science and Religion Conflict?

Echoes of this old conflict were heard again in the middle of the nineteenth century when Charles Darwin published his ideas on evolution and the descent of man. The issue once more was between ancient authority (in this case the Genesis-story of Creation) and the theory of evolution based upon observed facts.

The basic suspicion of religion by scientists centres around this matter of authority. For the scientist the only authority is perceived truth, towards which he strives by ceaseless observation and experiment. It irks him to hear statements made without any possibility of their being verified or established, and then to be informed when he challenges them, "Ah! this is where faith comes in." Nothing arouses his suspicion more than continuous demands for faith. The religious-minded man who has the ultimate faith in God, and the scientific man who has faith in the dependability of Natural Law or the consistency of Nature, can both defend themselves on strong ground, but all lesser faiths are regrettable necessities, justifiably held in a tentative way only until they can be replaced by knowledge.

The man who is both religious-minded and scientific is bound to affirm the unity of all truth. He is fully aware that the scientific method of approaching truth is a valid one and that it should be applied whenever possible. He is aware also that at the heart of religion he is concerned with another aspect of truth which cannot be verified by weighing, measuring, and observing as scientists do. The religious person *may*, however, have had a certain type of inner experience (called mystical) which offers him complete certainty. The experience may not adequately be expressible in words and therefore it can only be communicated very partially to others. It has, however, for the experiencer the indubitable stamp of truth, so that he could no more doubt it than he could doubt his own existence. The only evidence to others of such experience would presumably be in the difference of outlook in the life of the experiencer. It is also, of course, significant that the accounts given of mystical experience by individuals in widely separated backgrounds and centuries have remarkable elements in common. Truth of this kind is not apprehended through the senses and the mind as is scientific truth. It is experienced by that centre in the soul which says "I", when the mind is stilled. Ultimately all facets of truth must supplement each other and make a great unity.

WHERE RELIGION IS CRITICAL OF SCIENCE

Religion is critical of science on two broad grounds, (*a*) the assumption of materialism in the face of all the facts of experience, and (*b*) the incompetence of the scientific specialist to pronounce on the whole. Let us take these in turn.

Materialism I take to be the outlook which says that the things which we see, hear, and touch are real, while all else (including mind) is secondary and dependent on the physical world. Not all scientists are materialists, and the proportion of materialists is probably slowly diminishing. But this outlook is one which a majority of scientists hold, and have held during the last century, and in so doing they have influenced the outlook of the ordinary lay person. The religious outlook maintains that there is a reality more fundamental than mind itself: it is in fact only apprehended when the mind can be effectively stilled. It will suffice however to maintain the lesser viewpoint, that mind (which is an aspect or function of the Soul) is more fundamental than matter, and is not dependent upon it.

(1) The materialist who says that the things revealed to his senses are real and fundamental has some difficult problems on his hands. Take the subject of perception. We "see" the world with our eyes, which have sensitive retinae at the back of them on which the light falls. The light waves with which we see are, however, only a small range of wave-lengths out of the very wide range of electromagnetic waves known to science. Such waves range from the long radio-waves which may be miles from crest to crest, to short radio-waves as used in radar for example; they include infra-red waves, the small part which we call the visible spectrum ranging from red to violet, and beyond this are ultra-violet waves, soft X-rays, hard X-rays, and finally the extremely short wave-lengths of penetrating cosmic rays. Now out of all this vast range of waves only one small section is picked up by our eyes: to all the rest we are unresponsive because we have not evolved senses which are sensitive to them. Why is this? This question demands an answer from those who claim, as the materialist does, that the physical world is the basic reality. Suppose a race of men was born whose eyes responded to a different range of these waves, they would describe a very different world to the one we are familiar with. Which description would be truer? Could either claim to be adequate? The world which the materialist calls real and fundamental should surely

be beyond any doubt or confusion of this kind. Moreover, if the evolutionary process which produced the great apes and finally man, led to the survival of forms best adapted to their environment, why has the adaptation of the special senses been to so small a fraction of the environment? We can, of course, accept the theory of evolution without being materialists, but in this case we are obliged to hold that mind has played an important — indeed a fundamental — part in the whole process.

(2) The materialist thinks of man himself as a complex machine working as a unitary whole because of a system of physical and chemical responses. This machine has specialised parts which are called senses, and has developed a peculiar function called mind, to study the environment and decide how best to react to it. This is an extraordinary function for it interprets the electrical stimuli in one part of the brain as vision, similar stimuli in another part of the brain as hearing, in another part as touch, etc. Materialists do not tell us how or why. Moreover, this strange function called mind is usually hungry for sensations and is constantly stimulating the machine to secure the sensations which it likes. The materialist ought to tell us why it is that this function of the machine sometimes decides to take very little interest in the environment and entertains itself with mathematics or philosophy or puzzling over its own nature. In particular, we should be given some plausible reason why it sometimes leads the machine to destruction, quite deliberately, for the sake of satisfying something in itself which is describes as an ideal or a value. Is this pathological? If so, we should like to know frankly, and then we can ask the materialist to tell us why this so-called aberrant type of functioning has done infinitely more to enrich the world than the normal type of functioning.

(3) Sometimes materialism is expressed in medical terms. It is pointed out that changes in our physical state constantly modify our frame of mind. If the blood stream is toxic, if certain drugs are taken, if we inhale anaesthetics, then in varying degrees our state of mind changes. If certain parts of the brain are damaged then intelligent faculty is impaired. These are well-recognised facts: that *changes* in the state of the body-brain give rise to *changes* in the state of mind. It is obviously correct to infer that brain and mind are closely linked, but it is not legitimate to infer that mind depends *for its origin and maintenance* upon the brain. This is the assumption which the materialist makes, and it may or may not be true.

Other facts which must be taken into account are, that states of the mind can profoundly influence those of the body. Emotions such as anger, love, fear, etc. can alter blood pressure, respiration, skin resistance, etc. There is scarcely any organ of the body which may not be out of order, even though no organic lesion can be found, where the cause of the malfunction has not been shown to be in the mind. Anyone who has seen anaesthesia produced, or a blister raised on the skin, by planting this idea in the mind of a hypnotised subject, must admit the profound influence which mind can have on body.

The materialist making one assumption says, "When the body machinery is sufficiently disturbed so that it dies, the mind will necessarily perish too." But it is equally possible, making the assumption of the mind's independent status, to say, "When mind leaves a body which it has kept alive by reason of its intimate association with it, that body will die." Which assumption is correct can only be determined by further evidence of a different kind. For example, there might be evidence to demonstrate that a mind with its memories and other characteristics has survived the death of its former body. Such evidence is in fact discussed later in Chapter 12. We hold that there is as good evidence for some surviving minds as there is for dead bodies. The latter are known to us through the evidence of our senses interpreted by our minds; the former are known to us through our minds alone.

(4) We turn now to evidence which is crucial, which undermines, and will, I believe, finally convince all who study the data, that the materialistic position is untenable. The question we shall consider is: does mind need the special senses to gather knowledge of the world? Normally, we use eyes, ears, nose, and so on, to gather data in an encoded form (electrical impulses passing along nerves to the brain), which the mind interprets.* We have commented already on the limitations of the special senses which normally respond only to a small fraction of the total wealth of the environment. This suggests that the senses may be a restriction upon the mind's inherent power of gathering knowledge. The likelihood of this is reinforced by the careful research done during the last thirty years which has established the effect of extra-sensory perception. It has been shown that without using the sensory channels minds can, under favourable conditions, acquire knowledge of events in the world. This knowledge may be

* This commonplace view of perception is not, of course, the only one.

obtained both when it is present in another human mind, and when it is not. If mind is capable of this kind of activity perhaps hundreds of miles away from the body-brain on which it is supposed by the materialist to be dependent, we are bound to regard this supposition as extremely doubtful. Far from being a dependent relation, mind possesses powers which it can exercise without the limitations which space imposes upon material things. Not only has mind been shown capable of gathering knowledge of physical events at great distances, it has been shown that it can act at such distances (e.g. by influencing the fall of dice). It is clear that the mind's way of gathering knowledge through the senses and of acting through the neuro-muscular system, while it has certain advantages, is a restricted one, and not the only one. As Bergson once suggested, the brain may well be an organ of limitation.

While religion has grounds for being critical of scientists for their materialistic bias, both science and religion have in the past shown very little interest in psychical research — but for quite different reasons. Neither group has taken much trouble to examine its data or its claims. It has been easier to assume that it was not quite a respectable field of enquiry, having some vague associations with spiritualism, credulity, and fraud. The fact is that for about eighty years the Society for Psychical Research has investigated phenomena with due caution and has established the existence of phenomena which have implications of great importance for a balanced outlook on the world. The attitude of the materialistic scientist to these facts has been a most unscientific one: "We know already what is possible and what is impossible in the physical world. These things must be false because they strike at the foundations of our outlook." The attitude of most religious leaders has been a strange one in view of the fact that their scriptural records are full of happenings upon which psychical research has thrown a great deal of light. The religious leaders have probably thought it safer for the ordinary person to accept by faith what seemed strange and miraculous things in the scriptures, than to be encouraged to understand them and possibly in some cases to doubt them. There are signs of a changing attitude on both sides. A number of scientists and philosophers now freely admit the existence of psychical phenomena.* A number of leading churchmen have in recent years formed the Church's Fellowship for Psychical Studies.

* I do not wish to digress from the principal theme of this chapter to discuss the validity of the data of psychical research. For those to whom the data are unfamiliar,

The second broad ground of criticism of the scientists by religious thinkers is that they are prone to use their status as scientists to pronounce on philosophical matters. We know that today, scientists find it necessary to specialise in very narrow fields to advance their subject. They learn more and more about less and less. In any limited field of enquiry the specialist inevitably ignores qualities which from a wider standpoint he could not do. A scientist who is studying anatomy or physiology can make his study on any human body. He leaves out of his consideration all those data which distinguish persons: their intelligence, morals, religious outlook, racial background, etc. Any human body will do for his purpose. The chemist is a specialist on another level. Since the structure and properties of molecules interest him, he does not concern himself with living creatures. The physicist who probes into the interior of atoms, hoping to get down to the foundations of the physical world, has to ignore so much in his highly specialised field that, as a physicist, he is the least qualified person to speak to us of the wider significance of the world. Every more detailed study must inevitably eliminate something of importance from its purview. The analytical method characteristic of modern science, involves this breakdown process and must suffer the elimination of a wider outlook to arrive at a more detailed one in a limited field. The essence of materialism is precisely a limited and partial viewpoint purporting to explain the whole.

This argument is an important one: we shall therefore make the reverse approach, proceeding from the smaller to the larger view. A physicist speaks of fundamental particles such as protons, electrons, neutrons, mesons, etc., and from these he believes the ninety or more chemical elements are all constructed. Each of the chemical atoms has varying properties or qualities. None of these was present in the particles themselves: they are something new which has appeared, and arise from the relationships. If we now ascend the scale to molecules, we find that these possess new qualities which the atoms from which they were built did not possess. Still higher in the scale we come to living cells which possess qualities of a novel kind not found in the molecules which compose the cells, but which are a consequence of

---

or who, without study, have an attitude of incredulity towards them, I have suggested (*vide* Appendix) a number of books worthy of careful examination. My own studies have left me in no doubt about the existence of certain psychical phenomena and for this reason I refer to them in this chapter since they are very relevant to the matter under consideration.

relationship. We could proceed in steps to a complex structure like the human body and show that it possesses properties which none of its organs could claim. Greater wholes are always more significant than the sum of the parts, for the new relationships involve new and unpredictable properties. In the breakdown process which scientific specialism involves, these qualities of greater wholes are progressively eliminated. Materialism is one form of the fallacious view that we can understand the higher when we understand the lower: that wholes are in fact no more than the sums of the parts. The significance of this will be clear to the reader. If we want to know the "why" of existence, if we are seeking answers to the deeper questions about the world, we must take as our standpoint the highest level of wholeness that we can find. This means that our most reliable answers should be given by those rare persons whose insight and development combine the qualities of saint and sage.

SUMMARY

I can see no ground for conflict between religion and science when they are true to their own nature. In its essence, religion has to do with the mystical insights which come to man when he is functioning on his highest level. These disclose to him his true nature: his relationship to God. Science has to do with understanding the natural world which is evident to man when he is functioning on the level of his mind and senses. These are different levels of the functioning of man: they are complementary and not contradictory.

Chapter

2

HOW DID MAN COME TO BE?

Tell me, my friend, what has your life's experience taught?
Are you a man of dreams, or just a man of action?
Seek you to drown the truth with wine of mere distraction?
Or with the more corrosive opiate of thought?

Are you contented with dull prose of life's expression,
Or do you hear the poetry of Nature's voice?
There have been moments when you had to make your choice;
Chose you the ugly or the beautiful impression?

Some see in life a jungle of annihilation,
Others a counting-house for storing wealth within;
Some see a masque for columbine and harlequin,
And others a Gethsemane for meditation.

Tell me, my friend, to what illusions you have clung;
We can but hope to dream of light, whose eyes are bound;
In this dark forest of our hopes, what have you found —
Or am I speaking to you in a foreign tongue?
                                        Cyril Upton
                                  (*Musings in Provence*)

SCIENTISTS offer us an answer based upon their study of the Earth's
structure, of fossil remains found in different strata, of comparative
anatomy, and of a few skulls of primitive types of man which have
been found.

THE SCIENTIST'S STORY

We can only summarise the scientist's account, and it is as follows.
Ages ago, perhaps about five thousand millions years ago, there took
place an event which created the planets of our solar system. According
to one theory another star may have passed rather close to our sun
when both of them were in a gaseous state. As they were at a point of
near approach gravitational attraction may have drawn a stream of
matter out of the sun, and this breaking up, would condense into the
planets. According to a modern theory our sun was once a very
much larger spinning gaseous sphere than at present. In the con-

tracting process it rotated faster and became unstable. The planetary material was sprayed outwards, although it retained a magnetic link with the core.

For many hundreds of millions of years after this, no life of the kind we know could possibly have existed on earth, but with gradual cooling the liquid sphere would ultimately form a solid crust. At a later stage clouds of water vapour in the atmosphere condensed to form steaming oceans. Perhaps about two thousand million years ago in the warm seas of this ancient world, a complicated molecule started to show some of the characteristics of life. We need not stop here to discuss the criteria which distinguish the living and non-living, whether in fact this is largely a distinction of convenience for the biologist, just as lines of longitude and latitude do not exist but as a convenience for the navigator. The modern tendency is to see no very clear distinguishing mark. What are called viruses and genes may in fact be complex molecules which are starting to show living characteristics.

The first creatures were presumably single-celled, but the time came when colonies of cells formed, and at a later stage organisms consisting of many cells. The latter stage implies specialisation among cells in which different groups of cells take over various tasks. Some provided protection, others stability of structure, others would be concerned with food ingestion, excretion, and so on. It was as though "Nature" was making experiments to see what would work satisfactorily and what would not. Scientists, however, would not hold the view that there was anything conscious or purposive about this. They would say that creatures vary by chance or accident from each other. If any such variation conferred an advantage or benefit upon a creature in its struggle to survive, such creatures as possessed this would survive and multiply at the expense of those which did not. Natural conditions in the environment "selected" as it were those creatures best adapted to survive in the prevailing conditions.

At quite an early stage a radical and very daring experiment was made. Instead of keeping the hard parts of a creature on the outside of it, so as to protect the soft parts (shell-fish for example), the hard part was placed inside as a skeleton (e.g. ordinary fishes). From this point onwards, living creatures developed in two main divisions, the invertebrates (having no backbone), and the vertebrates (with a backbone). Both these streams of life have been successful. The insects are a particular example of the first division: it is estimated that about ten thousand different types of insect are found on the Earth's surface. The vertebrate division, in the course of many experiments, led through the fishes and amphibia to the reptiles and birds and mammals and finally to Man himself.

Plants evolved before animal life, and early invaded the dry land. There they diversified in great variety from humble lichens and grasses to great forest trees. Some two hundred and fifty million years ago, animal life which had until then developed in the sea successfully attempted an invasion of the land. Amphibia came first and after this developed the age of reptiles, remembered for the hugeness of some of its products. Mammals came later, and the primitive ape-like stock which ultimately led to the hominids might have been recognised perhaps one hundred millions years ago. The first real man, Homo Sapiens, may, however, not be older than one or two millions years. This age-long process of the advance of living creatures has been followed out in considerable detail by scientists, and their conclusions, which in broad terms are generally accepted, are described as the Theory of Evolution. It is usually the case that towards the great advances in our outlook, many scientists have made a contribution, and this is true of the evolutionary concept. The name of Charles Darwin will always have a special place of honour, however, for the two famous books *Origin of Species* and *Descent of Man* which he published just over a century ago. May we remind our reader again that the two master-keys of the scientist's theory are (i) chance variations which occur from time to time, and (ii) the operation of natural selection, which means that those creatures survive and flourish which vary in such a way as to afford them an advantage in the competitive struggle.

THE BIBLICAL STORY

The first book in the Bible presents to its readers what purports to be an account of Creation (in fact two accounts). Devout people once looked upon the story as though it were history: some doubtless still do. Modern man recognises that the Genesis story is in the language of poetry and myth, not of science or pre-history, and it is to be understood in this way. Whoever presented these accounts of Creation to a primitive nomadic people* was an enlightened man endeavouring to convey as much truth as they could hope to grasp in terms of pic-

* Probably they were adapted from the Babylonian mythology.

turesque myth. Those who read with insight can see behind the symbols and recognise the wisdom he is trying to convey. Consider a few of his statements.

"And God created man in His own image, in the image of God created He him." The truth which is here expressed and emphasised by repetition, has nothing to do with the outward appearance of man, but is a disclosure of man's inmost nature, the fact that there is a vital element in the soul which is the Divine spark or image. This is the incorruptible essence in human nature, and it is by virtue of this that man can be described as a "child of God" and possesses a status, which, so far as we can judge, none of the animal creation possesses. In virtue of this he possesses that God-like freedom to choose. In Browning's phrase, he is "a god though in the germ". This idea is one which Karl Barth and many modern theologians ignore or deny, when they talk of man as wholly lost, or unable to do anything to lift himself.

The myth draws an interesting picture of primeval innocence in Eden, yet in this paradise in a central place grows a tree of great significance called the "tree of knowledge of good and evil". To Adam and Eve is given the command, "Thou shalt not eat of it, for in the day that thou eatest thereof thou shalt surely die." Interpreting this on the superficial level, it might be regarded as an allegory of how sin and evil first entered into the world; that sin is disobedience to the commands of God and is inevitably punished; and that physical death, which God did not originally intend to be man's lot, came as a punishment. Much more than this is obviously intended. Adam and Eve represent all very primitive forms of man before the dawn of self-consciousness, when there was only an animal-like, unreflective, simple form of consciousness. At this stage there was no knowledge of the difference between right and wrong. After this event they acquired moral responsibility for their actions. From the superficial standpoint, the eating of the fruit of the tree might be described as "the fall of man", but from a deeper standpoint it is describing a stage in evolution, the birth of Homo Sapiens, free to make his choices, but obliged to accept the moral consequences of choice. He is driven out of the garden: there is no possible return to their former state of innocence. Now they have come to know the meaning of the opposites and they must choose their path. It was not so much physical death that they would now be called to face: even more it was the consciousness of alienation from that Being who had walked with Adam "in the cool of the evening".

It is interesting to notice that the old Sage who propounded the myth (and who had doubtless had to provide a code of sexual conduct for his people), used it to remind them that shame in regard to sex was linked with the same phase in development as that in which self-consciousness was born. The divine imprimatur was given to the wearing of clothing ("coats of skins"). The phallic symbol of the serpent was by no means fortuitous, but was used to inform them that herein would lie their greatest temptations, and here too they would have to accept responsibility for their actions.

"Cursed is the ground for thy sake; in toil shalt thou eat of it all the days of thy life." On the surface it is suggested that physical toil (in contrast with the leisure of Eden), has been prescribed as a punishment for wrong-doing, and it is possible that this primitive people liked hard work as little as many do today. The phrase "for thy sake" suggests a deeper meaning, viz., that that which man dislikes, pain, suffering, toil, and trouble, are to be the means by which he can tread the road of spiritual growth.

In one of the most interesting passages God is depicted as saying: "Behold the man is become as one of us, to know good and evil; and now, lest he put forth his hand, and take also of the tree of life, and eat, and live for ever: therefore the Lord God sent him forth from the garden of Eden." The implication is that immortality is something that man cannot be allowed to appropriate without effort. He must win his right to it and no short cuts will be allowed.

Ostensibly the Sage is offering answers to the questions which a primitive people must have put to him. Who made the earth? How did He do it? Why are there two sexes? Is there any reason to wear clothing? Why do we women find childbirth so painful? Why do we men have to work so hard? Why are there things we shouldn't do? He was conveying in symbolic form clues to answers more profound than they suspected.

THE CREATIVE PROCESS

If we are looking for answers to the ultimate questions we must look within ourselves as deeply as possible. How do *we* create? If a man builds a house, writes a poem, or paints a picture, what steps in the process can we discern? In the case of building a house, there are broadly three stages represented by the work of an imaginative kind by the architect, the detailed formulation of the plans by a draughtsman, and the execution of it in suitable materials by the builder. In creating a poem three similar stages can be recognised. The act of imagination or inspiration comes first. The process of ordering and working out is an activity of the mind. The setting out in words on paper gives it permanence and makes it available to others. Always behind the product which the senses appreciate we find activity of the mind which finds satisfaction in formulating thoughts and choosing words, while behind it is the stimulus of the creative imagination. Have these factors which we recognise in ourselves any counterpart in the great creative processes of Nature?

The biologist describes for us in a wealth of detail types of creatures which appear with the passage of time. In the Darwinian tradition he describes the appearance of novelties as due to "chance" variations. But is it not conceivable that imagination stimulating mind is the operative activity which lies behind and causes variation? Whether we postulate finite minds or something which may be called Collective Mind, or Planetary Mind, as responsible, need not enter into our speculation here. The point we are making is that if we recognise Imaginal activity as functioning behind the pageant of evolution, we should come into line with the small-scale creation as it is known and exercised by man. We should also have a natural way of accounting for three remarkable elements in the evolutionary process. (1) The first of these is the preservation of memories. The "know-how" of the process is preserved, not only in regard to Nature's successful experiments, but also in regard to the unsuccessful ones, which are never tried again. (2) The second feature is the wide variety of Nature's activity. It is by no means true that a single purpose has determined one line of evolution converging on Man as Nature's highest product. The development of the invertebrates has offered nothing in its countless experimental variety towards the structure of man. Even on the vertebrate line the side branches have had their own justification and developed for their own ends. (3) There is an aesthetic aspect in natural processes producing form, pattern, and colour, beyond that which might be regarded as calling for no comment. No one would confuse the results obtained by throwing quantities of pigment at a canvas and putting the pigments on in the usual manner. The product of chance and the product of imagination using the mind's skill are two very different things. It is of the latter we are reminded when we

35

look at butterflies, birds, deep-sea fishes, and many other natural products.

The scientist, speaking as a scientist, repudiates any knowledge of mind or imagination at work in evolution. He says, quite reasonably from the scientific standpoint: "As soon as you introduce these non-material and little-understood factors into the explanation of observed phenomena, you provide a convenient escape from all unsolved problems. I cannot test your hypothesis by my own methods. I must therefore stick to my own methods and study phenomena more closely to account for the things I cannot yet understand." Now the scientist as such is quite entitled to hold this position: indeed he is obliged to do so, and to push his techniques to their limit. But if he denies (or affirms) that mind and imagination may be operative factors he then starts to speak, not as a scientist but as a speculative philosopher. There are two things to be said to the scientist. First, that the evidence for certain psychical phenomena is now as good as that for natural scientific phenomena and it is foolish to ignore this. These facts point away from the cleavage of the world into matter and mind and therefore to understand the world properly the mind will have to be reckoned with and studied. Mind's power of psycho-kinesis may indeed be an important factor in the so-called chance cause of variation. Secondly, since an aspect of mind is its purposive activity, it is impossible to separate completely how-questions from why-questions. The scientist may claim rightly that he is interested only in the former, but even then he will find himself, as we have just suggested, called upon to face psychical factors. There is, however, no clear dividing line between the how and the why in some fields, and even more it is clear that scientists will be obliged to recognise the psychical energies of the world we live in.

THE COMING OF MAN

To the biologist man is the high point of a long evolutionary process, outshining all other creatures in his brain development. His survival (so far as factors other than self-destruction is concerned) is also favoured by the fact that he has not become too specialised. He can therefore adapt himself to a wide range of changes in his environment. To the Sage who wrote the creation-myth of Genesis, man was not merely the crown of the animal world, he was different in an important inner way from any other creatures. He expressed this idea in a sentence: "God breathed into his nostrils the breath of life and man became a living soul." He is given a status conferred by some additional factor: the possession of something god-like in his inner nature. These two viewpoints are not in conflict with each other, they are complementary. The scientist will say of course: "I know nothing about the soul." Nor is there any reason why he should, for his techniques are not such as would permit him to recognise it. The truth appears to be that man is the meeting place of two orders quite different in their characteristics, but related by the fact that the product of one order is made the vehicle of expression of the other. The first order gave rise to the physical body of man together with certain psychical and lower mental elements which are necessary to keep the body-machine running smoothly under control. This order in man is described, as far as its descent is concerned, by the evolutionary process of biologists. The other and higher order, of which we know little, which creates human souls, meets and blends with the first order in incarnate man. In Chapter 11 we express the view that the human soul consists of a quality of higher mind, and a new element which may be called Intuition or Buddhi (from a Sanskrit word meaning "enlightened"). This latter is an element in which insights and creative imagining are active. The soul has something at its centre of a still higher order which we may decide to call the divine spark or Spirit. The soul, which *is* the individual, has its own long evolutionary history behind it. When an individual soul associates with a human body in the process of incarnation, it brings to this new adventure, desires and tendencies, interests and latent capacities, and a store of wisdom which it has distilled from its past journeying. Some of these elements will be awakened in the course of life according to the nature of the body it is using (the hereditary factor) and according to the nature of the outer setting (the environmental factor). The soul's own memory of its past is nearly always completely submerged. Only rarely, and then usually fragmentarily, can the soul recall very much of its past. The author has, however, met a few people who have had such experiences. What *is* available, however, to a new incarnate personality, is that intuitive wisdom which the soul has distilled from its long past, and holds permanently within itself.

Everyone has remarked at times on the surprising contrasts between children of the same family. Doubtless bodily differences are adequately accounted for by the genetic re-groupings which take place in the fertilised ovum. What chiefly arouses comment is that children of the same parents, subject approximately to the same environment, may early manifest striking differences of temperament, sensitivity, interests, intellectual and artistic capacity, etc. Here we have evidence of the awakening soul which from birth until well into adult life is gradually infusing more of itself into the new personality. But an incarnate being is never more than a partial manifestation of the soul that is using this personality for purposes of its own fuller development.

The acorn has in its being a latent principle of oakness which can be awakened only if it falls from the tree, is buried in the soil, and subjected to the influences of this environment. So the souls of men at the beginning of their age-long pilgrimage through time have a wealth of possibilities latent within them. They must sow themselves (perhaps again and again) in physical bodies, and be subject to the influences of this physical order if their latent possibilities are to be unfolded. Sometimes we recognise intuitively that we have to deal with "old" souls or "young" souls. Some individuals make their impact upon us by their inner authority and the maturity with which they speak. In the case of others we know that they have far to go.

It may be asked whether anything is known about the origins of souls. It is probably wisest to say that we know nothing of the origin of souls and next to nothing of the origins of bodies. We think we know a little more about bodies, but such a judgment is superficial. I have speculated a little elsewhere about these matters.*

The biologist, expounding the theory of evolution, accounts in physical terms for the body and lower mind of living creatures. His account which is descriptive rather than fundamental is probably substantially true. It is, however, only half the story. The souls of men belong inherently to a different order of development of which the biologist as such, knows nothing. There are many different orders which I have called elsewhere* imaginals and sub-imaginals. The general principle underlying the whole process of manifestation is that higher orders make use of lower orders for purposes of their own development and fulfilment. More than this it is impossible to say within the compass of this chapter.

* See Chapters 8 and 9 of *Nurslings of Immortality*.

Chapter

3

CAN I *KNOW* THERE'S A GOD?

To find truth, or God, there must be neither belief nor disbelief. The believer is as the non-believer; neither will find the truth, for their thought is shaped by their education, by their environment, by their culture, and by their own hopes and fears, joys, and sorrows. A mind that is not free from all these conditioning influences can never find the truth, do what it will. . . .

When the mind has no motive, when it is free and not urged on by any craving, when it is totally still, then truth is. You do not have to seek it; you cannot pursue or invite it. It must come.

Krishnamurti

THIS is one of the most important questions we can ask. The theist says he believes in God; the atheist says he does not believe in God; the agnostic says he doesn't know, and he doubts if it is possible to know. Many scientists and philosophers, if they are not agnostic, think of God as a concept, a hypothesis of man's thinking, or perhaps with Aristotle as a First Cause. In contrast, many religiously minded people appear to take him for granted, and listen apparently without either doubt or surprise to preachers who tell them confidently what God thinks, likes, and expects of them. The enthusiasm and tenacity with which people "believe" some strange things is a reminder to us of the infinite capacity for self-deception of the human mind. Belief, even of a strong and definite kind, is one thing: knowledge is quite another. There is an important difference between them which we shall try to elucidate in this chapter. We are *not* now asking the question "Are there reasonable grounds for believing in God?" but the question "Can we *know* there's a God?" It will first be necessary to examine the question "How do we know anything?"

WAYS OF KNOWING

(1) One of the obvious ways of knowing things is by the use of our senses. You who are reading this book, are using the sense of sight in the process. You are aware of pages covered with words, and if you look around you will become aware of walls, tables, and chairs. You

maintain that this is all definitely reliable knowledge of your surroundings. The only people who might doubt you would be a few strange philosophers. For practical purposes you can rely on this form of knowledge. It "works", and everybody else relies on it too, in spite of any philosophic doubts they may entertain. We need not digress to discuss these doubts: all we are concerned to point out is that we cannot expect to know God through the use of our physical senses.

(2) There is another kind of definite knowledge which we possess: this is knowledge of our own sensations and feelings. We may feel the pain of toothache, we may feel angry or depressed, afraid or happy, and so on. Although no outward sign of these feelings may be apparent, we should disregard anyone who denied that we had such feelings, on the grounds that none of his senses disclosed them to him. We should reply, "These feelings are real enough to me." Can we know God in the way in which we know our feelings? I should say that the answer is both yes and no to this question. States of feeling are undoubtedly peculiar to, and very real to ourselves, although we may not be able to communicate them to others. In this sense the answer is yes. But feelings are often transient things and influenced by external factors. If knowledge of God fluctuated in this sort of way, I should regard it as very doubtful and uncertain.

(3) There is a deeper faculty which we call reason or intellect. This has been described as an organ of knowledge. It is rather like a machine which can carry out complicated operations provided raw material is fed into it. The laws which control its operation are the laws of logic, and the raw materials are idea sor various kinds of symbols. Wonderful systems of thought and frameworks of belief have been built up by theologians and philosophers, but they do not agree among themselves for two reasons: (i) either the words used have no clearly accepted meaning, or (ii) the basic underlying ideas or pre-suppositions which were originally fed into the machine and remain there unchallenged, are not generally accepted. Knowledge of this kind is not what we are seeking. There is all the difference in the world between a system of beliefs about God, and direct awareness of Him, just as there is a vast difference between a compendium of data about a person and friendship with that person. To Zophar's question, "Canst thou by searching find out God?" we would answer, "Not with the mind." Our experience has been the same as Omar Khayyam's:

Can I Know There's a God?

Myself when young did eagerly frequent
Doctor and Saint, and heard great argument
About it and about; but evermore
Came out by the same door as in I went.

(4) Within the structure of ourselves, at a higher and more interior level than mind, experience points to another level, which we may perhaps label Intuition or Insight. This level of ourselves does not use any sort of reasoning or mental process to attain its knowledge. Such knowledge flashes suddenly upon it like a light that has been turned on. This level of ourselves is a creative and imaginative one, particularly active in seers, inventors, poets, musicians, dramatists, and all creative artists. We say of such persons that they are inspired, since they appear to be more sensitive and receptive to truth and beauty than most of us. When afterwards, expression or formulation of these insights is given through the mind, many others who could not have arrived there by themselves make an intuitive response to it. They say, "I always knew it was so" or, "It rings a bell in me". Something leaps up to greet the insight presented by another.

Perhaps I may make a personal confession and say that for me several of Mendelssohn's works, and in particular the Trio No. 1 in D Minor, are much more than the expressions of emotional moods. For me they express insights into the nature of Reality. The same is true of passages in Wordsworth's *Ode on Intimations of Immortality* and Thompson's *Hound of Heaven*, and in certain other poetic achievements. I value them not merely for the beauty of their form and language but for the response they evoke to their insights.

This faculty of intuitive insight which many people possess, although doubtless in varying degrees, is one through which we might expect to have *some* knowledge of God. The sceptic will say, "Is it *knowledge*?" Since logical demonstration is impossible, all one can reply is that if knowledge is characterised by a satisfied response of the ego when it contacts truth, these intuited insights have as good, if not a better claim to this title than other ways of knowing. If valid they should not contradict the fruits of intellectual striving, although they are generally of a nature which intellect alone could not have produced.

(5) Beyond this level of ourselves there is sometimes given to a soul what is called mystical experience. In this may be conveyed authentic

41

knowledge of a clarity and immediacy which leaves no room for doubt or any uncertainty. In such experience the ego or centre in the soul is lifted up into momentary union with the Spirit (of which it is an aspect in exile). Examples of this will be given later. If intuitive knowing is like looking "through a glass darkly", mystical knowing is meeting "face to face".

WHAT GOVERNS INTUITIVE KNOWING?

I have come to the conclusion that any presentation of religion which affirms that knowing God is a widespread or commonplace experience is mischievous, liable to be misunderstood, and certain to do much harm. It is true that to the awakened soul something of the activity of God is revealed or disclosed in all Creation. Wordsworth, and many another, have found in Nature "a Presence which disturbed them with the joy of elevated thought". If we see a scene of great beauty, or catch a glimpse of the innocent wonder in the eyes of a little child, or observe some act of great self-sacrifice, we may be deeply moved by these experiences. In trying to express afterwards why we had such feelings, perhaps all that we can say is that something God-like has spoken to us through them. They have been sacramental because they have mediated what we believe to be a little of the divine beauty and love. The stimulus has come to us through our senses, but the intuitive level of ourselves has penetrated behind the outer appearance. Yet of such insights, and even of the more profound moments of mystical experience to which I have referred, it is true to say in the words of Job: "These are but the fringes of His ways, how small a whisper do we hear of Him." To talk lightly of knowing God is to debase the currency of words, and this makes for hypocrisy in religion. When I reflect on the sentiments of many hymns, the familiar discourse and trite phrases of piety which pass for public prayer, the platitudinous speech which is the substance of most sermons but which purports to disclose the "Mind of God", I am constantly shocked to think that religious people can acquiesce in such things. It would greatly help the cause of truth and increase the respect for religion if a new humility arose in which words were used carefully and sincerely.

How much any man can know on the intuitive level of himself depends on the degree of his development on this level, just as what he may know on the level of intellect depends on his development on that level. If a supreme work of Art is presented to a group of people, one or two will be deeply moved, one or two will begin to use the critical mind upon it, some will say it is very nice, and others will see nothing remarkable in it. Each has reacted according to his intuitive development.

It is interesting to notice that the personality of Jesus, outstanding as it was, resulted in a variety of reactions on the part of his contemporaries. Thomas, in a moment of insight, bowed himself to the ground and said, "My Lord, and my God." Judas, who had been for three years in the company of Jesus, had no such moment, nor had the members of his own family, nor had the Jewish hierarchy. "Is not this the carpenter, the son of Mary?" In the presence of so powerful a personality the intuitive limitations of the different persons were quite obvious, and there is no warrant for thinking that human nature is any different today. To *know God* in a small degree, must involve sensitivity and development on the intuitive level of a high order. To know God must be the most moving and overwhelming experience which man can imagine. What it may mean to have a sense of oneness with the Supreme Being, no human being can hope to conceive or express. Let men give thanks for their highest experiences, but remember in humility that "these are but the fringes of His ways".

SOME MYSTICAL EXPERIENCES

We have used the term *mystical experience*, and the reader may wonder what is meant by it. Occasionally there are inner experiences granted to people (they cannot be controlled or commanded), which bring with them an overwhelming sense of contact with what is ultimately and fundamentally Real. The emotional tones accompanying such experiences are expressed by the words bliss, harmony, joy, perfection. The sense of bondage within the walls of a separate self vanishes, and consciousness is greatly expanded and lifted on to higher levels of being. Sometimes the event is accompanied by intellectual illumination in which there is a clear awareness of a vast plan behind existence in which everything and everyone has a meaningful part. Immortality is usually self-evident and a great sense of Love and Wisdom pervades the whole. A few examples will perhaps convey to the reader the kind of thing we are referring to.

Case 1 (A Young Man of 20)

"Suddenly, in less than a second it seemed, came this 'feeling': a knowledge of oneness with ocean, sky, fish, birds, everything. The feeling was soon gone, but the impression has remained ever since. It was not intellectual or emotional, but the feeling of certainty was there beyond all other feelings. I am surer of this than of anything else in life. It left a deep happiness which lasted for some hours. All was completely impersonal. 'I was not there at all' is one way of expressing the feeling. I have used the words 'oneness', 'happiness', 'certainty', and so on. All are imperfect expressions, ludicrously so, of what I experienced. At this time I had not read of mysticism, but later when I did, I was much interested to read of similar experiences. This experience has left its mark on my intellectual life ever since."

Case 2 (Mrs. R. C.)

"I am an ordinary middle-class housewife and previously to this experience I had no knowledge at all of mysticism, nor had I read any books on the subject. I have always been eager to know all I could about the origin of man, who he is, why he is here; but I had a more or less open mind perhaps tending towards materialistic belief. Three years ago, at the age of 55, it became an obsession to me, this searching. I felt I *must* come to some conclusion . . . I read and read and read . . .

"I have always indulged in visual prayers on the few occasions that I rather shamefacedly indulge in prayer. . . . So it was not altogether surprising that on that August morning, my thoughts as usual fretting around this eternal problem of whether there was any purpose or meaning in the universe, I should find myself even in the midst of sweeping the kitchen floor, saying to myself, 'Well, let's try to imagine it all.' I proceeded to picture all that I had read about the beginnings of things and man's gradual emergence. As I watched, the pictures seemed to take life of themselves, as though it were taken from my own action, and I was merely an observer, not the creator of this amazing scene. Stranger still, an inner voice almost banteringly said, 'And do you think all this was accidental?' With that I dropped my broom and exclaimed aloud, 'Of course not. How could I ever have thought it was?' Then it happened.

"I felt as though something sneezed in my brain, as though some blocked channel had cleared and I felt *flooded with light*. With it came a joy that is ineffable. There are no words to describe it. I felt I had to go upstairs: I stood transported, looking out of my bedroom window. Opposite there was a lorry unloading some bricks, a workman in shabby grey flannel trousers, a beret on his head, a cigarette dangling from his mouth, stood rather dejectedly watching. I thought how beautiful he looked, the folds of his trousers seemed to make the most satisfying pattern. Everything I looked at had significance and beauty. There are no words to describe the reverence I felt for everything. I thought, now I know what it meant, that verse in the Bible, 'Now we see through a glass darkly, but then face to face.' Also, I know now that it is true, 'Perfect love does cast out fear.' A great gratitude filled me. I felt I was saved from some terrible wrongness, as indeed I was. When I came downstairs I found that hours had gone by, and yet it only seemed about fifteen minutes.

"This made a tremendous change in my whole outlook. For some weeks I felt a dynamic flow of energy and so much mental stimulus that it was difficult to sleep. For nights I would wake about 2 a.m. with thoughts whirling round in my head, so that I often had to get up and write them out. Perhaps the most valuable knowledge I gained was, that the strong desire for approval which appears to be the motive force for so many of our actions, good and bad, was not a desire for other people's approval, but came from an innate desire to be in harmony with this inner core which I now felt to be the Christ in me. Since a lot of my unhappiness had been caused by a strong desire to be liked and respected, and a refusal to accept the values of the people I lived among, this realisation meant a blissful cessation of conflict. For some weeks I lived as though walking on air. Every day brought new truths. Everybody was seen in a different light. All mankind was noble and lovable, only so mistaken, and needlessly unhappy. I longed to tell everybody of my wonderful discovery. It is hard to learn that it is impossible to communicate such experiences. . . .

"I feel I *know* now that this life is only part of a whole, and that there are higher forms of consciousness which may become the normal consciousness of man in the future, and of which we now just get a glimpse occasionally. Once before, I did have an experience under an anaesthetic — the same feeling of ecstatic joy, and particularly of *understanding*. I remember particularly the thought, 'So that's what it all means. How wonderful. I must go and tell everybody.' When I came round I told the doctor I had seen and understood the whole meaning of the universe. He smiled and said, 'What was it?' and I replied, 'A Great Light.' "

Case 3 (Mrs. G. W.)

"The occasion was the birth of our second child when, during the short period of the anaesthetic, I was free from my body. Immediately I thought, 'So this is how our spirits leave our bodies at death.' Yet I felt sure I had not died. I clearly saw the scene below with white-clad nurses and doctor around the table where my body lay. The joy and exhilaration of my freedom were beyond words. My spirit was caught up and reunited with the all-pervading Spirit of God, as a raindrop would return to a mighty river, *yet retaining its own identity*. I underline this, because it was the first of the surprises in store for me. As in Christian teaching, I had imagined our spirits returning to the one Spirit of God, but I did not think their individuality would be of any importance or would survive. Now I was returned to a seemingly infinite Divine Spirit, yet I felt more vibrantly alive and an individual than ever before. With my new intensified consciousness I understood to some degree the meaning of eternity. One breath in a lifetime was compared to one lifetime in eternity. My life on earth was as if I breathed in — birth: I breathed out — death.

"Eternity stretched on into infinity, and myself with it — truly an immortal spirit, travelling on, and *coming from eternity*. (This was my second surprise, for until now I had thought every baby born was a new soul.)

"Now I had a revelation of Love, and I thought, 'It is surely the meaning of Love as God loves.' Crowds of people of all races passed before me — black, yellow, honey-coloured, white, and red. I watched them pass and I loved them as if my heart would break. Acquaintances of my own passed, and people I liked least. I loved them and all mankind with a love beyond words, and longed to help them. Though it has not taken long to write, the revelation of Love was the most intense, deepest, most powerful, and seemed the most important part of the whole mystical experience.

"Now I was shown as if from a great height, a city with people hurrying like ants about their small affairs, their indifference and self-sufficiency seeming to enclose them like a hard shell, their hearts and minds tightly closed against the Love of God who yearned over them, striving to make contact with them. Then I was shown by a familiar illustration a man's real relationship to God. On a country road which I knew well there was an old ruin which had always appealed to my imagination. It was a two-storied shell of a building with high wide arched apertures where doors and windows had once been. Birds flew in and out, grass grew inside, the sun filled it and the winds blew through. Perfectly I saw it now, and I saw that man should stand like that shell of a building, filled, permeated, pervaded completely by the Spirit of God.

"Next I was able to understand that here we are not bound by Space and Time. Space was easy — just to think of a place was to be there. But Time was harder even for my extended consciousness. The illustration of timelessness was again a personal one and a very touching one. Our little daughter of $2\frac{1}{2}$ was an intelligent, unusual, droll child, and hardly a week of her babyhood had passed that I had not lamented the loss of each endearing stage. It seemed so wasteful that such perfection could give way to change and be lost for ever. Now I saw her as a baby, a child, a girl, a woman, and as an old, old lady. (This would surprise any mother, for she would not expect to see her child in old age.) It was as if her life were on a length of tape, not visual only, but whole and living. While one section was on view at a certain age in the physical world, here it was more like a composite picture. It was all there on the roll — past, present, *and future*. (This was more than a surprise, an utterly new idea which I could vaguely comprehend, that the future was inherent in the present, as also was the past.)

"The next revelation was a great consolation to me also. I was in circumstances of mental limitations and of restrictions of all kinds. I had a constant sense of loss about the world of ideas, intelligent companionship, higher education, high endeavour, research, etc., going on elsewhere. I did at this time over-reverence education. I was shown a vast ocean stretching to the horizon. On the shore there were men, some a little more advanced than others, but all with their toes in the water. These were our best brains, the world's scholars, its most learned men, on the fringe of the sea of All-Knowledge.

"Now I seemed to ask 'What of evil here?' And I saw that evil did indeed exist, but in some outer place, restricted and controlled, and that we, safely within the Spirit of All-Good, were insulated against evil.

"Now I was on a low cliff overlooking the sea, and I was conscious for the first time that I had a body of a light and airy kind. That I was physical in a physical world, there was no doubt, for I felt the sun warm on my face, and the breeze lifted the hair from my neck. The sea sparkled, great masses of white clouds sailed overhead. I stood in long grass so that where the swell of the sea met the land, a waving sea of grass began. The world was alive with movement, the air filled with vibration — of sound, light, colour, rhythm. I flung out my arms to it all, for here was the exaltation I had known as a child — felt more intensely now. I seemed to be identified with all created things, with the birds in flight, with the rocks hot in the sun. I was of the water, I was the grass bending beneath the wind, in the wind itself. There was a keynote in the vibration, but it was not my keynote. I felt that if my keynote could be struck on a mighty gong it would shatter my semi-physical body and I would be free indeed, if the fierce state of ecstasy, exultation and exaltation did not burst it asunder.

"Now I felt myself being drawn down as if by heavy weights. I came out of the anaesthetic with an appalling sense of loss, and one firm resolve — not to succumb to sleep. I went over and over the experience until morning committing it to memory in every detail. All the next day I felt separated from the physical mechanics of life, and when alone

D   47

I could actually re-enter the experience. I was definitely in a super-sensitive state. I read the first chapters of the Gospel of St. John, since when I have been trying to find in them what I found that day. I did not take it in at brain-level, but seemed to be inter-penetrated by the meaning as a sponge by air. As expected, after a sound night's sleep, I was right back on the physical plane, with my tremendous experience only a memory, but a vivid, alive, detailed one."

I shall comment briefly upon these three accounts, to which many more could have been added.

Case 1 is an example of what is sometimes called Nature-mysticism. The observing ego no longer sees the world as the mind interprets it, full of separate objects, but with the consciousness focused on a higher level than mind it participates in the formative ideas which lie behind the world. It is as though one were temporarily merged with the creative imagination of an artist before his inspiration had been expressed in forms.

Case 2 is fairly typical of a near-approach to what is called "Illumination". It is a momentary awareness or even union of the ego with the Spirit which lies beyond it (*vide* Chapter 11). The experience is often associated with a Light or Illumination, and the joy that results is beyond all ordinary description. There are frequently profound insights into life and the purposes which lie behind it.

Case 3 is remarkable in that it begins as an out-of-the-body experience and then moves higher to become a mystical one. An unusual feature of it is the clear delineation of a number of insights through the medium of illustrations or parables, as though a wiser or more advanced being was teaching the elevated ego what it was possible for it to grasp. The closing phase was probably astral-plane* experience once more, and it will be observed that the account says, "I was conscious for the first time that I had a body of a light and airy kind."

Such experiences as these which occasionally are granted to people are best understood as a glimpse by the ego of levels which lie higher than mind, which we have described as levels of the world of spirit. Some describe such experience as awareness of God, because the term *God* embodies for them the most sublime and awesome concepts.

---

* I dislike the term "astral", for it has nothing to do with stars! Unfortunately the term has had a wide use as a distinguishing label for that state of consciousness and the related world of awareness which follows death of the physical body. It corresponds probably to the heaven-world of Christian orthodoxy. With this apology I shall continue to use the term both here and later in Chapters 11, 12, and 13.

All those who have had such experience are agreed that language completely fails to convey the truth about it. As already suggested, if we are going to use language carefully, we should beware of accepting literally the ecstatic claims of union with God which are natural enough under the circumstances.

There are a few souls who appear to have achieved a state of more or less permanent Illumination. The Light is with them constantly, and there is no sense of self-hood in the sense that most of us understand the word. The exiled ego has no longer a sense of exile, but possesses a fully conscious awareness of being a centre of the Spirit's activity. There seem to be a few rare souls who have a consciousness of something beyond Illumination which is awesome, compelling in its wonder, and felt as something quite "Other" than belongs to ordinary human nature. This may be an awareness of a Divine Society.*

I had a friend who died in 1944, who, behind the façade of his outer life, had a deep interest in mysticism. He has occasionally communicated with me† through the writing of a sensitive, and on one occasion, replying to a question I had put to him, he wrote as follows.

"Too considerable a revelation of God would drive the most spiritual human being mad. The highly gifted mystic or yogi was never in his earthly life-time united with God. Actually, his little spark was blown on so that it became a tiny flame during the occasions he had mystical experiences. Only when the long journey through infinite time has been made, only when the human soul has been fully used for the purposes of Divine Imagination, and this soul is incomparably enriched by the strength of all the other souls in its Group, can it experience Union with Divine Imagination. To be on the level with God one has to become a god, and that full glory is not to be experienced by any human being."

Can we know there's a God? It is the ego, the centre in the soul which is concerned with knowing. With its instrument the mind, it can at best know *about* God. It can hold to beliefs and probabilities and say of a certain idea that it is reasonable. With its instrument the intuition, it can acquire insight, a penetrating sense that truth is near,

---

* The student may pursue these matters further in my book *Watcher on the Hills* (Hodder & Stoughton Ltd.).

† As I deal with the important question of survival of physical death in Chapter 12, I shall not digress here to defend my belief that this communication was substantially what it purported to be.

a quiet conviction about this that the mind has done nothing to produce and can do nothing to change. But in mystical experience, which no soul can command, but which may be granted by the Spirit, the ego is lifted up as it were and held for a moment in a full natural awareness of the glory of Spirit to which it belongs. This is *knowledge*, convincing and unshakeable. Knowledge of what? Shall we say in simple language, where all language fails, knowledge that God is. Beyond this point the way stretches into the infinite, and what a soul can know depends upon its god-likeness, for this is its capacity to know the Ultimate.

BELIEF AND KNOWLEDGE

Belief seems to me an attitude of the ego towards the conclusions of the mind's thought-processes, or towards statements which the mind accepts on the authority of others. Belief can never be satisfying in relation to ultimate things. Belief and doubt always go together: only the proportions of the two differ from one mind to another. The intuitive level of ourselves is a step nearer to the ultimately Real than is the instrument of mind. It seems to me that it must be identified with that level of the soul in which is stored all the wisdom distilled from past lives.* What we have called insight or intuitive perception is an illumination of the mind from this level, or possibly at times by some higher Being through this level. The mystic alone *knows* beyond any possibility of doubt, because his ego has experienced oneness with the Spirit, which is ultimately Real.

The *Last Lines* of Emily Brontë include several verses which show either profound intuition, or possibly mystically acquired knowledge.

> *With wide-embracing love*
> *Thy Spirit animates eternal years,*
> *Pervades and broods above,*
> *Changes, sustains, dissolves, creates, and rears.*

> *Though earth and man were gone,*
> *And suns and universes ceased to be,*
> *And Thou wert left alone,*
> *Every existence would exist in Thee.*

* To avoid interruption of the argument I ask the reader to suspend judgment on the question of a plurality of lives until it is developed in Chapter 14.

Can I Know There's a God?

There is not room for Death,
Nor atom that his might could render void:
Thou — THOU art Being and Breath,
And what THOU art can never be destroyed.

If your first reaction to reading these lines was a thrill, great or small, it was a response made from your intuitive level, because a fragment of this wisdom was already stored there. This is true, even though your second reaction (from the mind) was, "I wish I could believe that."

Can we do anything to attain the certainty of the mystic? Looking at some forty or fifty accounts of mystical experience, I can find no clear indication of conditions under which such experience may be expected to occur. Certainly some of the recipients were in dire need, but dire need is far more common than mystical experience. The latter has no obvious connection with quality of mind or intellect, age or sex, and one can only think that it is a grace of the Spirit granted to a soul when the Spirit wills. Every great religious tradition points nevertheless to certain paths or ways of living, which if pursued faithfully, lead the soul towards this possibility. It is considered that the soul which treasures such values as Love, Goodness, and Beauty, and expresses itself in self-forgetful service, in contemplation, or in both, is preparing itself for this end. Where the soul is itself the instrument as well as the subject of the experience there can be no easy and quick means of preparation. This is the pearl of great price which demands all that a man has in exchange. Many whose aspirations are high may have to be content to say for more lifetimes:

Yet, though I have not seen, and still
Must rest in faith alone;
I love Thee, dearest Lord, and will,
Unseen but not unknown.

CAN WE USEFULLY THINK ABOUT GOD?

Because higher realities are indescribable in language, not being disclosed to the senses, mankind has had to make use of symbols to stand in their place and remind him of their existence. The cross, the grail, bread and wine, are Christian symbols; the lotus, the wheel, and the stupa are Buddhist symbols; the flag, the crown, the orb, and the mace are symbols of State, and so on. While a symbol may have no resemblance whatever to the thing symbolised, an image may be regarded as being in some degree a vehicle of likeness, or the embodiment of some aspect of the reality. A mother nursing a child may thus be an image of Love.

There are many verbal images which help a worshipper to make more vivid to himself the sense of God. Such images are the Heavenly Father, the Divine Mother, the Good Shepherd. As aids to devotion, people of a certain temperament find such images of great help. The risks arise, not in the language and atmosphere of devotion, but in the field of theology, which is, or should be, truth-seeking. We have observed that the mind is an instrument of limited power and range. Its thinking is necessarily in categories of space and time, and its laws of operation are described as logical. It follows that it is only in so far as God manifests Himself within these categories that He can be spoken of. Here lies the real danger. Pride of mind has led to thousands of books being written, which are attempts to express that which is beyond mind in terms with which mind is familiar. It cannot be done without serious distortion. It is true that a picture in two dimensions can convey something of the three-dimensional world, but only because we have constant experience of the latter. How far language can expect to convey to the reader truth about God must depend upon his intuitive development or his mystical experience of Reality. Even at its best, language can only hope to convey hints about reality. We are therefore on the horns of a dilemma.

Christianity has at this point grasped one horn. It has taken the highest values known to human nature: wisdom, love, goodness, truth, and beauty. It has claimed that these were perfectly illustrated in the person of Jesus Christ, and has said to its followers, "God is like Jesus" or "God is the Father of our Lord Jesus Christ". In practice, this helps to make a sense of God real to many Christians, and certainly no nobler Image has been presented to mankind. The risks of this course, that part of the truth should be taken for the whole Truth, that the Image should be taken for the Reality, matured within the first century of Christianity. From being a living "Image" (Christ, who is the Image of God. 2 Cor. iv. 4). He became identified with God (In Him dwelleth all the fullness of the Godhead bodily. Col. ii. 9). Moreover, since we human beings only know of wisdom, love, goodness, etc., in so far as these values are embodied in persons, and since it is affirmed that these are embodied in the highest degree in

God from Whom they originate, the mistaken claim has been made by Christian theology that God is personal.

In stating this, the idea of God has been grievously limited. God may be the ultimate source of persons without Himself being personal. There may be a whole hierarchy of supra-personal beings in the universe, and God is embodied in, though not confined to, the Whole. He must not only be the whole of manifestation: He must include what is unmanifest (of which we can say nothing). After all, we don't even know a poet when we are familiar with all his poems; we know only one aspect of his manifestation. When God is spoken of as personal, the Image has been confused with the Reality. Since every positive statement made about God is a limitation upon Him, Christian theologians trying to use the logic of mind where it is inapplicable, find themselves constantly in difficulty and fall back on paradox. It is inevitable when this horn of the dilemma is chosen.

Gautama the Buddha chose the other horn. Seeing clearly, as he did, the utter futility and inadequacy of speculation about God, he remained silent, and encouraged his disciples to do the same. How few Christian theologians have understood this choice: they have preferred to foster the mistaken view that Buddhism has no belief in God! A high Buddhist authority from whom I enquired, wrote to me, "The idea of God is quite acceptable to us, but we do not encourage the use of the Word lest it should be tainted."

Inevitably, the luminous and compassionate figure of the Buddha became for many an *image* of That which cannot be expressed, and therefore a vehicle of salvation in whom his followers could take refuge.

In Hinduism we find the widest imaginable range of expressions about God. There are simple and popular forms of Hinduism apparently close to poly-theism. There are thousands of images presenting facets and aspects of the One. There is the purest philosophical Monism, speaking of the "One without a second". In its philosophical form of Vedanta it replies, "Not that, not that" to any description of the nature or attributes of God, realising that to affirm is also to limit and exclude.

God is the Supreme Mystery, and all the speculations of the puny minds of human beings are of little more significance than thistledown floating in space. Our best guides are the mystics, who speak from first-hand experience of higher levels, but say with one voice that language is inadequate to express their experience. Those who have seen "but the fringes of His ways" in their most exalted moments, have said such things as these: "I was aware of Love — Universal Love — Peace, Joy, Bliss, Ecstasy, to such an extent that it is impossible to express in words"; "It was the sense of the presence of an irresistible Power, wholly and utterly benevolent"; "Barriers were down; my aloneness had gone; I was at one with every living creature and thing"; "Somehow I *knew* that what I had experienced was Reality, and that Reality is Perfection".

If you want to know what to think *about* God, here are three voices through whom He was speaking:

"If ye, being evil, know how to give good gifts unto your children, how much more shall your Heavenly Father give His Holy Spirit to them that ask Him" (Jesus).

"God is Love, and he that loveth dwelleth in God, and God in him" (St. John).

"Howsoever men worship Me, so do I welcome them. By whatever path they travel, it leads to Me at last" (Krishna).

Think your own highest and noblest thoughts about God, and then know that they are not a thousandth part good enough to be the sublime Truth.

Chapter

4

AM I FATED OR AM I FREE?

... That noble fatalism which is a source of weakness in fools but of inspiration in the great.

John Buchan

I account it the highest wisdom to know this of the living universe, that there is no destiny in it other than we make for ourselves.

A.E.

FREEDOM is one of the most frequently used and least understood words. The politician uses it in speeches when the introduction of a little idealism seems appropriate. The Hindu saint uses it to describe that state of being towards which he aspires when he has overcome the illusions of the world. It is used by a young man when he cannot make up his mind which girl to propose to.

If the reader looks back over his own life, and traces its course forwards from early years, one of his observations will almost certainly be, "How much of it just happened — without my willing or consciously planning it!" We were born in a certain year within a particular period of history. We were born in a certain country to two particular parents out of the millions of possible ones. As a result we grew up in a particular home and were subject to a unique set of influences which will affect our outlook for the whole of life. The school we were sent to was chosen for us, and the atmosphere there was one that others had created. We were told what to do and what not to do. As we look at the picture of life it is obvious that about many things we had little or no freedom of choice. The greater part of our early life was determined for us by others, and the bit of freedom we possessed was largely to choose how we would react to this situation.

In adult life we appeared to have a little more freedom of choice: perhaps to say yes or no to a given offer, to live in one place rather than another, to marry one person rather than another. But once this choice was made we found ourselves again facing an environment not made to our design or moulded to our interests, and into this we had to fit. It influenced us a great deal, and perhaps we influenced it a little. We got caught in a round of things from which escape was almost impossible. From time to time there came series of events, often seemingly trifling in character, but leading to momentous changes. Perhaps it was a letter, a meeting, an accident, a disease germ, an impulse, but the whole direction of life was changed again. Looking back, they may seem to have been insignificant things, and we exercised no conscious control of the issues.

I remember a young medical officer who had returned after several years of service in the last war, relating to me a remarkable series of experiences which had befallen him. The details do not matter now, and I can only imperfectly recall them. It appeared that in the early years of his active service, he had frequently tried to arrange a transfer here or a change there, or his selection for a particular task. In about half a dozen instances which he detailed one after the other, it was clear in the light of later events that had his wish prevailed, he would almost certainly have lost his life. This came home to him very forcibly at last, and he said to me, "Can you wonder that after this, I attempted no more wangling? I decided that I would accept what would come to me." He might indeed have quoted Wordsworth:

> *I deem that there are powers*
> *Which of themselves our minds impress*
> *That we may feed these minds of ours*
> *On a wise passiveness.*
> *Think you 'mid all this mighty sum*
> *Of things for ever speaking,*
> *That nothing of itself will come*
> *But we must still be seeking.*

In his well-known poem *Into Battle* Julian Grenfell describes the same wise passiveness which is not outwardly very different from Fatalism.

> *Through joy and blindness he shall know,*
> *Not caring much to know, that still*
> *Nor lead nor steel shall reach him, so*
> *That it be not the Destined Will.*

Something which may be described as the Destined Will or Fate, is often at the back of men's minds. Soldiers in the war among falling shells or bombs would say, "It'll get me if my number's on it." The

Mohammedan speaks of the inscrutable Will of Allah. The alternative terminology which appeals more to modern man is to describe it as Chance. This is another way of saying that the causes are inadequately known, and in any case are so numerous that we cannot make any forecast of their outcome.

In 1912 the *Titanic* sank on her maiden voyage across the Atlantic. It struck an iceberg in foggy weather and one thousand four hundred people were drowned. Shall we say that it was the Destined Will, unavoidable and inscrutable, or shall we say that it was the unfortunate result of innumerable natural causes and faulty human judgment which all unwittingly converged on this result? In neither view is it suggested that any of the passengers contributed towards the result except by being there at that place at that time. It happened *to* them and not through them. It was part of the givenness of things. When they chose to travel it was not a *consciously* significant choice, because the resulting issue was not present to them.

Neither by postulating a Destined Will, nor by calling it Chance, do we add anything to our understanding of the event. The term "Destined Will" is simply personalising "that which in fact happens". It may comfort us to think of it as determined by some Power who wills it; but since this Power is inscrutable, we are not explaining anything. Likewise when we use the term Chance, we are admitting that we do not know all the contributing factors (some of which may be free choices by persons), so that once more, this is a label to cover our ignorance. Both views might have substance in them, e.g., a powerful Will might make use of so-called chance factors to effect its purpose. But how can we know?

Is there any other way of looking at events? I think there is, and it is expressed by the Eastern idea of "karma" which is generally linked with the concept of a plurality of lives (see Chapter 14). Karma is really the moral law "Whatsoever a man sows, that shall he also reap" operating on all levels of the world. It says that thoughts and actions sown by a person, will inevitably sometime, somewhere, yield a harvest which returns to the sower. It is not a question of rewards and punishments, but of inevitable consequence. From this viewpoint, what we are determines what happens to us. Events and persons are drawn into our orbit of life by reason of trains of karmic consequence which we have ourselves set going somewhere in our long past. We are masters of our fate and captains of our souls. It is no fate external to ourselves which we have to meet, but always something for which we — regarded as enduring souls — are responsible. At the same time, it has to be recognised that we do not live and never have lived in isolation. We manifest in a web of relationships so that our karma is inter-linked with that of others whom we have influenced, and who have influenced us. We may reap effects which others linked with us have sown, and we may contribute to causal energies which affect others. This view (discussed further in Chapter 14) avoids the incredible supposition that God places one newly created soul in a position of advantage and another in a position of extreme disadvantage, and in effect, tells them both to make the best of it. Undoubtedly the concept of a law of karma is helpful, but it is delusive to imagine that when we supply a new label we resolve our difficulties. It is easy to be glib and say, "It is the working of karma," as though we have provided an all-inclusive explanation. At the same time, the concept is one which makes a contribution of a useful kind, in that it recognises causal chains operating between a series of incarnate lives. That there *is* some kind of karmic pattern in existence for each individual born into the world, is evidenced by the facts of pre-cognition. This is so important, and bears so obviously on the question which heads this chapter, that we shall look at it now before we try to suggest any answer.

KNOWLEDGE OF THE FUTURE

One of the most remarkable conclusions of those who have devoted much study to the mind's lesser-known powers, is that there is a deep level of the self at which what we call the future can be foreseen. Such an idea would, not so very long ago, have been called mere superstition. The laboratory work of Rhine, Tyrrell, Soal, Carington, and many others have put the facts beyond dispute. Long before modern statistical methods and laboratory experiments had established the fact, observers such as Osty and Richet had reached conclusions based upon a lifetime's study of more dramatic data. Since these are of more interest to the reader, I shall give one or two examples to illustrate the subject.

It is familiar knowledge that a good sensitive or medium in trance will frequently "thought-read" the minds of the sitters and give back to them memories, fears, desires, hopes, etc., often not distinguishing their different nature. Occasionally, however, a sensitive appears to establish a deeper rapport, and may present to a person not only reliable data from their memory, but a forecast in considerable detail of things yet to come, where these are of such a nature that no process of inference can account for them.

(1) From *This World and That*, p. 159–60, Payne & Bendit (Faber & Faber Ltd.):

"The swarthy black-eyed woman asked me in the usual way to cross her palm with silver, then she lightly touched my finger-tips for a moment, shut her eyes and poured out a torrent of speech. Her character reading was astonishing; and she mentioned without hesitation a number of incidents in my past life. She was particularly clever in her analysis of my psychic abilities, seeing both their weaknesses and their strength.

"Eventually she began to tell the future. It sounded incredible, not to say impossible. She sketched correctly the kind of professional life I was then living and said it would change radically. 'You will marry a man who is either a doctor, or who is in a profession associated with sharp bright instruments.' She went on adding various details about him. . . . She then foretold a number of events that would lead up to this. Then, guessing my doubts, she said, 'You don't believe me, so I am going to tell you three unimportant things which will come true within the next seven days. When they do, you'll remember what the gypsy said, and you'll see that in the next few years the big things will happen too.'

"She then told me that I should very shortly receive a gift of stones; that I would also be given a ring; and that, on some very stony ground, I should find two sprays of white heather where no other white heather grew.

"I said nothing of all this to my hostess, but that evening while I was dressing for dinner, she came into my room bringing a box of unset cairngorm stones beautifully cut. She said, 'I got these for you last Christmas, but you will remember that I had 'flu and was too ill to send them off. So here they are.'

"Three days later a registered parcel arrived from London. It contained an old ring and a note from a friend who said, 'I meant to leave you this ring in my will, but I don't see why you shouldn't have it now, so I am sending it at once.'

"Then on the fifth day we were out for a picnic, and on our way home, as we went through a desolate pass in the hills, my hostess said, 'There's a fine cairn just at the top of the hill. Let's climb up and have a look at it.' I had nearly reached the top of the rough and stony track when I saw, growing in solitary beauty, two sprays of white heather. There was not another scrap in sight."

Mrs. Bendit says that the larger issues all developed as foretold.

Air-Marshal Sir Victor Goddard who commanded the Royal New Zealand Air Force in 1942–3 has published an account of an adventure of his for the truth of which he vouches. It involves a remarkable precognition in a dream of events which happened within the following forty-eight hours. I give below a much abbreviated form of the main features.

(2) Sir Victor Goddard was in Shanghai in January 1946 about to fly home via Tokyo, Pearl Harbour, and Washington. He was attending a cocktail party in Shanghai, given in his honour on the evening prior to his departure, when he overhead a conversation between two Englishmen behind him. It was something like this.

"I'm very glad this party is really on tonight!"

"Of course, old boy, but why shouldn't it be?"

"Well, wasn't it laid on to welcome Air-Marshal Goddard?"

"It certainly was. What of it?"

"We haven't met him. We never shall. He's dead!"

"Dead? You don't mean that! He couldn't be. Ogden would have put off the party."

"Yes, that's what I thought. But he is dead. Died last night in a crash — hell of a crash. Yes, he was killed — no doubt about that. Not a hope. Bad show!"

Sir Victor turned slowly round to see who was speaking with such conviction, and found that it was a British naval Commander who, glancing up a moment later, and seeing Sir Victor, staggered back as if he had been struck, and made a most profound and confused apology. In reply to questions he said he had had a most vivid dream the night before (or was it this afternoon?) which he could only believe was true. He went into detail. The crash took place on a rocky shingly shore, in the evening and in a snowstorm. He was not sure whether it was in China or Japan, but the plane had been up over the mountains in cloud for quite a long time. The plane was an ordinary sort of transport passenger plane, probably a Dakota. On board, in addition to Air personnel, there had been three civilians (two men and a woman), all English. The Commander gave his name and ship, talked a little about Dunne's book *An Experiment with Time* and hoped that the Air Marshal would not fly for a couple of days at least.

Sir Victor was not unduly perturbed, for he knew that there would only be air-crew on board.

A little later in the evening, the Hon. S. B. who had been given a lift up to Shanghai asked Sir Victor if he could possibly continue on to Tokyo, and this was agreed to. In the evening Sir Victor was the guest at a dinner-party given by the British Consul-General when a servant came up with a radio-message from the British Foreign Office to the latter. It was a request that he should visit the High Commissioner in Tokyo as soon as possible, and he naturally asked the Air-Marshal if he could possibly have a lift. Later in the evening another radio message came for the Consul-General. It was from Tokyo, presuming that he would be coming by air, and asking if he could possibly bring with him a stenographer. . . . It was difficult for Sir Victor to refuse.

They were all on the tarmac early next morning, and the Air-Marshal describes his feelings, which he had necessarily to keep to himself. The weather report was sufficiently good and there was no adequate reason for delay.

The full detail of the flight is not essential. The weather deteriorated far more rapidly than could have been anticipated, and towards evening, with the fuel supply getting rather low, they were in dense cloud and uncertain of their position. There was no radio response from Tokyo, and they circled round pending a decision as to the best course of action. They had been in heavy cloud with only occasional breaks, and it seemed clear that an emergency landing would have to be attempted, if a possible place could be found. They came down low, and after much searching found that only one place seemed even possible. It was a beach of less than three hundred yards of shelving shingle interspersed with rocks. At each end it had black crags and broken rocks. It was a remote chance they were taking, but there was no alternative, and with great good fortune they made a crash-landing in a snowstorm — without serious injury to anyone.

The Air-Marshal wrote a letter to the naval Commander giving him an account of this experience. The letter took a considerable time to catch up with him as his ship was on the move. In reply to a question the Commander said, "No, I can't say that I actually saw you dead, but I certainly thought that the crash was a killer. Glad it wasn't. And I hope you won't blame Dunne for what didn't happen!"

Dr. Eugene Osty has left on record many of the experiments he did with sensitives, several of whom appeared to have a most unusual ability to get in touch with the necessary deep level of the subject's mind, and foretell with accuracy the future pattern of the life. Dr. Osty did not regard his experiences as supporting a rigidly determined future, but says:

"Foreknowledge is variable knowledge, constantly and progressively elaborated; like life, it is evolutionary and living." It is as though at any present time there is a foreseeable future, but that this is not a static unalterable thing. The foreknowledge appears to be less detailed when the event is distant than when it is close, and this is what might be expected if there are limited alternatives depending on free choices of some of the participants in that future. Osty gives an example, which is quoted below.

(3) From *Supernormal Faculties in Man*, p. 175 (Methuen & Co. Ltd.):

"Two years before the event a sensitive had predicted a narrow escape from death for Dr. Osty. 'Oh! peril of death after a while . . . perhaps an accident . . . but you will be saved, your life continues.'

"Four months before the event he was told, 'Take care, you will soon have a serious accident. I hear a violent shock . . . a loud noise . . . you will be very near death. . . . What luck! You will take no hurt. I see a man bleeding on the ground; he is moaning, and all around him some things are strewn, I can't say what.'

"Dr. Osty's account of the event itself is as follows. 'I was going at an easy pace in my car, when a drunken baker driving furiously, pulled the wrong rein and collided. The shock was such that the shafts which struck the frame of the front glass were shivered to pieces, and one wheel mounted the bonnet and crushed it in. My friend — who was with me, and I also, were struck with amaze at the suddenness of the accident, and our good fortune in being unhurt. Turning round we saw the horse galloping off, the cart in the ditch, wheels uppermost, and the baker stretched moaning and bleeding in the middle of the road with a number of loaves of bread scattered round him.' "

Osty remarks that he has himself never come across precognitions of events other than where the person was himself connected with it. In other words he is suggesting that it is not an impersonal future which can be tapped, but the future pattern of a life. The implications of these facts are profound, and we cannot discuss them in any detail here. We must not jump to wrong conclusions and assume that since some things can be precognised therefore everything is predetermined. We have stressed rather that it is a fluid future with which we have to deal: one that is in the making, and to which personal choices contribute. This is perhaps the difference between past and future.

What we are interested in at present is that the fact of precognition demonstrates that there is a life-pattern in existence, and this brings significant evidence to support the ancient idea of karma. It need not be interpreted as a Destined Will imposed upon us, but may more reasonably be regarded as the unfolding destiny which we have created in our past lives and are still creating, in our relationships with others by our words, thoughts, and actions.

KARMA AND FREEDOM

The question "Am I fated or am I free?" is answered by saying that both are true. The large element of "givenness" in life, about which we had no choice, is what has been called karma. We distinguish karma from the fatalistic Destined Will, because the basic thought is that we have ourselves created this karma in our past. There is a principle of continuity linked with the soul of a man, which makes him ultimately the master of his fate. We are constantly influencing the future. Again and again the karmic pattern presents us with points of real choice, and this is where freedom comes in. It is freedom within a living and changing pattern. Such points of moral choice affect the future pattern and are opportunities given to us to progress. We may have failed somewhere in the past to choose wisely: we have taken a wrong turning. So possibly in quite a different setting and outward form the same essential choice is presented to us again and again, until we have wisdom to choose wisely.

It may be helpful to point out that this same intermingling of givenness with freedom is found in all games of skill. There are fixed rules which limit and define a game as cricket, for example, but within this framework the batsmen and bowlers have freedom as to where they will send the ball. Either without rules or without freedom there would be no game of skill.

Freedom is in essence a divine attribute. The ego which is the centre of the soul, has this quality. It is the divine spark which has freedom and, like a seed once sown, it is capable of growth. By right use of it the soul enlarges its freedom at the expense of karma, and the very advanced soul unites those god-like qualities of Love and Wisdom which are found in the perfect man. The perfect man is completely free and is not bound to any karma. The animal-man is tethered by a very short rope, having won no further freedom beyond the original divine endowment (which remains latent). Every right moral choice which we make and act upon enlarges our area of freedom: every wrong choice diminishes it.

Let us return in conclusion to the question of the one thousand four hundred people who lost their lives in the *Titanic* disaster. Was it their karma to do so, or was it truly a chance event which interfered with their karma? It is an impossible question to answer since both "karma" and "chance" are interpretations of happenings which include within themselves factors of which we are ignorant. We do not know the karma of these people, and when we speak of chance we are recognising that the causes contributing were so numerous or little-known that their outcome was unpredictable. We have seen that the facts of precognition support the idea of karma, but we have to remember that no individual's karma is isolated: it is a region of network which includes the karma of many others in it. I find it difficult to suppose that the karma of one thousand four hundred people — men, women, and children — was such that they were all gathered together, as it were, for this particular end to their physical life. In a world where human relationships interact with each other and with physical laws, some souls (and occasionally many souls) suffer because of the ignorance, errors, or foolishness of other souls, and because physical laws are what they are. The principle of karma may be broadly true without any compulsion to assume that this ending of life was necessarily a part of their soul's karma. It may have been an unintended interference with the pattern. We must not, however, allow physical tragedy to loom too large in our thinking, as it must to the materialist. From a higher and truer viewpoint we can appreciate the relative unimportance of such events which affect the physical body, in a universe where immortal souls are all that really matter.

Karma and chance (in this sense) may both be true. We must beware of treating possibilities as though they necessarily excluded each other. Above all, in such speculative fields as these we must avoid being dogmatic.

Chapter

5

WHY DO MEN SUFFER?

The Infinite Being is not complete if He remains absolutely infinite. He must realise Himself through the finite; that is, through creation. The impulse to realise comes from the fullness of joy; but the process must be through pain. You cannot ask why it should be — why the Infinite should attain truth by passing through the finitude; why the joy should be the cause of suffering, in order to come back to itself — for it is so. And when our minds are illumined, we feel glad that it is so.

When we fix all our attention to that side of the Infinite where it is pain and death, where it is the process of fulfilment, we are overwhelmed. But we must know that there is the positive side; that always there is a completeness along with the incomplete. Otherwise, there would be no pity in us for the suffering: no love in us for the imperfect.

. . . But this much we have known, that there is a love which is greater in truth than pain and death. Is not that sufficient for us?

Rabindranath Tagore
(*Letters to a Friend*, p. 65)

SUFFERING is universal, and perhaps its constitutes man's chief problem. Men look at the world as the Buddha looked at it two thousand five hundred years ago, and are often inclined to agree with his judgment, "All existence is Sorrow." There is suffering in birth and in death, and between these events few people can claim to be long free from it. The pageant of Nature in which living creatures prey on each other and must do so to live, adds to the perplexity of those who think about life and seek to justify the ways of God to man. The anguish of millions of people in Europe who were separated in the last war from those they loved, and often never knew their fate, is a vast pyramid of suffering which cries to Heaven and challenges man, if he can, to believe in a loving God. While there are beauty and love in this world — and we can never forget them — the problem of suffering demands our best thinking if the human situation is not to lead us towards pessimism and despair.

At the beginning it is necessary to point out that pain and suffering are not the same thing. Pain belongs to the physical body; suffering belongs to the mind. Pain has a function to fulfil in that it provides a warning that something has gone wrong with the body's organisation: thus it offers us useful information. Having served us in this way, pain is rightly regarded as an evil from which to escape, and a man may do so through pain-killing drugs, through hypnosis, or through medical or surgical aid. Suffering is a state of the mind, not *necessarily* connected with pain. There may be no pain of the body, but suffering may be acute. On the other hand, a person may be in pain with or without suffering. We usually consider, however, that where pain is intense or prolonged it will give rise to suffering, because the mind's attention tends to be anchored to the body's pain. The mind is then unable to live its normal life of thinking and feeling, and this deprivation leads to a feeling of isolation and loneliness, which we shall find to be of the essence of suffering. Pain presents man with its own problems and we shall look at these first, so that we can set them aside and look at the problems of suffering itself.

THE PROBLEM OF PAIN

We have to face the fact that because we are souls incarnate in physical bodies, we have to meet and endure the hazards inseparable from physical existence. These hazards take many forms: accident, disease, lightning, storms, earthquakes, floods, etc. Such events of the physical world may bring pain and death to man, but we should not blame God for this except in so far as we presume to claim that the physical embodiment of souls was itself unjustifiable and deplorable.

If lightning strikes a man, electricity is only doing what it is compelled to do by the laws of its own nature, viz., it is seeking the path of least resistance as it runs to earth. It is because there are such laws, reliable laws, that all the harnessing of electricity to the service of man has been made possible.

Similar remarks apply equally to all the processes of Nature which are evident in storms, earthquakes, floods, etc. The extreme winds which we describe as a storm are the inevitable result of physical laws which are operating all the time. These maintain the world in a physical condition which makes life possible upon it. If law were capricious and unreliable, the body of knowledge which we describe as science could never have been acquired, and human life — if it were possible — would be far more hazardous. So long as we possess physical bodies and live in a physical world, we must accept as inevitable the risks and hazards consequent upon that fact.

There are many people who share this view, but are troubled by the problems which disease raises. Different types of disease are too numerous for us to look at them all, but let us take cancer and malaria in order to see what sort of problems they raise in men's minds. The cause or causes of cancer are still unknown in spite of an enormous amount of research. When the discovery of them has been made, we may surmise that treatment and prevention of cancer will quickly follow, and mankind will have been delivered from one of its greatest scourges. We know that in cancer the processes of growth and cell-division which are normally under control, have got out of control. The physiological conditions which govern the growth and multiplication of cells are every bit as fundamental in the world of living things, as are those physical laws which we have been talking of, which make for the inhabitability of the physical world. We know rather less about the physiological laws than the physical ones, so that it is not possible yet to describe the precise conditions which cause uncontrolled growth. But even when we can do so, may we not expect cancer to be a hazard in the world of cells, in the same way that we expect lightning, storm, and flood to be hazards in the physical world against which complete protection is impossible? Someone may say that the world could have been made otherwise, presumably that we might all have been born with knowledge equal to coping with every hazard and contingency. This possibility is doubtless a pleasant exercise of the imagination; but the beings in such a world could not be human beings like ourselves. In the only world we know, no aspect of knowledge has been inherited. We are endowed with certain instruments of knowledge, with curiosity to seek for knowledge, and with the power to make our own discoveries.

If we consider those types of disease which are due to invading micro-organisms, we may take malaria as an example. The malarial parasite must have slain millions of people, and it still causes widespread illness. It may be said that the particular mosquito which carries it is one which the world could well have done without. "Why did the Creator permit such things?" says the ordinary man. I don't think he pictures the Creator as releasing creatures into the world from time to time, regardless of whether they are pleasant or noxious to humanity; but in a general way, he assumes that an all-powerful Creator might have exercised a discriminatory veto in the evolutionary process, in the interests of man.

The process called evolution by which more advanced types of creature arose from simpler forms, is clearly one in which there was inherent, from the beginning, a basic element of freedom to develop, subject to certain underlying laws. This is clear when we look at the process. We see "Nature" trying out experiments. Some of them were failures and perished. Some provided valuable information, aiding the development of other better types. Successful methods were remembered and used; failures were in future avoided. Throughout the whole process we can observe an element of freedom which has extended right down to the lowliest organisms — and, as we go up the scale, is most marked in man.

It is possible to imagine a world in which all would go well for a privileged being in it because no alternative was present. It would be a very different world from ours; its inhabitants would not be human beings; and its coming-to-be would not be by evolution. It is man's own freedom to choose, and the effort he has had to make to gather knowledge, which have made possible his growth of character. Without these conditions he would not have been human: with these conditions, he has god-like potentiality. As we know only too well, man has misused his freedom and brought upon himself untold pain and suffering. The same freedom in lesser degrees runs through the whole range of creation, and this also has led to abuses and the conflict of interests between man and some of these creatures. We should bear in mind, however, that although some micro-organisms are inimical both to man's welfare and that of other creatures, by far the majority of micro-organisms play a beneficent part in the total scheme of Nature. Indeed, man himself could not live on the planet without the services of some of them.

We have to pay a price for freedom and this price is the possibility of suffering and pain. There is no problem here for the man who does not believe in freedom or in God. For the man who does, his problem consists in reconciling this kind of world with a God of Love. He may be able to effect this reconciliation if he can (1) come to realise that the experience of earth is leading to some august destiny which will justify the travail of the way, and (2) come to realise that this God of Love is not a powerful Being outside the experiment, but is Himself deeply involved within it. The roots of suffering therefore go down into the ultimate reasons for Creation.

Why Do Men Suffer?

Let us now look at that distressful state of mind which we call suffering. Its most characteristic feature is that the self feels lonely and isolated. Consider some of the ways in which suffering may arise. We shall begin with some lesser ways and pass on to others of an overwhelming kind.

(1) *Loss of Possessions*. In a physical world such as ours, it is natural that men should seek to possess things. Psychologists talk of an acquisitive instinct, which doubtless led primitive man to store food and skins against a time when they would be unobtainable. In this we can see an instinct subserving the end of man's preservation. The desire to acquire has, of course, run to extremes in our society, so that there is no longer the issue of survival involved, but the satisfaction of security, pleasure, and power. Shall we say then that the person who takes pleasure today in owning an attractive house, a beautiful garden, some good pictures or an extensive library of books or records is a low fellow? Something depends on how we came to possess them, but everything depends on *how* we possess them. Are we attached to them to such an extent that they are an extension of our personality which we could not do without, or do we sit lightly to them, and are we glad to share them? If we are *attached* to them, we suffer if they are taken away. If we can enjoy them without attachment, then our serenity is unchanged if we lose them. It was a clear recognition that suffering arises because people are attached to things which pass away which formed one of the bases of the Buddha's teaching. It was the same note which Christ struck when He said, "Lay not up for yourselves treasures on Earth, where moth and rust do corrupt and thieves break through and steal . . . for where your treasure is, there will your heart be also." In spite of these ascetic notes, neither Gautama nor Jesus advocated asceticism: both took, and pointed to, a middle path.

There is a story told of the Buddha, that there came to see him a man of great wealth and also great philanthropy, to ask whether he would not be wiser to give his wealth completely away and don the yellow robe. Seeing his sincerity the Buddha said, "I say unto thee, remain in thy station in life, and give thyself with diligence to thine enterprises. It is not life and wealth and power that enslave men: it is their attachment to life and wealth and power."

Likewise there is a story told of a young man of integrity but with

69

great possessions, who came to consult Jesus as to the wise course. Seeing that he was attached to his possessions, the advice given to him was, "One thing thou lackest, sell that thou hast and give to the poor, and come, follow Me." He went away sorrowful: the demand was too high.

(2) *Destruction of Work.* Few people can face the apparent destruction of that which they have laboured to create, with equanimity. In a passage of great insight, the famous Hindu classic the *Gita*, says, "Your concern is with action, but not with the fruits thereof." In effect, it is saying that all right deeds and actions should be performed by men as an offering to God — for no other reason than that they are right. The doer should neither be elated by success nor depressed by failure. The person who is attached to results is like the person who is attached to things. Both pass away, and their passing brings suffering.

In his biography of Edward Grey of Fallodon,* British Secretary for Foreign Affairs in the years preceding the first world war, G. M. Trevelyan tells of the many misfortunes which came to him in the last quarter of life. He was a countryman at heart, but a deep sense of public duty held him captive to the dusty ways of Westminster. When he left office he was too blind and ill to enter into the life which he loved. In 1906 Grey had lost, through an accident, his first wife, to whom he was deeply devoted. In 1922 he married again, but after six years his second wife died. In the same year his brother Charles was killed by a buffalo in Africa. Trevelyan continues:

"And besides these private strokes, Grey lived to see his hopes for the pacification of the world shattered, America withdrawn into herself, Europe armed to the teeth, and Germany under the Nazi regime. He foresaw a grim future for mankind, the more so as he had less than no sympathy with the increasing mechanisation of life.

"But his private afflictions and public disappointments never broke his courage or soured his serene and constant spirit. Neither in his letters nor in his talk was there any cry of personal pain or even of impatience. He was unfailing in his quiet humorous observation of life, and his determination to make the daily best of what was left. All who saw him went away cheered and elevated by the strong even current of his talk, delightful, easy, humorous, sustained without effort, high above the level of his griefs."

* *Grey of Fallodon*, G. M. Trevelyan (Longmans Green & Co. Ltd.).

(3) *The death of Loved Ones.* The death of someone we love removes from us their physical form, and leaves us feeling bereft and sad. So long as we are incarnate beings who have therefore to be concerned with the physical world, this sense of loss is inevitable, although it need not be fraught with suffering. It is important to come to terms with death before we are compelled to face it for ourselves or in others. If love is of the body alone, no immortality of love can be expected. But if love is an energy of the deeper self, sustaining relationships between one soul and another, it is essentially untouched by death, or by any separation of the two bodies. A mother loves her baby, she loves the toddler, she loves the growing child, the adolescent, the youth, the mature adult, and so on; but in each new appearance which is so precious to the mother, the former appearance is lost. What does she really love? If it is the outward form, one would expect the process of the child's growing up to be a strange mixture of sorrow and happiness. This is not the case because the mother knows it is the *same* person whatever outward changes take place. If the logic of this is fully realised, we can see that love does not belong to the outer form, but is attached to this only because it is the present expression of the underlying person or soul. The real bond is a relationship of souls, and this lies behind the physical level. No one need fear that in the after-death state he will be cut off from those for whom he feels deep affection.

(4) *Loss of Hope.* In the old legend of Pandora's box, it will be recalled that the forbidden lid was opened, and all the evils and troubles that afflict mankind were released from their captivity. The lid was quickly shut again, but only one creature remained in the box, and this was Hope. If hope is lost, then indeed all joy has gone out of existence and there is nothing to live for. It is into these depths that some men and women sink, feeling alone, cut off from all who might understand, in utter darkness and despair. This is suffering of an acute and tragic kind.

(5) *Loss of God.* Assuming the existence of God (*vide* Chapter 3), such loss is intrinsically impossible, but the feeling may be real enough in a man's darkest hour. It is acute suffering to feel cut off from communion with one's fellows, and have to face in one's own soul a sadness that cannot be shared: but so long as a man can hold on to some faith in God, he cannot be wholly in despair (the story of Job commands our admiration because he was just such a man). There

appears, however, to be a darkness of the soul in which even this can vanish, and then we meet suffering in its most acute form. The suffering of Christ on his cross was such that apparently He felt utterly forsaken, even by the Father who had been so real to him throughout His life. The same sense of utter desolation has been described by some mystics who have called it "the dark night of the soul". They have known great spiritual heights, and the depths they are then called to face seem the blacker by contrast. Memory and reason seem to be no help in this desolation. All is lost except for some faint whisper of the inmost self which bids it hold on. The soul does not know that this also is God.

WHAT IS SUFFERING?

We have looked at some causes of suffering. There may be others, but the examples given cover in their range of intensity all that human nature can meet. They have in common a sense of isolation. The soul feels partially or completely cut off from man and God. The emotions are in turmoil and reason fails to help much except in the minor forms of suffering.

Linked with the fact of suffering are some of man's deepest problems. Is it inevitable that man should suffer? What ends does it serve? How should we meet it? Is the world just? Why did Christ suffer? We shall try to suggest answers to these questions in the next few pages.

It is significant that just as the soul's sense of isolation and loneliness is the basic cause of suffering, the converse truth is that in the ecstasy and bliss of mystical experience the soul has the sense of belonging to a great unity. The range of suffering between acute suffering and mystical bliss seem to be bound up with an individual's measure of awareness of his relationship to the Whole — to God, or what I have described elsewhere as the Divine Society.* To feel cut off from this is suffering: to feel united with this is bliss.

I think the great poet and mystic Tagore, was expressing this truth when he said:†

"When we do not see ourselves in the Infinite, when we imagine our sorrow to be our very own, then life becomes untrue and its burden

* *Watcher on the Hills*, p. 28 (Hodder and Stoughton Ltd., 1959).
† *Letters to a Friend*, p. 80 (George Allen and Unwin, 1928).

becomes heavy. I understand more and more the truth of Buddha's teaching that the root of all our miseries is this self-consciousness. We have to realise the consciousness of the All, before we can solve the mystery of pain and be free."

Many devout people have held views about the relationship of God to suffering, which are impossible to maintain in the face of facts. We should clear away these ideas first.

(1) Belief in a kindly Providence who protects from harm those who trust in Him, and is relatively unconcerned about others. There is no justification of any kind for the Psalmist's view, so palpably contradicted by the experience of life:

"A thousand shall fall at thy side, and ten thousand at thy right hand, but it shall not come nigh thee. Only with thine eyes shalt thou behold and see the reward of the wicked. . . . There shall no evil befall thee, neither shall any plague come nigh thy tent. . . ."

The Psalmist was living in a world of make-believe with the notion of a tribal God, to whom he attributed the all too human weakness of protecting his friends (the good), and letting his enemies (the wicked) take what was coming to them. In this life there is no reliable relationship between goodness and freedom from suffering on the one hand, and wickedness and inevitable suffering on the other. What sort of goodness or morality would it be which was built upon enlightened self-interest? I believe there is a profound principle of justice or karma which undergirds the world, and results sometime, somewhere, in the return to the thinker or doer of the consequences of his activities, but this bears no resemblance whatever to the Psalmist's conception.

(2) Belief that pain and suffering are sent by God as a discipline or test of character. Such an idea (obviously contradicting the one we have just discussed) is equally erroneous. It is prepared to attribute to God activities which, if they were perpetrated by men, would be regarded as callous, malevolent, and deserving of condemnation. What about children born with imperfect bodies and brains, or children struck down by disease from which they suffer pain and slowly die? Are these tests of character? The falsity of such a view is evident from the praise we give to the efforts of medical science to eliminate

such pain and suffering, and from the satisfaction we all feel when new advances are made.

(3) The belief that suffering is a consequence of sin or wrong-doing. This is one of those dangerous generalisations which contain both truth and error. We have already affirmed our belief in a principle of moral justice in the world, in the light of which some pain and suffering are linked with sins and mistakes. But it is equally true that it would be ridiculous to ascribe it all to this origin. If a liner sinks or if two trains collide and hundreds of people are injured and killed, why should we suppose that such events have necessarily a moral cause within the sufferers? We know that some suffering arises through love. Noble souls have often taken suffering upon themselves in order to help others to reach firm ground again. So long as souls are related to each other in bonds of love, this sympathy must always hold within itself the potentiality of suffering as well as of joy. If a wiser soul is compelled to stand aside and watch another taking the wrong path, this is a situation fraught with suffering for the former. St. Paul recognised this when he wrote, "Love suffereth long and is kind."

THE DEEPER CAUSES OF SUFFERING

A view which is widely held and often expressed is that it is difficult to reconcile the suffering of the world with its control by a God of Love. The underlying assumption is generally, that being an omnipotent Being, God could have made things differently had He chosen to do so. We have already discussed this view and shall briefly reiterate our position. Doubtless the Creator of the Universe has set going a great variety of experiments in the evolution and growth of consciousness. On our Earth, He has given us, within limits, the power to develop our latent possibilities in freedom. True freedom is necessarily freedom to go wrong as well as to go right. Few people who have thought seriously about the alternatives would wish it to be different. J. S. Mill once said, "No one would choose to become a cow, even if he would be a perfectly happy cow." It is the accumulated consequences of "going wrong" which have made the fear-ridden, anxious, sick world we live in.

Let us remember that the most significant consequence of misusing our freedom is that we become isolated within the growing walls of self: we cut ourselves off from the great Unity of the whole, which is

God. Suffering is inherent in this, and perhaps it is a merciful provision which we often forget. I have just used a phrase, "The great Unity of the Whole" to remind us that God is not some absent Power far above His creation. This is an aspect of the truth, of which the complementary aspect is that He has also partly sunk His Being *in* creation. Man, Nature, and God are all bound together at a deep level, so that the welfare of any part affects the welfare of the Whole. There is no completely isolated suffering and no completely isolated joy. The human experiment is one in which we cannot contract out of this Commonwealth of unlimited liability. In the great drama of human life there are, broadly speaking, two kinds of people: those who *care* for others and those who are indifferent. The former give themselves in self-forgetful service along the road of suffering to help others to arrive. This is redemptive work. The world has seen this from time to time in figures of heroic stature, but the greater part of it is unknown and unrecorded. Such souls, known and unknown, are the salt of the earth, and without their continuing efforts among us the world would long ago have run to destruction.

There is a remarkable passage in the New Testament which reads: "For it became Him, for Whom are all things, and through Whom are all things, in bringing many sons unto glory, to make the author of their salvation perfect through sufferings." It is remarkable because it expresses the insight that without suffering there cannot be perfection for human beings. The fullest sensitivity to God, the most intimate relationship with the Whole, can be known only by those who have known what it means to feel cut off from it. What was true of so great a figure as Jesus, is true also of ourselves. In a poem *The Man to the Angel*, George Russell (A.E.) pictures the man saying:

> *They are but the slaves of light*
> *Who have never known the gloom*
> *And between the dark and bright*
> *Willed in freedom their own doom.*

> *Pure one, from your pride refrain:*
> *Dark and lost amid the strife*
> *I am myriad years of pain*
> *Nearer to the fount of life.*

Chapter

6

IS THERE ANY TRUTH IN BEING
"SAVED" OR "LOST"?

I will arise and go to my father, and will say unto him, Father, I have sinned
against heaven, and in thy sight: I am no more worthy to be called thy son:
make me as one of thy hired servants. And he arose, and came to his father.
But while he was yet afar off, his father saw him, and was moved with
compassion, and ran, and fell on his neck, and kissed him . . . and said
let us eat and make merry and be glad, for this my son was dead, and is alive
again; he was lost, and is found.

Luke xv

THERE has grown up within the Christian Church a terminology which
must be practically meaningless to the outsider. Whether it has
meaningful content for most of those who use it, is another matter.
One of these terms is "salvation", which is presumably a state of
being "saved". But saved from what?

The language of piety has strange emotional tones, so that while
a member of the Church of England might feel some embarrassment
if he were asked, "Are you saved?" a member of the Salvation Army
would probably reply enthusiastically, "Yes, glory be to God.
Hallelujah." The term *salvation* has been spoiled by fervent evangelists
who have always supposed that people were to be found only in two
categories, the saved and the lost, and that their own success was
measured by the number of transfers they could effect from the latter
category to the former. How simple to see the world in black and white!
How satisfying to be the bearer of good tidings to the souls of men that
whereas they were lost and would perish (if indeed they did not linger
for ever in the torments of hell), now, by affirming their faith in Jesus
Christ, they could be sure of the joys of heaven! This sort of nonsense
has done more harm to Christianity than can be easily be computed.
It has alienated not merely persons of ordinary intelligence but also
persons of ordinary kindliness. Organised Christianity has in fact
suffered far more from those who imagined they were its friends than
those who believed they were its enemies.

In the books of the New Testament we find the terms "saved" and
"salvation" in frequent use and meaning something definite to the

users. St. Paul affirmed that his work and preaching were motivated by the hope "if I might save some of them". Jesus used the term when He described His own life-work, "The Son of Man came to seek and to save that which was lost." Used in this context, the term appears to describe a state of spiritual wakefulness and aspiration in contrast with one of spiritual blindness and absorption in the material order of existence.

The term is also used in connection with sin or sinners, as when Paul declared that "Christ came into the world to save sinners". If it is clearly recognised that the state of sinning is really a "lostness" or alienation from God, the two senses in which the term is used converge. As this recognition is not general there is a popular but wrong conception of the term. A logically minded person asks "to save sinners from *what?*" The answer is obviously not "saved from further sinning". This would be manifestly untrue as a matter of experience. Equally untrue would it be to say "saved from the consequences of sin". When trains of consequence are set going on the physical level, these are frequently irreversible. Fervent evangelists would probably wish us to believe that the answer is "saved from hell", but this view is unsupported by the attitude of Jesus, and today, evangelists who present the medieval picture of a hell where an offended deity punishes the wicked are rightly laughed at. There may be hell in some states of mind, but this is not the hell which they and their predecessors, as guardians of morality, have portrayed with such fervour. If we hope to find meaning in the term "salvation" we must find it in different ideas to these.

Enlightened Christianity lays emphasis on sin because its chief and most tragic consequence is this, that it raises a barrier between man and God so that communion is no longer even possible. Enlightened Buddhism lays emphasis on ignorance: ignorance by man of his true nature, by which he is cut off from Divine being. The sin is ignorance, and the ignorance is sin. Salvation has meaning in relation to such a state, whether the Saviour is Jesus Christ, or Gautama the Buddha, or Socrates, or many another who in some degree has opened blind eyes. What men need to be saved from is the pervading sense of futility and meaninglessness, from ultimate despair as the things they crave for turn to dust and ashes. Jesus described Himself as having come "to seek and to save that which was lost". Are not most individuals, and humanity as a whole, in that bewildered

77

state of spiritual ignorance most simply described by the term "lost". Is there any widespread sense of a spiritual goal? Do men know where their busy living is leading them to — for what destiny they are bound? On the contrary, they are for the most past lost in material existence and superstition, bemused by the delusions of mortal life, lacking in any sense that this business of earthly life is a fragment of a meaningful pattern.

The teaching of Jesus to His age and ours, rightly understood, offers a way of salvation to men. It offers meaning and value to life because it relates it to a spiritual order, which Jesus called the Kingdom of God, meaning, the rule or reign of God in the hearts of men. Although His teaching embodied virtually nothing about man's further destiny or the specific part in it that terrestrial existence was designed to serve, it could have left no doubt in the minds of those whose ears were opened, that human beings with their problems were very dear to the Heavenly Father Who cared for them in all their joys and sorrows. The luminous quality of His own life spoke to them in a language they could understand. He disclosed the Eternal in the present moment of Time — the only point at which it can ever be apprehended. He unveiled for His own and for succeeding generations the spiritual possibilities of every man. When he referred to Himself in the third person it was as the Son of Man — an older and wiser Son, no doubt, but still, one of the family of Man.

He taught many things in parables about the Kingdom of God. It is within men. It does not draw attention to itself. It works like leaven. It is the treasure most worth possessing. In an interview given to the friendly and admiring Jewish teacher Nicodemus, He said to him that unless a man was born anew he shouldn't expect to see the Kingdom of God. Unless in fact he was born both physically *and* spiritually, he couldn't enter into it. The account suggests that Nicodemus was somewhat mystified, but Jesus left him little room for misunderstanding. "Listen to the wind, Nicodemus. Its origin and destination are alike unknown to you. It is not under your control: you cannot see it with the eye of sense, but you cannot deny its effects and operations here. You are aware of its effects. In the same way there is a world of spiritual Reality, wrapped in ultimate mystery to you. You cannot see it: you know nothing of its beginnings or its goal, but you cannot deny its effects and operation. The man who is spiritually awake knows this well." Natural man knows the physical world through his physical senses: he *cannot* know the spiritual world unless his spiritual senses are awakened. When this happens it is as dramatic and significant as physical birth. In a few sentences Jesus presented a commentary on the state of mankind which every great religion describes in its own way. Buddhism speaks, for example, of "entering on the stream".

The fact is that a man may be competent and distinguished in the eyes of the world and yet be a person in whom no flicker of awareness of the spiritual world has ever arisen. Such a man may be described as once-born. Another man who has even momentarily glimpsed a spiritual order can never be content thereafter to remain as before. His outlook has been changed by that glimpse, so that however slow his response he is aware that he must one day follow to its source the gleam he has had. The gleam may have been very transient, "small as a grain of mustard seed" in the words of a parable, but its consequences are as significant as those of birth. The existence of a new world has been disclosed to him. He is no longer "lost": he is at least saved from aimlessness and futility.

It is all simply portrayed in what is perhaps the world's best known short story — the parable of the Prodigal Son. In effect Jesus said to men, "God is like that Father".

SALVATION BY FAITH?

I do not think it is necessary to strain after a definition of faith. The ordinary person knows what faith is, through having exercised it in many situations of life. He exercised faith when he made some choice and acted upon it, even though reason could not demonstrate its correctness. He has had to show faith in the expert (perhaps a physician or surgeon) when he was impotent to act or decide. He has had to trust a person when no proof of his honesty or competence was possible. Broadly speaking *faith is an attitude involving commitment of one's self where there is no rational security; it is an attitude of confidence sustained by the higher intuitional levels of one's self.*

There is a theological doctrine expressed in the phrase "salvation by faith", the content of which is popularly understood to mean that salvation is secured by an individual who has faith in Jesus Christ. The basis of the doctrine is in such Pauline texts as, "Believe on the Lord Jesus Christ and thou shalt be saved," and "By grace are ye saved through faith; and that not of yourselves: it is the gift of God, not of works, that no man should glory."* Unfortunately the simple and intelligible conception of faith in Jesus Christ as being a total and voluntary commitment to His spirit is not at all what most theologians mean by this doctrine. The ordinary man has a good idea what Studdert-Kennedy meant when he described faith as "betting one's life there's a God", but I am sure he recoils mystified from Tillich's statement, "Faith is a total and centred act of the personal self, the act of unconditional, infinite, and ultimate concern."

I must ask the reader's patience while I try to expound in a few sentences what most modern theologians mean by faith. It has been suggested to me that Bishop Gustaf Aulén might be taken as a fair representative and where I use quotation marks below, they are from his books.† As he uses the term faith it is always to be taken as synonymous with "Christian faith" which is directed towards God through Christ. It is not, as one might suppose, an expression of man's attitude to God. That is only a subsidiary part of faith. Apparently the primary feature of the relationship of God and man is God's revelation of Himself in Christ, and according to Aulén, this "dominates and subdues a man" so that for him "God is the centre in which life is dominated by God alone". If this man "turns and commits himself to God" this is the response. This response to God's initial act constitutes the theologian's *faith*. If one points out that if "God dominates and subdues" a man it is paradoxical to talk of a free responsible "yes"; we are told that "the divine revelation can only be apprehended by the eye of faith". Aulén specifically says, "Faith is altogether a work of God, but it is at the same time man's choice and decision." This sort of paradox (and there are many such, which apparently constitute the content of Christian Faith) is described as "religious" paradox, in contrast with metaphysical or logical paradox. It is thereby regarded as being immune to criticism, for if you cannot accept it you lack the "eye of faith".

To the reasonable person it is obvious that if God does everything then man does nothing, and the last vestige of what is ordinarily understood as faith has gone. By such a view the whole onus is put on to God. We are back at a Calvinistic doctrine of election which is wholly incompatible with the teaching of Jesus and God's love for all men. The basic fallacy arises from having no right understanding of

* Ephesians ii. 8.   † *The Faith of the Christian Church* (S.C.M. Press).

the structure of Man. Aulén chooses to regard man as a being wholly separate and different from God with no divine spark within, no latent divinity, no immortal soul. He is inherently "lost" in his inner nature and can do nothing about it. It is thus an act of pure grace that God enters into human life to redeem it.

We reject this view of Man (see Chapter 11) as apparently the writer of the Epistle to the Romans did when he wrote, "The Spirit himself beareth witness with our spirit that we are children of God; and if children, then heirs; heirs of God and joint-heirs with Christ." A conception of Man as related to a divine centre within himself, in which God is immanent, eliminates all these so-called "religious" paradoxes. Let us consider one or two others to illustrate the point.

Aulén says, "God stands as a judge in a radical opposition to sin, but at the same time enters into communion with sinful man." With the recognition of the divine spark within, this is no paradox. Tennyson could write of man:

> *He ever bears about*
> *A silent court of justice in his breast*
> *Himself the judge and jury, and himself*
> *The prisoner at the bar.*

On this view, when a man sins the barrier is raised between the divine spark within and the lower levels of himself. He has cut himself off from the divine centre (the "Father" of the parable). It is not without significance that in the parable of the Prodigal Son no mention is made of judgment. The prodigal judges himself: he has cut himself off from the Father. When he is yet a great way off, but returning, his Father sees him and runs to meet him. There is no mention of rebuke, only of compassion. The phrase of Aulén's, "God stands as a judge", is too anthropomorphic. It smacks of Jewish legalism rather than Christ's teaching.

Take another of these so-called religious paradoxes, "It is obvious to faith both that divine power *is* sovereign and that it is engaged in a continuous struggle under historical conditions against that which is opposed to it." Suppose we recognise the divine spark of God as immanent in man, then man's heart is the battle-field of this continuous struggle between higher and lower. Accepting the divine power as power of Love, we can believe both in its sovereignty and yet in its continuous conflict with the lower self, because there are some methods which Love cannot use. It must respect the freedom of another to choose for itself. To return to the parable of the Prodigal Son, the Father in spite of his love, exercised no restraint upon the prodigal's journey to the far country. If his heart and mind were already there what virtue was preserved by keeping him at home? The Father's love remained sovereign even when to outward appearances it was defeated — for it won in the end. The Divine Love respects man's freedom to choose his way.

With the strange conception of faith expounded by Aulén, based upon a wrong view of Man's structure, we must reject the doctrine of salvation by faith. If we are prepared to take the more general and popular view of Christian faith that it is an act of total commitment to the spirit of Jesus Christ of one's life, then it is indisputable that this has been for very many all down the ages, a Way of Salvation. But to proclaim this as a dogma, as of necessity the *only* Way is to offend against the spirit of Jesus Himself. If it were true it would lead us to say that non-Christian people of the world, no matter how great their spirituality or saintliness, were among the "lost". This is nonsense. Whatever theory one may hold about salvation, this at least is fact: the great saints and mystics are not confined to any one religious tradition. They appear in many traditions, and are beyond the point where labels matter. Many roads converge on the Mount of God, and the travellers along these many roads are expressions of the One Spirit.

THE STRUCTURE OF MAN

The nature and structure of Man will probably engage man's interest and enquiry long after the chief questions about the physical world have been answered. As long as Christian theology ignores such help as is now available from the fields of Jungian psychology, psychical research, and mysticism, in understanding man's nature, it will continue to wallow in "religious" paradoxes. We have presented in Chapter 11 an outline of a suggested structure which is based upon evidence from these fields. At this point we are merely concerned to suggest that it offers a much more satisfactory basis for understanding what salvation may mean. If the reader will turn to p. 142 he will see that men must be recognised as participating in many levels which are all Real in differing degrees. Such levels are not clearly defined nor are they separate: we are dealing with a whole, but to try and understand the many functions of this whole, we have attempted this crude analysis. The physical level is the lowest expression of Reality, as far as we know, but it is not *un*real. The central point of individuality labelled "ego", in virtue of which we may be described as children of God, is an exiled spark of the divine level labelled Spirit. By its exile it establishes a new centre of selfhood, but it is no longer *consciously* a part of the great Self or Spirit. In the mystical experience of Unity of which we had some examples in Chapter 3 there is temporarily a conscious awareness by the ego of its true nature. The "channel" between Ego and Spirit, normally closed, is open in mystical experience (the Spirit itself beareth witness with our spirit that we are children of God).

Ordinary man, "once-born", absorbed in the interests of material existence, is in a state of blindness as to his true nature. To describe this state of lostness, Gerald Heard has used the phrase "strangulated consciousness", and this strangulation is presumably somewhere on the mental level at that point where the permanent soul and the transient personality can be distinguished. The soul is then largely cut off from an effective link with the personality except through the lower mind which interprets the data of the senses. This is the state of lostness of men who are immersed in the futile and unsatisfying pattern of mere physical existence, and suppose that this is all there is to life. To emerge from this state the first step is a realisation of one's lostness, a yearning leading to an aspiration by the personality to contact the soul. The way of ascent which makes for wholeness, or the removal of this "strangulation" is expressed in a different terminology in different religions, but the underlying process is the same. Hinduism offers the various yogas; Christianity offers prayer, moral discipline, and loving service; Buddhism recommends non-attachment to the world and the practice of the noble eight-fold path, and so on. This wholeness of soul and personality (Jung's process of Individuation) can be achieved by man's effort, but mystical experience and *a fortiori* a permanent state of Illumination is a grace of the Spirit. When this latter state is reached the Ego is no longer only a centre of individuality: it is the perfect instrument of the Spirit, surrendered to its greater purposes. Egotism has gone though the Ego remains. "I live, yet no longer I, but Christ liveth in me," said St. Paul.

83

None of us lives in isolation. On all levels of ourselves we have possibilities of communication. We influence others and are influenced by them. In terms of the diagram on p. 142 we may say that separateness is at its maximum on the physical level where two bodies cannot occupy the same space at the same time. As we pass up the scale of Reality, relationship and inter-penetration become increasingly important factors. It may well be that on some of these higher levels the great helpers of mankind are making their greatest contribution to our welfare.

THE NATURE OF SIN

The term "sin" is peculiarly a religious one and implies that man has some relationship to God which is impaired by the act of sinning. This relationship, for the ancient Jews, was very much a legal one. The law of God was contained in the books of Moses and the Prophets. Offences against these laws were a matter of constant concern to them and appropriate expiation for offences, consisting of rituals and sacrifices, were a large element in their ordinary life. There was a marked obsessional character in all this religiosity, and the burden placed upon people was so oppressive that Jesus, in a mood of compassion, once said, "Take my yoke upon you and learn of me: for I am meek and lowly in heart; and ye shall find rest unto your souls, for my yoke is easy and my burden is light."

The disciples of Jesus, Paul and other leaders of the early Church, found it very hard to rise above their Jewish background to the universal and timeless teaching which Jesus gave them. Although He reminded them that "no man putteth new wine into old wine-skins lest the wine will burst the skins", this very activity cannot fail to be noticed in the writings of the New Testament. John the Baptist is reported to have said of Jesus, "Behold the *Lamb* of God that taketh away the sin of the world." This was clearly the beginning of a theory intended to bridge Jewish customs and Christian belief. No one pursued the process of theorising more vigorously than St. Paul, and the theologians of the Church have continued ever since. The old Jewish wine-skins still have an air of sacredness about them, and are still being patched.

A number of statements about sin are attributed to Jesus in St. John's gospel. Although it is unlikely that they are the precise words of Jesus, they are the interpretation of the spirit of Jesus by a mystic who understood it better than perhaps any of his contemporaries. Jesus made it clear that sin arose in the conscious choice of a lower way when a higher one was seen to be present. "If ye were blind, ye would have no sin: but now ye say, We see: your sin remaineth." He indicated also that the most tragic consequences of sin were the effects on the doer. "Everyone that committeth sin is the bondservant of sin. And the bondservant abideth not in the house for ever." Through this image, familiar to His hearers, of the different relationships of servant and son to the householder, sin is presented as the cause of moral slavery, and ultimately of banishment from God.

Basically, all sin is self-centredness: putting oneself in the centre of the picture and relegating all others to the periphery. It is a denial of the unity of all selves on a deep level, just as love is the affirmation of this unity. The soul of the saint embraces wide vistas: he does not know where his soul ends and his brother's begins. The soul of the sinner is imprisoned within narrow walls of selfishness which sin has built. They isolate him from the fellowship of man with man and all with God. The most tragic aspect of all this is the sinner's blindness and self-delusion. In the beginning a wrong choice may have been clearly understood to be such, but the way of lower choices diminishes sensitivity to this recognition. The illusion of freedom remains without the reality, and in the end the sinner cannot see beyond the limiting walls of self.

Of course in addition to these inner consequences of sin there are trains of outward consequences set going, previously described by the term karma. We do not live in isolation, and our sinful acts affect others, causing them perhaps injury, suffering, or loss. On the physical level chains of effects arise. Although it may seem to the superficial eye that these are soon over and done with, so that both good and evil deeds are swallowed up in the gulfs of time, the principle of karma says: "No: there is no escaping them. They ultimately return to bless or chastise the one who caused them." To change the metaphor, the karmic seeds which are sown may lie latent for a long time — perhaps for more than one life — but ultimately they will germinate and give rise to situations which have to be faced. Outwardly these situations may appear different, but they contain in essence the same moral issues and we have to learn to face them rightly and worthily. Herein lies a key to much that is presented to us in life. Perhaps we find ourselves in a situation of suffering: it may be what we have brought on ourselves in the past; it may be an opportunity the soul has sought to advance; it may have been voluntarily undertaken to help another. We must face it with courage and unselfishness and fortitude. We may have been given a chance to pay some karmic debt, to make amends, to overcome some weakness, to help another, to widen the bounds of our soul's freedom. Happy are those who recognise that life offers to us a series of opportunities, whether we like or dislike them at the time, through reacting rightly to which, we may unfold the latent greatness of the soul.

FORGIVENESS

In different language but with a common purpose, every great religious teacher has stressed the importance of treating others as we should wish to be treated ourselves. Since a wrong done to another raises a barrier against relationship, penitence by the wrong-doer and forgiveness by the wronged person is the only way to a restored relationship. This is psychological and spiritual truth apart from any particular religious beliefs.

In Christianity and those religions which describe God in personal terms as the Heavenly Father, or the Supreme Person, moral law is regarded as an expression of His nature, being His commands to mankind. A wrong done to another person is therefore not merely inter-personal, but is a violation of the moral law and therefore a sin against God. We have already mentioned two-fold consequences of sin. Subjectively, a barrier is raised between the sinner and God so that any communion is impossible. Objectively, trains of consequence are set going which have to be reckoned with sometime. Forgiveness is concerned with the subjective consequences. The words of Jesus offer assurance that God's forgiveness is always forthcoming provided there is sincere repentance and that the effort is made to set right the relationship where another has been wronged. "If ye forgive men their trespasses, your Heavenly Father will also forgive you. But if ye forgive not men their trespasses, neither will your Heavenly Father forgive your trespasses."

In the light of this emphasis it is not surprising that one great division of the Christian Church has made confession one of its sacraments; in others, there is a ritual in which penitence, confession, and absolution (by a priest) play a recognised and important part in worship. This formalisation represents a strange attitude towards the nature of forgiveness. If its essential element is the restoration of relationship, or at least the removal of any barrier which would make that renewal impossible, one would have supposed the approach to this must be one of spontaneity as well as sincerity. Moreover one would have supposed that it should be at the level of the soul and God, not at the level of a prescribed ritual in which others are involved. To make of confession a duty, or even part of a regular service of worship, savours more of a legalistic process than the restoration of a relationship between the worshipper and God. If the preservation of human relationships (say between husband and wife) required a prescribed weekly confession, the nature of which would inevitably become rather repetitive, instead of the spontaneous language of love, it is easy to see what a travesty of the character of such relationship could easily arise.

In those religions which do not personalise God the existence of evil is just as fully acknowledged and the consequences of wrong-doing are taken care of by the universal law of karma. The mystical unity of all selves, or the recognition of the One Self in all, means that any offence against another is an offence against one's self and against all. The evil-doer is regarded rather in terms of ignorance than of sin (although, as we have said, these are really twin aspects of the one truth). He is immersed in the darkness of ignorance as to his true nature. He is cut off from knowledge of the unity of which he is a part. Instead of treading the narrow path which leads to the gradual dispersal of his spiritual ignorance and delusion, he sinks further and further into the darkness of isolation. Through suffering and effort he must some day make the long journey back towards the light of freedom, from the fetters of ignorance. The divine Self, which never left him, will be re-discovered along that road.

It is a matter for surprise that in the teaching and doctrine of the Christian Church more emphasis seems to have been placed upon the theorising of St. Paul about sin and salvation than upon the teaching of Jesus as we have it succinctly and sublimely in the Parable of the Prodigal Son. (One wonders if St. Paul had ever heard of this parable.) All the essential insights are there. Sin is putting one's self in the centre: "Father give me the portion of goods that falleth to me." The consequence was separation from the Father: "He took his journey into a far country." It may have been a hunger of the body which started him thinking: it was a hunger of the soul which led to his returning. "He came to himself" and took the road back to the Father's House, not to say "I am hungry" but to confess "I have sinned." "The Father saw him when he was yet a great way off, and had compassion, and ran to meet him." It was a tender and unconditional welcome in which the relationship was restored. The Father made no reference to the past; He pronounced no judgment; He didn't "pardon and absolve" him. He made no mention even of forgiveness, for language was not used to sully what Love had made clear.

Was this salvation by faith? If so it was faith that the Father still loved him. I should call it salvation by Love. Was there a "price" to be paid? The price was suffering, and the Father paid it during His son's absence. The son would pay it too, as he came to know through growing sensitivity what it had meant.

Chapter

7

HOW AM I TO REGARD JESUS CHRIST?

Oh, be prepared, my soul!
To read the inconceivable, to scan
The million forms of God those stars unroll
When, in our turn, we show to them a Man.
Alice Meynell

IT is impossible to write objectively about this great Figure. Jesus has been the object of devotion of innumerable people through twenty centuries. He has been equated with God by orthodox theologians. Even to discuss Him is to tread the razor's edge, for all too easily a writer will find himself accused of irreverence. If he is a humble man he will probably accuse himself of presumption.

Apart from these involved emotional factors, we are all aware that language itself is an imperfect instrument to convey spiritual truth. It was never designed to convey man's highest insights or mystical perceptions. These are things which can only be known in experience. Even though the poet's tongue can convey something of them, it can only awaken response in another person to the extent to which the latter's experience of life can fill those words with significance. When people are confronted with a great work of Art, if they dare to express a critical judgment, then out of their own mouths the inspired work judges them. This is even more true of a great soul: in such a presence the commentator is himself under judgment. These are some of the reasons why it is so difficult to write of Jesus the Christ.

RECORDS

We are not particularly interested in this book with questions which have interested scholars and produced a mass of scholarly literature. A few relevant facts may be of some interest to the reader.

Our knowledge of the life and teaching of Jesus is almost entirely derived from the first four books of the New Testament, which are called gospels (meaning "good news"). As long as those who actually heard the words of Jesus were alive, an oral tradition may well have

89

been thought sufficient. When the first disciples became fewer and scattered the need for written records must have been felt. It seems probable that at least one written collection of the sayings of Jesus had been made: this is a hypothetical document called "Q" by scholars. Its existence is inferred because of many similarities in the words of Jesus quoted by both Matthew and Luke. It seems likely that they drew from a common source. The first gospel to be written was Mark's, and its chief source of information was probably his recollection of Peter's teaching and preaching. A likely date for its compilation is thought to be about A.D. 65. It contains fewer of the sayings of Jesus than the others, and looks much more a narrative intended for the Gentile reader. In some New Testaments the reader will notice a gap left after Mark xvi. 8. This is because the end of the gospel as it originally was, is considered to have been lost, and what follows this point is thought to be a later addition.

The gospels of Matthew and Luke were compiled perhaps twenty years later than Mark's. Luke was believed to be a physician and was closely associated with St. Paul's circle. He was also the author of the Book of Acts. In contrast, Matthew's gospel makes constant reference to the life of Jesus as fulfilling Old Testament prophecies. It may safely be inferred that his gospel was primarily intended for circulation among Jews who had become Christians. St. John's gospel is a still later compilation dating perhaps from about the end of the first century. It is by no means certain that it was written by John "the beloved disciple". While it adds to our knowledge of the life and sayings of Jesus, it has a mystical and philosophical character not found in the other three. The sayings may quite possibly not be exact words of Jesus, but rather words ascribed to him as the expression of His spirit by an advanced mystically inclined soul. If the writer had any particular reading community in mind it was probably the Greek-speaking world.

It is scarcely necessary to say that none of the first century manuscripts have been found. Not many early copies could have been expected to survive the Diocletian persecution in A.D. 303. Until about seventy years ago the two oldest manuscript copies of the Bible were the *Codex Vaticanus* (dated about A.D. 350), and the *Codex Sinaiticus*, now in the British Museum. The search for ancient manuscripts in more recent times has brought several important discoveries to light and we may mention one or two. In 1892 two

Oriental scholars of Cambridge found in the monastery of St. Catherine on Mount Sinai a Syriac translation probably made in the fourth century, and believed to be from a Greek text of about A.D. 150. In 1931 the announcement was made of three well-preserved third-century papyri covering a considerable part of the New Testament. They were found in jars dug up from an old Coptic graveyard in Egypt. The oldest known fragment of a New Testament manuscript consists of five verses of St. John's Gospel (John xviii. 31, 32, 33, 37, and 38) found on a papyrus from Oxyrhynchus in Egypt by Grenfell and Hunt in 1897. This fragment has been dated as A.D. 150. Such discoveries as these, and more recent ones, when compared with the texts of the great fourth-century Codices, have given scholars considerable confidence in the latter.

Such facts as these, while in one sense an interpolation into this book, may serve as a reminder that Christianity had its beginning in historical events, the records of which were doubtless copied again and again. It is of course likely that the original texts had many things added to them by copyists and other self-appointed interpreters. It is likely that later documents came to incorporate legends found in the oral traditions. Although it may prove impossible ever to answer accurately the scholars' question as to how far we have a completely authentic account of the historical Jesus, honest minds which read the accounts we possess are in general agreement that there shines through them the picture of a truly God-conscious man — perhaps the noblest who ever walked the earth.

The great value of these records is not to be measured in terms of their historicity (although I believe they enshrine a core of historical events), but resides in the timeless challenge they present to the hearts of men. They show what human life was meant to be like. They show the height to which the Father expects His children to rise. They show how a fully God-conscious man reacted to all human experience, with love and wisdom perfectly blended. We have in them a mature disclosure of the divinity latent in man: the Eternal revealed in Time.

INCARNATION

It seems likely that the birth of Jesus may have been about 8 B.C. to 4 B.C., but the precise year is a matter of no consequence. Likewise, it will be appreciated that the scriptures offer no indication of the season of the year at which the birth took place. Early in the fourth century the celebration of Christmas was arbitrarily placed on December 25th. The choice of this mid-winter date, as it is for the Northern hemisphere, happily symbolises in the turning point of the year, which is the beginning of the ascendency of light over darkness, a turning point in the fortunes of humanity. Christmas is rightly an expression of unqualified rejoicing, and there can be few who would wish to take away from it the romantic mythology which has entered into its celebration. There is an account of shepherds on the hills of Bethlehem whose sensitivity was so raised that they became aware of angelic hosts in the familiar everyday skies. There is the story of the Magi, who saw an unusual star (probably a Nova) which led them to undertake a long journey to pay their homage to the Child. There is the account of Simeon's visit to the temple, when he recognised the Child's greatness immediately. There is the record of Herod's malevolence and his attempt to destroy the Child — a ruthless gamble of the forces of evil to frustrate an event so filled with significance for humanity. According to Matthew an angel appeared to Joseph in a dream, and according to Luke the angel Gabriel appeared to Mary, announcing the virgin birth that was to be.

Some may regard these events as historical, some as wholly legendary, some as an inextricable mixture of history and legend. The last view is the one I am disposed to take: but are such opinions of any importance? The poet's expression of truth is different in its character from the scientist's and the historian's. The poet may properly use myth, legend, and paradox to convey his insights. To judge the vehicle of expression by its rationality, its historicity, or its scientific validity is to miss the central core of truth. Humanity pays tribute to its greatest figures in the very fact that legend comes into being and weaves its way into their history. Similar legends gathered round the Buddha's birth in the sixth century B.C. It is said that the coming Buddha chose carefully the time, the country, and his future Mother. There is the legend of an immaculate conception, and that his Mother had dreams and visions of her son's coming destiny. When he was born she named him Siddartha ("He who has fulfilled his purpose"). The vision of Simeon is paralleled by that of Asita, a Himalayan sage who arrived at the palace and asked to see the Boddhisatva who had been born. The legend says that he smiled and then wept. He explained that he smiled because he foresaw that the child would become a Buddha, but he wept because he would not live to see the day.

The stories which surround the birth of Jesus, like all such, are significant because of their insights. Here was cause for earth and heaven to rejoice (shepherds, wise men, and angels). All would recognise His greatness. He would be a unique revelation of the Eternal (the immaculate conception and the star). A star that "went before" the magi and "stood over where the young Child was" is clearly poetic licence. Much else may be: does it matter?

LIFE AND WORK

So much has been written about the life, work and teaching of Jesus that it is impossible to say anything new. Familiarity with the records has possibly dimmed for many people the moving challenge of His life. In contrast with a situation in which millions now adore Him, His earthly life must have been a particularly lonely one. Outwardly He enjoyed the fellowship of His disciples; inwardly He was alone, yet as He said, "Not alone, for the Father is with me." Of His mission, was He sure, even at the end, that they had understood it? He moved among people of every kind, farmers and fishermen, women and children, publicans and taxgatherers, lawyers and rabbis, always able to see beneath the surface. He loved the struggling goodness, the inner aspiration, the buried seed of faith, and He felt a great compassion for the multitudes who to Him seemed as sheep without a shepherd. His life was an unqualified illustration of His affirmation that He was doing His Father's work, and that even as His Father cared for them, He cared too. Preaching long after the death of Jesus, Peter paid Him the simple and sublime tribute, "He went about doing good."

Jesus undoubtedly possessed psychical powers to a remarkable degree. There is no need to ascribe the miracles attributed to Him to growing legend and myth. Last century the self-assured scientific mind was prone to see in the record of miracles evidence of the unreliable character of the records. In the light of psychical research we can take the view that such powers as He demonstrated may well have been quite natural to Him. Such powers are recorded from time to time as possessed by other advanced souls. His concern seemed to be that when He used them to help people in need he would not fasten any fetters on their freedom to choose their own path.

What Jesus taught men in language of remarkable simplicity was what mortals most need to know for everyday life. Metaphysical questions He left strictly alone. If a man doubted his value in the sight of God, he was told that not a sparrow fell to the ground without the Father's knowledge. If a man thought he was forgotten and of no account, he was told that the very hairs of his head were all numbered. If anyone thought he was too wicked to deserve the love of God, he was told of a Father who kept a loving vigil for the time when he would turn his steps homewards, and as soon as he came in sight hurried to greet him. When He saw ordinary folk struggling to live, with little leisure and many cares, burdened further by the professional purveyors of religion, His compassion welled up and He said, "Come unto Me all ye that labour and are heavy-laden, and I will give you rest."

His teachings on values challenged contemporary judgments, and they equally challenge those of today. The world respects power: He said it was the meek who would inherit the earth. The world strives after wealth: He said it was hard for those with wealth to enter the Kingdom. The world says "Love your friends and hate your enemies": He said love was always right. The world values publicity and desires recognition, honours, and acclaim: He said "Do good secretly." At every point of life His teaching contrasts with worldly wisdom, and well might Chesterton comment on the way of Christ that it was "not true that Christianity had been tried and found wanting: it has been found difficult and not tried". He still moves far ahead of us in His standards and values.

HIS DEATH

It is not at all surprising that He was put to death. What he taught challenged to its foundation the religious power, the pride, and the legalism of His day. The religious leaders of the nation worked for His death, and their plea before Pilate "If thou let this man go, thou are no friend of Caesar's," was characteristic hypocrisy, although shrewd psychology, for they touched Pilate's repressed fears for his own position. By everything that Jesus was and said, the priesthood of Judaea stood condemned. He was too dangerous a man for them to leave at large. If, as might appear from the narratives, Jesus at first hoped that the truth He proclaimed would work a miracle of change, even in them, it is also clear that He came to recognise it would not. He foresaw the end, but He foresaw also that in His death He would be sowing seed which would yield a harvest for generations unborn. Therefore — and this again contrasts with all worldly wisdom — He took no steps to avoid this end.

There is a remarkable and significant account given in St. John's gospel, of a deputation of Greeks who came to see Him shortly before the events which led up to His crucifixion. From a land with a tradition of culture and philosophic interests, we may surmise that these men came to invite Him to teach in their country. It was an alternative to crucifixion. When He heard of this, He spoke with moving insight of the need of the grain of wheat to fall into the ground and die if it is to bear a harvest. In a few sentences of immortal power He summed up the whole mystery of sacrifice: that suffering is the measure of love, and the measure of all spiritual achievement; that in complete self-losing is complete Self-finding; that by giving to the death, and to outward appearance losing all in defeat, there is a rising to more powerful life, and the guarantee of victory.

Yet it was clear that for a moment He was troubled. It may have been a natural human shrinking from the ordeal of death by crucifixion. Perhaps it was a momentary doubt whether the purpose for which He had lived would be better served now if He went to live in Greece, than by His death in the near future. He would be trusting His mission to the limited insight and understanding He had managed to evoke in the hearts of a few disciples. Whatever caused this troubled moment, it passed again as He prayed, "Father, glorify Thy Name." The reassurance came to Him, "I have both glorified it and will glorify it again."

"The cross signifies," says Radhakrishnan, "that progress is achieved not by those who fight for it, but by those who suffer for it."*

And so the world's best man deliberately chose to go to His death.

RESURRECTION

He had predicted this to His disciples, but it is certain that none of them realised what He meant until the event itself broke upon them. The narrative of the events which accompanied and followed His death is probably familiar. The first three gospels agree in recording an

* *Eastern Religions and Western Thought*, p. 108 (O.U.P.).

unusual darkness over the land between noon and three o'clock. They record that as He died, the veil in the temple was mysteriously rent from top to bottom, and that just before this He had cried out with a loud voice. Only Luke records that He said, "Father, into Thy hands I commend my spirit." Matthew goes into more narrative detail, recording an earthquake and a number of apparitional appearances. All of them say that the Roman centurion was very impressed and disturbed by what he saw. Matthew and Mark record that he said, "Truly this was a Son of God." Luke's version is "Certainly this was a righteous man."

The time will come when it will be generally recognised that the physical order exists only as a precipitate of mind, and that a powerful mind's agony and release will inevitably be reflected in paranormal happenings.*

The accounts of events following His death differ in their detail but are significant in their agreement. There was a visit of some women to the tomb at sunrise on Sunday: the great stone at its entrance had been rolled away. There was a vision of angels reminding them of the predictions Jesus had made. There was the profound impression made upon Peter and John by the absence of the body and the disposition of the grave-clothes. These, together with many appearances of Jesus in a fully materialised body† to those who loved Him are impressive testimony. The reader may not know that there are accounts given from time to time of meetings with advanced beings who can materialise a physical body when they wish and dematerialise it at will. In this scientific age such reports are naturally treated with reserve, but it is unwise to dismiss them as impossible in the light of the little we know. With some knowledge of psychical research and in face of all the evidence that He was a very advanced soul, nothing in the resurrection accounts leaves me surprised.

To those who loved Him and witnessed these things, there was naturally a complete change of outlook, from a mood of complete despair after they concluded that His death was the end, to unspeakable joy when they realised the full implications of what had happened.

If the miraculous elements in the narrative prove a stumbling block to the reader, he should study the data of psychical research before

---

* Cf. *The Imprisoned Splendour*, pp. 257-8, R. C. Johnson (Hodder & Stoughton, Ltd.).

† Matthew xxviii. 9; Luke xxiv. 38-43; John xx. 20; John xxi. 4-14.

coming to a conclusion. If he remains unsatisfied he still has to account for a psychological "miracle". Something happened which changed the outlook of a group of shattered and depressed men and women into one of assurance and the joyful conviction of a mission. What was it? It led many of them to a martyr's death.

WHAT THE CHURCH CAME TO BELIEVE

The story of the early Church is recorded in the Book of Acts, and it is probably most effectively told in one of the modern translations.* It is a story of enthusiasm, of conviction, and of sacrifice. A prayer of Ignatius Loyola, prayed many centuries later, might well have been constantly on their lips:

"Teach us, good Lord, to serve Thee as Thou deservest: to give and not to count the cost; to fight and not to heed the wounds; to strive and not to seek for rest; to labour and not to seek for any reward save that of knowing that we do Thy will."

They were a happy people. They felt an intense sense of brotherhood because of their common loyalty to Jesus. What they came to believe about Him is expressed by the bold preaching of Peter to the Jews.

"Let all the house of Israel therefore know assuredly, that God hath made Him both Lord and Christ, this Jesus Whom you crucified."
"God hath raised this Man to His own right hand as Prince and Saviour to bring repentance and the forgiveness of sins to Israel."
"He is the one appointed by God to be the judge of both the living and the dead. It is to Him that all the prophets bear witness."

Paul echoed the same theme in his arguments with the Jews, frequently quoting and explaining passages to prove the necessity for the death of Jesus and His rising again from the dead. It is clear that while much of this exposition was directed towards convincing the Jews that Jesus fulfilled their early prophecies, a conception was beginning to grow up of the cosmic significance of Jesus as having a unique relationship with God. Scores of passages could be quoted to illustrate this, but one from a letter to the Church at Philippi will suffice.†

* E.g. *The Young Church in Action*, J. B. Phillips (Geoffrey Bles Ltd.).
† Philippians ii. 5–11.

"Christ Jesus: who, being originally in the form of God, counted it not a thing to be grasped to be on an equality with God, but emptied Himself, taking the form of a bond-servant, being made in the likeness of men; and being found in fashion as a man, he humbled himself, becoming obedient even unto death, yea, the death of the cross. Wherefore also God highly exalted Him, and gave unto Him the name which is above every name; that in the name of Jesus every knee should bow, of things in heaven and things on earth, and things of the world below, and that every tongue should confess that Jesus Christ is Lord, to the glory of God the Father."

The deification of Jesus is already obvious, and this led to the great theological controversies and dogmas. It led for example to the doctrine of a Trinity, in order to try to reconcile these beliefs about Jesus with the strict monotheism of the Jews. It led to endless difficulties and complexities in the doctrine of the two natures of Jesus — human and divine.

JESUS' VIEW OF HIMSELF

The difficulty, if not impossibility, of determining this is obviously that we have to rely on the writers of the gospels whose own views would lead inevitably to an interpretation of the words of Jesus which they recorded many years after they were spoken. Probably we shall never know what words are attributable to Jesus Himself, and how far the writer's interpretation has entered in. St. John attributes to Jesus such words as, "I am . . . the door, . . . the bread of life, . . . the light of the world, . . . the true vine," etc. Are these the result of devout meditations by the writer of this gospel? It may well be so, for we feel that the writer understood deeply the spirit of Jesus.

If we turn to the synoptic gospels where perhaps we might think the task was a little easier, there are many sayings which indicate that He was aware of a close and vital relationship with a Higher Being to Whom He constantly referred as His Father, and in relation to Whom He described Himself as a Son. He clearly felt this relationship most satisfactorily depicted in language as that of Father and Son. The terms are intended to convey the sense of perfect understanding and of unity which existed between them.

"All things have been delivered unto Me of my Father, and no one knoweth the Son save the Father; neither doth any know the Father save the Son, and he to whomsoever the Son willeth to reveal Him." (Matthew xi. 27.)

Following the question of Jesus to His disciples, "But who say ye that I am?" and Peter's declaration, "Thou art the Christ, the Son of the Living God," Jesus said:

"Blessed art thou, Simon Barjonah, for flesh and blood have not revealed it unto thee, but my Father which is in heaven." (Matthew xvi. 17.)

At the same time as there is this sense of an intimate relationship amounting to unity with the Father, there are sayings attributed to Him which proclaim His unity with mankind.

"Inasmuch as ye did it unto one of these my brethren, even these least, ye did it unto Me." (Matthew xxv. 40.)

"Whosoever shall receive one of such little children in my Name receiveth Me; and whosoever receiveth Me, receiveth not Me, but Him that sent Me." (Mark ix. 37.)

These relationships are obviously something more than language can properly express, as is the case with all mystical relationship. When Peter affirmed that Jesus was the "Son of the Living God", Jesus rejoined that this insight must have been granted to him by the Father. It was not a human deduction. When, on the other hand, a reverent questioner once addressed Him as "Good Master", Jesus rejoined, "Why callest thou Me good? There is none good save One, even God." The fact is that nowhere does Jesus offer us definitions or proceed to enter upon metaphysical discussion. Nowhere does He discuss the idea of God: His term is the "Father". He takes a questioner with his limited conceptions, but does not discuss his limitations. He adds such terms as He thinks the questioner will understand in order to convey to him a little more of the truth.

When we turn to the gospel of John there is an abundance of statements put into the mouth of Jesus about Himself and His relationship to the Father.

"The Son can do nothing of Himself, but what He seeth the Father doing."

"No man can come unto Me except it be given unto him of the Father."

"I and my Father are one. . . . Though ye believe not Me, believe the works; that ye may know and understand that the Father is in Me and I in the Father."

99

"I came out from the Father and am come into the world: again I leave the world and go unto the Father."*

In the prayer of Jesus which constitutes Chapter xviii of St. John's gospel we have a petition for all His disciples, several times repeated, "That they all may be one; even as Thou Father art in Me, and I in Thee, that they may be in us." The language of this gospel is that of a mystic who has meditated deeply upon the life and thought of Jesus and come to view Him in His eternal significance. The constantly recurring theme is the essentially mystical one of the Unity of Father and Son, and the profoundly moving prayer is that all who follow Him may consciously enter upon the same sense of Unity.

When this is interpreted in the objective and rational language of theology, rather than regarded as a necessarily imperfect expression of mystical insights, we arrive at the formulations of orthodoxy. The Father is equated with God, the Supreme One, while Jesus becomes in a unique sense the Son of God of the same nature and attributes ("very God of very God" as the creed puts it). All this in logical terms becomes incomprehensible. The personal may mirror something of the supra-personal, but it cannot be equated with it. The finite may reveal something of the Infinite, but they can never mean the same thing. The Jesus of history may disclose something of the timeless and eternal "One", but to identify Him with the One in a logical as distinct from a mystical sense is to corrupt language and distort meanings.

Those who defend such orthodoxy frequently claim that no other figure of history has ever used such commanding language and spoken with such authority as to say he was the "Way, the Truth, and the Life"; or was "One with the Father". On the contrary mystics in their highest moments have used similar expressions, finding the language of Union with God the only adequate way of trying to convey the wondrous state. The feature which distinguishes Jesus is that this sense of Unity with the Father was fully conscious and continuous.

WHO THEN IS JESUS?

If we are not content to leave the relationship as mystical, and therefore inexpressible in language except symbolically; if we insist

* John v. 19–27; John vi. 65; John x. 30 and 38; John xvi. 28.

on having a theology of His person which is to be logically defensible, we must look with fresh presuppositions at the problem.

(1) Why should it be assumed that between man and God there is a great gulf empty of conscious beings? I am aware that Biblical tradition and medieval theology have written of angels and archangels and the hosts of heaven, but such concepts have never been taken seriously or developed to a point which would make apparent their relationship to God and man. No one has ever suggested that such ideas are relevant to theology. Why should we assume that man is the crown of God's creation? May not Jesus have been a higher Being who accepted responsibility for his planet?

(2) If we start to think cosmically rather than in planetary terms, the Supreme Being is One who is concerned with the Universe which modern astronomy discloses on its physical levels. We live on a little wayside planet which is revolving round a star. This star is one of a hundred thousand million which constitute our galaxy or "island universe". The largest telescope which man possesses has shown that hundreds of millions of galaxies exist. We know of no limit: why should we expect any limit if we think of God as infinite? Theological thinking remains at this point completely anchored to the medieval conception of the world. In this picture the Earth was the centre of the universe, with sun, moon, and stars a part of the kindly provision, the decorative backdrop, for the home which the Creator had provided for man. Is it surprising that with this outlook, Jesus, regarded as God's fullest revelation of Himself to man, should be deified and regarded as having a uniquely important relationship to God?

We are not merely drawing attention to the physical vastness of the universe as demanding a change of viewpoint. It certainly does. But if matter is a precipitate of Mind, the universe is a living Universe of Mind, and behind Mind lies Spirit. Life fills it: life doubtless in vastly different forms from anything we can conceive. Is it not likely that experiments in creative consciousness beyond all our imagining — but aspects of Divine Imagining — fill the depths of Space and Time?

It is astonishing to observe how man stands on the little hilltop which he calls truth, which he has ascended slowly and with many setbacks, and thinks he is on the summit of Truth. Always there are explorers who go farther and show his little summit to have been but a foothill of the majestic peaks which lie farther ahead. Of course it is interesting for the theologian to trace the concept of God from the minds of primitive Jewish tribes in Old Testament times up to the lofty concept of the early Church. But if he then affirms that a conception formed nineteen centuries ago, and sublimely reflected in the Figure of Jesus, is the final word, he is back in the old traditional groove once more. Jesus is still vastly beyond us, but we pay Him no devotion He can accept if we do not put Truth first.

> *Crown Him the Lord of Truth,*
> *The past He leaves behind,*
> *He reigns in His eternal youth*
> *And loves the honest mind.*

What do we, puny creatures of limited mind, know of the Universal Mind? All that it is important to know, say the orthodox. Happy people to be so sure of Truth!

(3) Is it not possible, even probable in the light of the universe in which we live, that the "Father" with Whom Jesus felt Himself to be related in so close a way is not to be identified with the Supreme Being? This identification is commonly made without any alternative being considered, and from this identification arise all the metaphysical difficulties which no reputable theologian professes to have solved. Suppose the "Father" is a finite Being, a Spirit of goodness, love, wisdom, and power, far beyond our understanding: a great Being, guiding, redeeming, and directing our solar system (or even part of our galaxy, or even perhaps the whole galaxy). In our ignorance suppose we assume the last of these. We must then remind ourselves that our universe is known to contain hundreds of millions of galaxies. The great Being, our "Heavenly Father", must be a One-Many.* He must be an evolving One-Many, though better not described as an imperfect One-Many. Such an adjective only has meaning in relation to a definition of perfection, and this we cannot offer. Moreover one does not describe a boy as an imperfect man, even if one attempts to describe a perfect man!

In fact as soon as we start to analyse we go astray. We abstract the religious concept of a "One" (perfect), and a "Many" (imperfect) from the truth of a One-Many, and it is better not to do so. Jesus had clearly a conscious awareness of His unity within this One-Many. I have elsewhere applied the term "Divine Society" to those members of this One-Many who have reached full awareness. They all know

* *Watcher on the Hills*, p. 123–5, R. C. Johnson (Hodder & Stoughton Ltd.).

"I and my Father are One". The mystical language put into the mouth of Jesus by St. John is natural to all of them. In this sense Jesus is truly divine and a Son of the Father (the Divine Society). "He that hath seen me hath seen the Father" is true for all conscious members of this Divine Society who are in a perfect understanding and harmony of relationship at this high level.

We ordinary human beings are members of this evolving One-Many but with a vast distance yet to travel before we reach the heights. We are all pilgrims on an infinitely long journey in evolving consciousness. From this viewpoint new depths of meaning are found in the prayer of Jesus "that they all may be One; even as Thou Father art in Me, and I in Thee, that they also may be in Us".

Such a viewpoint is consistent with the Hindu doctrine of the Avatar: that from time to time as is necessary, the Divine Society manifests itself in a human form. It is consistent with a statement made by Gautama, "I am not the first Buddha who has come upon earth, nor shall I be the last." Any Avatar being a member of the Divine Society, can do no other than present to men the one Truth, which it embodies, adapted in its emphasis and by the limited vehicle of language to the necessity and understanding of the Age in which He appears.

"Truth is One: men call it by different Names."

Chapter
8

WHAT AM I TO THINK ABOUT OTHER RELIGIONS?

My brother kneels, so says Kabir,
  To stone and brass in heathen-wise,
But in my brother's voice I hear
  Mine own unanswered agonies.
His God is as his fates assign,
His prayer is all the world's — and mine.
  A Song of Kabir

The majority of readers of this book were probably born in a country nominally associated with the Christian religion. They would probably claim a formal allegiance with this faith. Even the small minority who would claim a vital allegiance with it as being the faith by which they live, would seldom be found holding it as an intelligent choice made after sympathetic study of the other religions of the world. Similar comments would equally apply to members of all other faiths. The accident of birth led us to be born into one of these religious traditions, and if it proves itself to be vital, i.e., offering a framework of belief into which can be fitted a man's experience of life and intuitions, then he becomes a faithful adherent. He is disposed to defend and maintain its rightness, and all too easily his attitude to other religions becomes one of superiority. It may take the form of a kindly tolerance on the assumption that his own faith embodies fuller insights than the others, or it may become uncompromisingly hostile on the assumption that it possesses the fulness of truth and offers the only way to God. In the latter case, those who find in other religions a framework for *their* insights, or a mode of expression for *their* deeper aspirations are deluded souls who have not seen the light which shines benevolently on themselves.

Can this really be true? Does the intolerant person seriously ask us to believe (if he is an adherent of the Christian faith) that Socrates, Gautama, Asoka, Nanak, Kabir, Milarepa, Confucius, Lao-Tse, Sankara, Ramakrishna, Sri Ramana, Gandhi, Tagore, and a thousand others were benighted travellers not on the road to God, while he, baptised and confirmed in the Church of England and repeating the

Apostles' creed every Sunday, is saved by faith? (My question is put in terms of the intolerance I know, rather than the intolerance I don't know — but similar remarks are true of all the faiths.) Surely, as the Indian philosopher Radhakrishnan has said,* "The truth of a religion is not what is singular and private to it, is not the mere letter of the law which its priests are apt to insist on and its faithful to fight for, but that part of it which it is capable of sharing with all others." Many devout Christians are seriously troubled at this point. They read in the Scriptures the words of Peter, "And in none other is there salvation: for neither is there any other name under heaven, that is given among men, whereby we must be saved." Their commonsense tells them that such exclusiveness would condemn some of the greatest souls who have ever lived on earth. In any case they know that this spirit is quite unlike that shown by Jesus Christ. We must look at this dilemma.

IS CHRISTIANITY THE ONLY WAY?

As long as it is a part of Christian orthodoxy that Jesus Christ was God in human form, not in the liberal sense that the divine is manifested in every man but in the unique sense implicit in the Trinitarian doctrine, I can see no logical alternative to Peter's exclusive attitude, that Christianity is the only Way since God in human form has shown it to us. After all, if the words of Jesus are identically the words of God, the only relevant enquiry is to determine whether particular words can be reliably regarded as an expression of His mind. If this is demonstrable, then it is utter presumption not to accept and act upon them. If Jesus is the "only-begotten Son which is in the bosom of the Father" (the "Father" here being identified with the Supreme Being); if Jesus Christ is identifiable with the Greek Logos so that "without Him was not *anything* made that was made", the issue is clear and admits of no doubt. All other great souls, whether founders of religions or not, past, present, and to come, are but as candles to the sun. The little light they had was borrowed light, scarcely to be distinguished from the darkness when the sun appeared.

But if Jesus was an Avatar (in the Indian sense), *a* Son of God, a member of the Divine Society which is responsible for our galaxy perhaps, on all its levels of Reality, then our attitude need not be less

* *Eastern Religions and Western Thought*, p. 34 (O.U.P.).

worshipful and reverent, but it can be different. If a member of the Divine Society incarnates from time to time, when our planet's need becomes great, in order to teach men and to reveal through his person more of the sublime and illimitable Truth and Beauty, it is nonsensical to ask of these Persons, whether one is greater than another. Members of that Society live in an ineffable Unity. The differences which scholarly study may recognise and discuss are not differences of the Spirit, but differences of approach to the special needs of the age in which they appeared. These needs were met in the best way for that time. If a Christian claims that from this standpoint there has only once been an incarnation of a member of the Divine Society, he is laying claim to knowledge which I do not think any human being can possess. As well might a first-form schoolboy pass an opinion on the relative ability of Newton and Einstein.

Consider these words put into the mouth of the divine Krishna

"Whenever spirituality decays and materialism is rampant, then O Arjuna, I re-incarnate Myself."

"To protect the righteous, to destroy the wicked, and to establish the kingdom of God, I am re-born from age to age."

"The ignorant think of Me, who am the Unmanifested Spirit, as if I were really in human form. They do not understand that My Supreme Nature is changeless and most excellent."

"But," says a devout Christian, "what are we to make of some of the clear claims of the Scriptures?" Peter's affirmation has been quoted. To this we reply that it is time we recognise seriously how *relative* all humanly proclaimed truths are. Peter was speaking to a Jewish crowd with a certain background of thought and tradition. They had a particular background of prophecy: they were looking for a Messiah to be sent by God — and all their dreams and hopes were wrapped up in this event yet to be. Now Peter had seen the light of God shining through the person of Jesus Christ. He recognised that He was the fulfilment of their ancient prophecies, and it was natural that Peter should use the highest and noblest language to convey this to them. He was a preacher, not a metaphysician. Paul uses the same unqualified language when he says that God "raised Christ from the dead, and made him to sit at His right hand in the heavenly places, far above all rule and authority, and power and dominion, and every name that is named, not only in this world, but also in that which is to come". These men were human like ourselves. They were children of their age and racial background, limited by the thought-forms of their time (as we are ourselves), and they were making a response to the impact upon them of one of the greatest souls who has ever walked the earth. Why should we suppose that the sincere utterances of men who were making a great contribution to the outlook of their generation are not relative truths but ultimate truths, binding upon ourselves? If Christianity is to make an impact upon this modern world it will have to free itself from the dead hand of the past and trust itself to a new inspiration of the Spirit.

If a devout Buddhist makes his way to spiritual heights and finds in the teaching and example of the Buddha a framework for his experience and an inspiration for his living; if an Indian sitting in meditation on some hill-slope, cave, or temple pavement, *knows* that he is one with the All; if a Sufi raises his heart to the Ineffable, and *knows* he is accepted of God, what right has anyone, Christian or otherwise, to claim an exclusive Way? All such claims speak to me of a love which is not big enough and a mental attitude tethered to a particular tradition. If such persons claim to be Christians, I can only say that they do not remind me of the matchless love, tolerance, and grace of Jesus of Galilee.

I am going to assume that most of my readers have had little opportunity to study sympathetically other religious traditions than their own. I propose therefore to take Buddhism and Hinduism and make a few comments. My purpose is simply to arouse some interest and appreciation of other viewpoints.* May I stress two things as a preliminary. First, that I am presenting only a few glimpses. Secondly, that I am not concerned with popular forms or particular sects, but only with a few of the greater insights.

BUDDHISM

In the sixth century B.C. about the same time as some of the great prophets of Israel, while Zoroaster was teaching in Persia, and Lao-Tse and Confucius were living in China, there was born to the king of a small tribe whose territories were on the slopes of Nepal, a son called Prince Siddartha. The tradition is that although he was brought up within a palace, in surroundings which provided everything the

---

* I warmly commend as an introductory study Professor Huston Smith's book *The Religions of Man* (Mentor Books).

senses could desire, an unrest which could not be stilled grew within his soul. It is recorded that by chance he had three encounters — with an aged man, with a leper, and with a funeral procession — and that his reflection upon these incidents brought home to him the suffering of humanity. Believing that there must be some meaning in the flux of change, some abiding Truth that would relieve this suffering, he took a vital decision in his twenty-ninth year, and set out to find it. One night, when all in the palace were asleep, he said a silent farewell to his wife and little son and slipped out into the darkness. He changed his clothes for those of a beggar and became a wanderer in search of the truth that would save mankind. With utter disregard of comfort and health, he gave himself to religious practices such as fasting, meditation in solitude, and extreme asceticism, but in spite of a seven-year search he failed to find the truth which he knew must exist. Finally, on the night of the full moon in May he sat down under a Bo-tree to meditate, and vowed that he would not rise until he had found that for which he had so long searched. With the dawn he attained Enlightenment. He rejected the temptation to pass on to higher levels of existence (Nirvana), and turned his face with great compassion to humanity. These are some of the things he taught.

(1) The doctrine of the Middle Path. Equally futile and vain are the pursuits of the two extremes: earthly pleasure and possessions on the one hand, and asceticism on the other. The wisest path is between the extremes, and it demands from men purity, complete control of self, and inner discipline. "If a man conquer himself he is a far greater conqueror than if he conquers a thousand men in battle." To others however, one should show great tolerance and compassion.

(2) The doctrine of the four noble truths. (*a*) All existence is sorrow. (*b*) Sorrow is caused by desire for and attachment to transient things. (*c*) To conquer sorrow this desire and attachment must be eliminated. (*d*) The way to do this is by practising the noble eight-fold path. Gautama expounded this path in detail. He saw that life was full of sorrow because men fastened their affections upon things that would not last, but pass away. The thirst for sensory existence was to him an indication that men were unaware of their true nature, Spirit, and this spiritual ignorance was for him the root problem. The path of salvation must therefore lead to inward knowledge of the true self. This state is in its fullness called Enlightenment.

(3) His emphasis being on self-discipline in thought, word, and

deed, he did not encourage speculation about the after-life, or upon metaphysical themes. He himself offered no teaching about God, not because he knew nothing, but because he realised how far beyond human understanding the truth of such matters was. He maintained a reverent silence on the principle "He who speaks does not know: he who knows does not speak."* Because of this he has been described as an agnostic, or even an atheist, which is a complete misunderstanding.

One of the concepts of Buddhism which has been little understood (and sometimes deliberately misunderstood) in the West, is that of Nirvana. This word means literally a "blowing-out" or "extinguishing". Since Nirvana is the highest state of man's spiritual attainment as man, it has been wrongly supposed that Buddhism is pessimistic, regarding man's highest destiny as extinction or nothingness. On the contrary, that which is extinguished is not the Spirit of man, but the egotism which would preserve the boundaries of a private and personal self. This high state of consciousness is that which Hindu mystics refer to as Freedom or realisation of the One Self in all, and which Christian mystics refer to as the Unitive Life. Gautama deflected many attempts which were made to induce him to describe it more fully. He affirmed that Nirvana was a state of consciousness "incomprehensible, indescribable, inconceivable, and unutterable". All that he would say further was, "Bliss, yes bliss my friends, is Nirvana."

(4) He accepted two basic teachings of Hindu thought, reincarnation and karma. He saw clearly that the fetters of karma bound men life after life to the wheel of sentient existence, and that only by dispelling the fundamental ignorance in man (of his true nature as Spirit), could this otherwise endless round be broken.

(5) One of his teachings which has drawn criticism and further misunderstanding is that of the absence of a permanent soul. What, I think, the Buddha wished to convey was that the soul should not be regarded as a vehicle of finer "substance", eternally separate from all other souls, but rather perhaps as a flow of consciousness individualised but yet part of a greater Whole. The categories of language applied to non-sensory concepts convey very easily wrong impressions.

A sonnet which Matthew Arnold wrote of Shakespeare might equally well have been a tribute to Gautama.†

* Tao Tê Ching.
† I am indebted to Professor Huston Smith's book for this thought.

Others abide our question. Thou art free.
We ask and ask: Thou smilest and art still,
Out-topping knowledge. For the loftiest hill
That to the stars uncrowns his majesty,
Planting his steadfast footsteps in the sea,
Making the heaven of heavens his dwelling-place,
Spares but the cloudy border of his base
To the foiled searching of mortality:
And thou, who didst the stars and sunbeams know,
Self-school'd, self-scann'd, self-honour'd, self-secure,
Didst walk on earth unguess'd at. Better so!
All pains the immortal spirit must endure,
  All weakness that impairs, all griefs that bow,
  Find their sole voice in that victorious brow.

Anyone who has looked at the development of Buddhist thought will see that it comprises a complex system of metaphysical ideas. Gautama has suffered from this as much as Jesus. Their own teachings were profound but simple and essentially practical. "What victories could Heaven give us," said Gautama, "we must be conquerors here on earth." "If I told you earthly things and ye believe not," said Jesus, "how shall ye believe if I tell you heavenly things?"

The life of Gautama as a wandering teacher with a band of disciples, covered at least forty years, and it is believed he died at about the age of eighty. His outer setting was by no means placid or free from conflict. Although a cousin Ananda became a life-long and devoted disciple, another cousin Devadatta attempted not only to kill him, but to frustrate all his work. The Brahmins of his day, like the scribes and Pharisees of Judaea, were violently opposed to his teaching that the same essential Spirit manifested in all men. Ascetics also bitterly resented his condemnation of their excesses. On one of his journeys messengers came to tell him of the massacre of his own people by a neighbouring tribe. Yet he moved among the sorrows of life with a heart of compassion, pointing all who would listen to a way by which they could come to know the Truth that would set them free to rest serenely above the flux of passing things.

With the passing of the Founder and the enthusiasm of the first few generations, all religions split into divisions and sects. The main division of Buddhism is into two schools, Hinayana (or Theravada) and Mahayana. The countries of Burma, Ceylon, Thailand, and Cambodia, belong to the first school, while elsewhere in much of Eastern Asia the second predominates. The first school remains closer to the early teaching which stresses that man's quest for Enlightenment is essentially a solitary quest depending on his own effort and self-discipline. Its demands are therefore met most satisfactorily by retreat from the world, typified by the monk's full-time devotion. The Mahayana school places more weight on the example of Gautama's life of compassionate service to mankind. It therefore recognises that his quest need not be solitary, but that he may have the help and grace which flow through the Buddha.

One of the doctrines of the Mahayana school is that from time to time other great figures qualify to enter Nirvana, but following Gautama's example they turn back to become helpers and saviours of mankind. These are the Bodhisattvas, of whom it may be said, as Matthew Arnold wrote of his father:

> *But thou would'st not alone*
> *Be saved, my father! alone*
> *Conquer and come to thy goal,*
> *Leaving the rest in the wild.*
>
> . . .
>
> *Therefore to thee it was given*
> *Many to save with thyself;*
> *And at the end of thy day,*
> *O faithful shepherd! to come,*
> *Bringing thy sheep in thy hand.**

In recognising this compassionate interest in mankind, Buddhism is given a form which those engaged in worldly avocations can appreciate and follow. There are of course other differences between the two schools. Thus, Mahayana has a place for ritual and prayer, while Hinayana advocates meditation in solitude. The former is therefore much closer in its beliefs and practices to Christianity than the latter.

Those Western theologians who misrepresent Buddhism as a moralistic religion leading to the goal of extinction are not merely wrong: a little psychological understanding would have shown them that if this were true it would be inconsistent with the fervour,

* Matthew Arnold, *Rugby Chapel.*

enthusiasm, and devotion which led to missionary enterprise and carried the Buddha's message widely over Asia. Rabindranath Tagore has reminded us that:

"The preaching of the Buddha in India was not followed by stagnation of life, as would surely have happened if humanity was without any positive goal and his teaching was without any permanent value in itself. On the contrary we find the arts and sciences springing up in its wake, institutions started for alleviating the misery of all creatures, human and non-human, and great centres of education founded. . . . And that power came into its full activity only by the individual being made conscious of his infinite worth."*

HINDUISM: THE GITA

All religions have their crude, ignorant, and debased forms, and Hinduism is no exception. In its enormous variety of cruder forms there are thousands of image-cults with their minor gods and goddesses and sacred animals. In its highest form Hinduism was the gradual creation of saints and mystics, who, two or three thousand years ago, were searching for truth. Many of them lived very frugal lives in the caves, forests, and hills of ancient India, and some of the dialogues and teachings which passed between these sages and their bands of disciples has been preserved for us in the Upanishads. Some two hundred of these scripts are known, but they are difficult for the Westerner to read without a commentary and a good understanding of the outlook. They embody what we should describe as religion, philosophy, psychology, and mysticism.

The *Bhagavad Gita*, the authorship of which is unknown, crystallises much of this thought, and may be ranked among the world's greatest books. Perhaps it dates from about the fifth century B.C. but it is probable that it includes many later additions. It is a small book comprising eighteen chapters and about seven hundred and twenty verses, which I suppose could be read through easily in two hours (although this would not be a profitable way to read it). It should be studied with a commentary and perhaps in more than one translation. Like all great scriptures it may embody some history, but this is of little importance compared with the value of its insights, ideals, and perceptions of truth. Such works are Myth in the highest sense of the

* *Creative Unity*, pp. 70, 73, Rabindranath Tagore (Macmillan & Co. Ltd.).

word, concealing yet disclosing to the sympathetic mind "truths which break through language and escape".

The ostensible setting is a battle-field on which opposing armies are marshalled awaiting the signal for battle. The reader's sympathy is with Arjuna the leader of one of the armies, whose chariot is drawn up a little way in front of his troops ready to lead them into battle. He is in a mood of great dejection as he thinks of the slaughter which is imminent. He starts to talk to his charioteer who turns out to be no less a person than the Lord Krishna himself in human form (Krishna is regarded as an Avatar by Hindus). In this situation Arjuna asks Krishna for guidance, and the Gita presents his teaching. It is a philosophy of life, teaching about the meaning of existence, what life is for, how far action and duty should rule men, where true wisdom lies, and who he (Krishna) is. At times it presents abstruse metaphysical ideas: at other times it becomes intensely practical. The battle-field is really the age-long battle-field of the human soul where the great Opposites are contending with each other. Good is fighting evil, love is fighting hate, the outgoing energies which immerse souls more deeply in matter are contending with the ingoing energies which are striving to lift the soul back to its high estate.

Arjuna is clearly a type of the thoughtful awakened soul, and his concern about the coming slaughter, which is the immediate issue, is the starting point of Krishna's teaching. He points out that physical death is but a surface event.

"There never was a time when I was not, nor thou, nor these persons were not; there will never be a time when we shall cease to be.

"As the soul experiences in this body, infancy, youth, and old age, so finally it passes into another. The wise have no delusion about this.

"As a man discards his threadbare robes and puts on new, so the Spirit throws off its worn-out bodies and takes fresh ones."

Krishna tells Arjuna that it is his duty to *act* in this situation. He then follows up this advice with a philosophy of action, the essence of which is embodied in two verses.

"To action alone hast thou a right, but not to the fruits thereof. Let not the fruits of action be thy motive, nor yet be thou enamoured of inaction.

"Perform all thy actions with mind concentrated on the Divine, renouncing attachment and looking upon success and failure with equal eye."

This philosophy looks behind all outward action to the motive which impels it and sustains it. A man should do his duty faithfully, caring neither for gain or loss, praise or blame, but offering his faithful performance as a sacrifice to God.

The two doctrines of the Avatar, and of a plurality of lives, are introduced by Krishna. The latter remarks that the same wisdom which he is teaching Arjuna he had taught to Viwaswana, the founder of the Sun dynasty, and Arjuna naturally expresses great astonishment. This evokes the reply from Krishna:

"I have been born again and again from time to time; thou too O Arjuna! My births are known to me, but thou knowest not thine."

It is one of the beliefs of Hinduism that until a soul attains that wisdom which enables it to see through the fantastic pageant of human life and know that it is *Maya* (the Illusory, not the ultimately Real), it will return again and again to earthly incarnation. The twin doctrine of karma is also expounded by Krishna. He points out that it is quite possible to live and act in the world without generating any more binding karma. If action is "freed from motives of desire" then it does not enmesh the doer further in the world of illusory existence. A sage or wise man can live in the world with the necessary detachment because he sees through the snares of desire.

One of the great affirmations of Hindu thought is expressed by the phrase "That art Thou", by which is meant that the essence of every human soul is one with the Divine Being. The "Atman" which is this central point in man is identified in its nature with the "Brahman" (the Supreme Being). This daring declaration must have been the fruit of mystical experience by Indian saints and sages. It goes beyond the Christian teaching that the souls of men are creations of God, by affirming that the central essence of each soul *is* God. Multiplicity in all its forms is said to be a phenomenon of the world of appearance (maya): the Reality is the one Self in all. It is an uncompromising monistic position.

Philosophical Hinduism has always been concerned with the way by which man's soul can extricate itself from the illusions of the sensory world and realise truth. To this end various forms of yoga are described to suit different temperaments. These are techniques or disciplines by which the approach can be made. Bhakti yoga is the way of complete devotion or love towards God; Karma yoga is the way of action or works done as a sacrifice to God; Gnana yoga is the disinterested search for wisdom; Raja yoga is the way of mind-control or meditation. Speculative theology is discouraged in favour of the path leading to immediate mystical experience. To those who would define the Ultimate, its word is "Not that: Not that". It realises that all positive statements are dangerous in that they become limitations. One cannot say anything about God without implying that He is not something else: it is therefore preferable to retain a reverent silence.

If the greatness of a religion is confirmed and illustrated by the appearance within its culture of men of outstanding spiritual stature, then Hinduism of the last century can show us Sri Ramana, Sri Ramakrishna, and Mahatma Gandhi.

SOME REFLECTIONS ON RELIGIONS

In so far as religion is mystical — and this is the core of all the great religions — there is a conscious awareness of the Spirit. The ego breathes for a moment its native air and knows its unity with the Whole. Such experience cannot be communicated to others except allusively and inadequately, but it is from this that all true religion has sprung. Once the soul has been illumined, it can never view mundane existence as it did before. It now has knowledge rather than belief, certainty rather than faith, and life is henceforward viewed in the perspective given to it by that glimpse of underlying Reality.

As soon as religion leaves the subjective level, exposition of the new outlook to others has to wrestle with the problem of communication. How can the ineffable truth be presented to others who have not known this Illumination? It cannot, except by parables and symbols, and the most powerful symbol is the illuminated person of the Founder. Here we meet the fundamental problem of all socialised and organised religion. We can only communicate on the level of mind through the imperfect vehicle of language. Poetic expression is a better and more subtle vehicle than intellectual formulation, because it is emotionally toned, is less defined, and is designed to awaken intuition rather than inform the mind. The religions of the world are never content to leave matters thus: they desire to have creeds and codes that can be handed on from one generation to another. Such frameworks are preserved by the faithful and venerated as almost sacred. They are defended with weapons of intellectual verbiage, and often with considerable fervour, and in the course of doing this, antagonism is frequently felt towards other frameworks. This is always a saddening spectacle, for it shows how far removed from the mystical essence of religion are these outward forms of expression, and how little the defenders realise the true nature of religion. It is as though half a dozen parties of exploration should go out to explore a vast and infinitely varied continent, and on returning should quarrel among themselves because their accounts do not agree. I do not hesitate to say that if the great mystics of all religions were brought together they would feel in a perfect unity with each other. With no impeding sense of egotism they would not even be aware of personality as a form of separation. They would know themselves one and all as mediators of the same Infinite Truth.

> *Children of men! the Unseen Power, whose eye*
> *For ever doth accompany mankind,*
> *Hath looked on no religion scornfully*
>   *That man did ever find.*
> *Which has not taught weak wills how much they can,*
> *Which has not fall'n on the dry heart like rain,*
> *Which has not cried to sunk, self-weary man:*
>   *"Thou must be born again!"*

Chapter

9

SHOULD I ACCEPT ANY AUTHORITY?

If we here speak and write, it is but as guides to those that long to see: we send them to the Place Itself, bidding them from words to the Vision. The teaching is of the path and the place: seeing is the work of each soul for itself.

Plotinus

THE role of authority is familiar to us all. Broadly speaking it arises in three ways. First, wherever organisation develops there follows the delegation of responsibility and authority. Authority is conferred in the interest of efficiency, and it is outwardly marked by rank or position. Examples are innumerable: in the army, in government, and in business. Secondly, there is a kind of authority which is recognised, not conferred: this is the authority of the expert. He is listened to with respect because of his wide knowledge or experience. Thirdly, there is a source of authority in venerated tradition. This is often subtle and not closely defined. Its roots are emotional, not rational, and they frequently go back to a distant past. "This is how the subject has always been viewed"; "This is what the great so-and-so thought." This great man was probably no wiser or more intelligent than some of his successors, but time has magnified his virtues and obscured his weaknesses.

These kinds of authority have all played their part in organised religion. Consider the authority conferred by organisation. When the head of the Roman Catholic Church makes certain official pronouncements he is declared infallible. Consider the following claim made on behalf of the church by an eminent Roman Catholic writer, Father Martindale:*

"A Catholic considers that he has cogent reasons for holding that the Roman Church is guaranteed by God to teach him only what is true, and to command him only what is right. He has then but to discover what she teaches and commands, and will proceed to believe the dogma and obey the command, not only when he has no feelings

* *The Faith of the Roman Church.*

117

about the latter but when his feelings may be in a perfect tumult of opposition. . . ."

If conferred authority is challenged, the second kind of authority may be invoked, the authority of the expert. It is pointed out that in every field of learning there are scholars and life-long students whose weight of specialised knowledge is so great that by common consent their views are authoritative in their own field. Now in matters of religious belief the Church says: we are the experts. Is it reasonable for any individual to suppose that his opinions can carry any weight against a unified pronouncement made by the doctors and best scholars of the Church?

Some divisions of the Church do not go so far as this, but invoke the third source of authority, venerated tradition. In this case, the Bible is generally regarded as an infallible guide to belief and conduct. The quotation of texts or passages is generally considered a way of proving a point or settling an argument. The writers of the New Testament books are not regarded as able and sensitive men, capable like ourselves of making mistakes, but authorities from whom it is impious to differ.

In this chapter we are going to consider the question whether there is any need or obligation to recognise any authority in the matters of religion. The Roman Church would certainly say that it is both needful and obligatory. The Protestant Church, by and large, would say it is needful but not obligatory. Some groups (such as the Society of Friends) would deny both and claim that the only authority they can recognise is the "inner light" which each man possesses within himself. All mystics would share this viewpoint although many Christian mystics have found their spiritual home within the Church.

In forming a judgment in this matter it should be remembered that religion differs from all other fields of man's concern in that it deals with a relationship, not between man and his neighbours, between man and Nature, or between man and the State, but between man and a spiritual order. Its central element is the growth into consciousness of the link between man's soul and God. It is essentially mystical. It is true that religion will influence the whole of a man's life, intellectual, emotional, and physical; it will influence his outlook, his actions, and his relationships with his neighbours — but all this will flow from his inner experience. It is inevitable when generalising, that we do less than justice to some branches of the Church. Broadly, however, it is true to say that the Christian Church has been rather suspicious of its mystics. It has not been content to guard the holy fire as a worshipping community which can witness to certain common experiences and insights. It has claimed to tell men what they *should* believe, and in matters of morals what they should do. As we look back over past history we find the Church has used at times almost every weapon which held out hope of coercing men into conformity with its views. The kindly reader may be disposed to say that we are now living in a different age with a very different spirit: that various divisions of the Church are tolerant of each other's views, and tolerant of free opinion expressed by individual laymen and clerics. With regret, I take leave to doubt this. There are signs of movement in this direction, but change of heart is a very slow process and there is a long way to go. The chief difference in this connection between our modern age and those which preceded it arises from two factors. First, the widespread character of elementary education among the generality of people has diminished the power of the Church. Intolerance no longer produces the same results. People can now read for themselves, to some extent they can think for themselves, and to a large extent they are not at all interested in what the Church thinks. Secondly, in the democracies, secular power rather than ecclesiastical power is dominant in all but a few backward countries, and men may therefore exercise freedom of speech without the same fear of persecution or ostracism.

Lord Acton was responsible for a much-quoted dictum: "Power corrupts; absolute power corrupts absolutely." History shows that this has been as true of the Church as of secular institutions. With shame we must face the fact that the distinction which modern man makes today between Christianity and Churchianity is the nemesis of past ages of the abuse of power.

THE SPIRIT OF JESUS

Jesus never set Himself up as an Authority. It was those who listened to Him who said that He spoke with authority — and not as the scribes. He spoke with the first-hand authority which the mystic possesses. W. R. Maltby* has very truly written:

---

* *The Significance of Jesus*, pp. 30–1 (S.C.M. Press, 1929).

"He respected as no other has done, the sanctity of the human personality, and He died rather than invade it, as He died in order to win it for God. 'Behold I stand at the door and knock' — that is His word. It is not there that others are content to stand. Kings and captains have battered the door down. Priests have claimed the right of entry. Parents stopped at that door have disowned their children. Only the Son of Man, following the way of the Father refused to do us any violence, and had patience and humility to stand at the door and knock."

At the beginning of His life as a wandering teacher, it is recorded that He faced three temptations. He was conscious of having unusual psychic powers at His disposal, powers which He used from time to time to read men's minds and heal their bodies. He was fully aware that great danger was inherent in an unwise use of them. The first of the temptations, "Command that these stones be made bread", was a subtle appeal to His compassionate nature, to eliminate hunger and sordid poverty by their use. He declined to do this, knowing that men might then follow Him to satisfy their physical needs. Those who followed Him must do so in freedom because they wanted the spiritual food He could give, not because they wanted the food of the body. In the second temptation it is said that He was offered the kingdoms of the world on condition that He did homage to the Satanic power that ruled them. In plain language, the temptation was to use the world's methods to achieve its submission; to use force and temporal power for the end of just and benevolent rule. This has always been a temptation to good men holding high ideals and pursuing noble ends. The temptation is to believe that the nobility of the end justifies the use of inferior means to attain it. All experience shows that if the wrong means are used, the original goal is modified and the result is compromise. Jesus therefore rejected the use of temporal power as a means towards a spiritual kingdom, for He knew that men could never be coerced into spirituality. The third temptation, to throw Himself down from the pinnacle of the temple, and offer to the crowds the evidence of a miracle that He spoke with authority as a messenger of God, was rejected for the same reason. A man who could use his psychic power to defy the force of gravity would certainly have been regarded as having the divine imprimatur upon his teaching by those Jews who were always seeking after a sign. In each of the temptations Jesus chose to respect the freedom which God had placed within the soul of man and rejected the use of any kind of force, physical or psychical, which would have restricted men's power to choose freely. He maintained this attitude throughout His life, and though He used His paranormal powers to help others, He was careful to see that on occasions where spiritual issues were involved they were not influenced by paranormal happenings.

Two recorded incidents typify His profound respect for the intellectual integrity of people. St. Luke gives an account of two sorrowful and puzzled men who were walking from Jerusalem to Emmaus after the events of the crucifixion. They had been followers of Jesus, and the turn of events which culminated in their Master's death had left them not only deeply depressed but intellectually bewildered. It would have been easy for Jesus to have appeared to them as they had seen and known Him, and this would have put their hearts at rest, even though it would have left them more bewildered. It was characteristic of His concern for their mental integrity that He should choose first to show them how the puzzling events of the preceding week made a meaningful pattern, and that He should *then* disclose to them the fact of His survival.

The other incident equally eloquent of His concern at the same point, was His treatment of Thomas the doubter. He had heard from the other disciples that they had "seen" Jesus, and in the light of such astounding claims he concluded that it was more likely that his colleagues had been deluded than that a man whom he had seen crucified and placed in a tomb, was two days later alive in visible form. He asked for first-hand evidence as the condition of his accepting the fact. It was a perfectly reasonable request, and it was granted. Jesus clearly had no inclination to demand faith from Thomas, when He was in a position to offer him the evidence of his senses. But Jesus did use the occasion to make a significant observation. "Because thou hast seen me, thou hast believed. Blessed are they that have not seen me and yet have believed." His action had been an indication that He was not hostile to scepticism, nor was He reluctant to provide sensory proof. His observation was, however, a reminder that the latter is not always possible, and that there are other more "blessed" ways of knowing than the senses offer.

Jesus saw a world as God had made it, with freedom to go right or to go wrong, freedom to believe or to disbelieve, freedom to live as though power and possessions alone mattered or to live sacrificially, and He gave His own unhesitating assent to the wisdom that permitted this. "The Son," He said, "can do nothing but what He sees the Father doing." His teaching method was so to illumine the truth that it became each man's own discovery. Again and again, after some simple parable, He would say, "He that hath ears to hear, let him hear." This, says Maltby, was equivalent to saying to them, "God has given you minds: use them!"

At no point has the historic Church been more conspicuously untrue to its Founder.

THE HUMAN CRAVING FOR SECURITY

Many people are haunted by the deeper questions of existence; many are hard-pressed by the circumstances of their lives, and they crave for "security of belief". It is an emotional need transferred to things of the mind. The Roman Church offers such security to its members with confidence. In effect it says, "There is no need for you to puzzle over problems of faith or doctrine, or over matters of life and destiny. These issues have been studied by the wisest minds within the Church, and we offer you reliable answers. Leave behind all your doubts and vain questioning: we offer to you all that is necessary for your comfort and salvation."

The Protestant Church, in its many divisions, steers a variety of courses between dogmatic teaching and the freedom of the individual to form his judgment. I recall the challenging words of Emerson, "God offers to every man the choice between truth and repose. Take which you will, you can never have both." This is a wise saying, for Truth is a *living* reality, and when men start to organise it the life ebbs slowly away. I find myself in full sympathy with Lessing when he said, "Did the Almighty, holding in His right hand truth, and in His left hand search-after-truth, deign to proffer me the one I might prefer, in all humility, but without hesitation, I should request search-after-truth."

I am not prepared to hand over to any other person, though he be very wise and learned, or to any institution however ancient or sure of its position, my inalienable right to search for ever-growing and ever-expanding truth. I believe the craving for security in belief is one which arises from within ourselves, and can only be met adequately from resources which are within ourselves. It seems to me that it is far more important for a soul in evolution to believe a few things, because it has struggled, thought, and suffered to discover and possess them, than it is for it to have a comfortable and orderly faith which it has adopted second-hand from any source outside itself.

Tennyson expresses all this perfectly:

> *Perplexed in faith, but pure in deeds,*
> *At last he beat his music out.*
> *There lives more faith in honest doubt*
> *Believe me, than in half the creeds.*
>
> *He fought his doubts, and gather'd strength*
> *He would not make his judgment blind;*
> *He faced the spectres of the mind,*
> *And laid them: thus he came at length*
>
> *To find a stronger faith his own;*
> *And Power was with him in the night,*
> *Which makes the darkness and the light*
> *And dwells not in the light alone.*

SHOULD I BELONG TO A CHURCH?

In the light of what has been said of the Church as an institution, the question arises for every religious-minded man and woman, "Should I belong to a Church?" If such a one is a humble follower of Jesus Christ, attempting to apply His spirit and teaching to the issues of life, should he become a member of one of the neighbouring church congregations?

Bishop Stephen Neill may be regarded as speaking for most of the Church's theologians when he writes:* "To those who ask whether it is not possible to accept Christ and to dispense with His Church, we must answer, in the light of the New Testament, that it is impossible."

If this is true — and I do not accept it — it is certainly remarkable that the teaching of Jesus Himself gives no clear indication of it. As Bishop Neill admits, the word "church" occurs in the gospels only twice, and both instances are in St. Matthew's gospel. Their context strongly suggests that the passages in which they are found are not

* *Christian Faith Today*, p. 171 (Pelican Books).

reliably attributed to Jesus at all. The constant teaching of Jesus is about the Kingdom of God and its nature. This Kingdom, we are told, is within us. The concept of the Kingdom of God is not by any means to be identified with the Church, which might be described at its best as an instrument or agency of that Kingdom, and at its worst, as a hindrance to it.

The early Church very naturally considered that all followers of the Way of Jesus should and would join their community. They were in a minority, and indeed, through the early centuries of persecution it would have been difficult if not impossible to be a Christian, and not make this avowal. But the situation today is different, and modern theologians who hold that "the Church is an essential part of the Gospel" are obviously echoing the views of the early Church, not the views of Jesus. It is certainly true that Christianity has social implications and a community aspect: no one would wish to dispute this. A Christian who withdrew from the world, other than with the motive of more effectively serving his fellows through it, and after it, could scarcely be regarded as a follower of Jesus, who "went about doing good". "He that loveth not his brother whom he hath seen, how can he love God Whom he hath not seen?" But the recognition of this essential Christian attitude is by no means identical with joining a particular church community or becoming a member of any church. The alternative to joining a church is not withdrawal from life or neglect of self-discipline. A man may acknowledge the Lordship of Christ and strive to serve his fellows in the same spirit as his Master, and I reject as mere dogma any statement that if he were not a member of the church he was not a true Christian.

The desirability or expediency of membership of a church is quite a different matter to that of necessity. A person who is honest will have to face and answer several questions. How far is the Church in the contemporary world aiding the coming of the Kingdom of God in the hearts of men? Is the Church a venerable institution which has made its chief contribution to the world's need and has now outgrown its usefulness, or has it still an effective contribution to make, even though its thinking and outlook need reform? Is there any serious recognition of the need for a radical spring-cleaning in its theology, so that the huge gulf which separates the Church from modern man may be bridged?

A practical question which is sometimes proffered by religious-minded people, not fundamentally antipathetic to the Church, is "Why should I attend a church each Sunday and there have inflicted on me a futile, often irrelevant and boring sermon?" If the Church is described as a "witnessing community", it is pertinent to ask "To what, and to whom is it witnessing?" If it is described as a "worshipping community" the relevant question is, "Do I find true worship easier within a church or outside it?" These are not questions to which a swift and easy answer should be given. To do this would have little value and would probably present unwise and untrue generalisations. The sincere seeker will have to discover his own answers. It seems to me that the sensitivity and orientation of a man's soul towards God is the supremely important thing, and this can neither be achieved or preserved without self-discipline. If a person decides that he will not avail himself of such aids as people within the Church find it gives to them, I should not wish to offer any criticism of this decision. I would merely wish to tender the suggestion that it is necessary to preserve a discipline of prayer or meditation on the one hand, and of social service on the other, so that one does not fail to keep in touch with spiritual realities, in a world which values them very little.

Chapter

10

IS THERE ANYTHING IN PRAYER?

Be as the bird that halting in her flight
Awhile, in boughs too slight,
Feels them give way beneath her and yet sings
Knowing that she hath wings.

Dante

THE popular idea of prayer is that there is a God Who is able to hear and answer petitions made to Him, provided the petitioner is sincere, and asks in faith. To the religious-minded person this idea of prayer would be considered quite inadequate. He would say that prayers of petition were only one aspect of this important activity of the Christian life, and that to be worthy of the name prayer should include many aspects. Some of these are: adoration of God, praise and thanksgiving for the blessings of life, penitence by the worshipper for his failures and sins, intercessions for his fellows, and then petition for himself. Such a view probably expresses the mind of the Christian Church, and is the usual practice in its worship.

It should be remarked that all such praying, whether it is private or corporate, takes place as an activity on conscious levels of the mind. Extending far beyond this are types of prayer which involve deeper levels of the mind, and ultimately involve some of the levels beyond mind. Here prayer, as usually understood, changes into various forms of meditation and contemplation, and leads on to forms of mystical experience. In this chapter we are confining our attention to prayer in the commonly appreciated sense, and we shall begin with some of the questions which constantly arise in the minds of those who are interested in prayer.

IS PRAYER REASONABLE IN A SCIENTIFIC AGE?

When we describe our Age as a scientific one, we are probably thinking of the enormous advances in knowledge due to research, and of the impressive applications of this knowledge. Behind the features which give to our modern civilisation its main characteristics are the

126

key ideas of science. One such idea is that we live in a law-abiding universe, and that all physical events are governed by the law of cause and effect. As new factual knowledge has come to light, men found that it led them to Natural Law and thus to an ability to use Nature's energies for their own ends. By and large, these activities and laws of Nature appear to be independent of the observing minds. They are the same for all scientists everywhere. In a word, they are regarded as objective. It is true that in the last forty or fifty years scientists have found phenomena in which the observing mind plays a significant part, but important as these may be in their implications, let us set them aside for the present.

While scientific research has been proceeding in the West at an increasing tempo, the observer himself has been little studied and remains a fundamental mystery. Of his own nature and structure Western man has scarcely started to think: his psychology is largely a science of behaviour and is still young and naïve. Modern contributions such as that of Dr. C. G. Jung are but beginnings in this vast field. Apart from psychology, studies of lesser-known human faculty made by psychical research societies and individuals in the last seventy-five years have disclosed that the mind of man has powers of perception and action beyond the familiar field. Though as yet little understood, the human mind is certainly the seat of powers which have been labelled telepathy, clairvoyance, precognition, psycho-kinesis, etc. In a world in which these are facts to be reckoned with, there is no justification for supposing that prayer is necessarily a superstitious activity. Whatever else prayer may be, it is certainly the use of the mind in a special way and for special ends. Certain kinds of prayer may turn out to be closely related in their mode of operation to some of these little-understood powers of mind.

DO PRAYERS INFLUENCE GOD?

Some such question is a fundamental one. It must have arisen in the mind of any person who has ever tried to pray or thought of prayer. It is a deceptively simple question for it raises several others. Can God be influenced at all, if He is all-knowing? If the answer were yes, would it be wise ever to use such prayer, since God is also considered all-wise and all-loving? We cannot hope to say whether prayer might influence God unless we ask what sort of a God it is that we believe in.

If we think of God as a Supreme Individual "out there", while the person praying is an almost negligible individual "here", the idea of influencing God is an incredible one. Astronomers have picturesquely suggested that the number of stars in the universe is possibly of the same order as the number of grains of sand on all the sea-shores of the world. Perhaps on this scale a man might be thought of as an atom in a particular grain of sand. There is no hope for man in this kind of thinking which is conditioned by our senses.

Suppose, however, that God is thought of as an all-pervading Spirit, manifesting Himself in different degrees on different levels of Reality, and on any one level in infinite variety. The physical level of the world we live in is then only one level of the manifestation of God, but we do see something of Him in the mud and in the stars. On the higher levels of Reality which we shall discuss further in the next chapter, there are different orders of manifestation of God, and man himself participates in these levels. On such a view our attitude to prayer can be a very different one. Instead of regarding ourselves as insignificant specks apart from God, we can begin to realise in ourselves the fact of God immanent. Since man himself participates in the Reality on these different levels, his concern must be to make conscious an awareness of the God Who is already there, especially on higher levels of himself. When the Spirit breaks through to the centre of his consciousness then there dawns upon him a supreme experience, for in that moment all sense of egotism goes and he realises his unity with the Whole.

On such a view prayer is a method, a technique, a practice, by which a man of sincerity and persistent devotion may come to know the heights and depths of himself. This is not "influencing" God in the sense of the question at the head of this section: it is an increasing discovery of Him and communion with Him. Someone may say: are we to believe then, that this spark at the centre of the soul is of the nature of Spirit — of God Himself? The answer of all the mystics is yes.* It is a drop of the great Ocean, one in its essential quality and nature as far as its latent potentialities are concerned. These have yet, even in the finest men, still to unfold and develop, so that Browning spoke of this centre in man as "a god though in the germ". It is the

* Gerald Heard in *The Third Morality* (p. 244) says, "It is not that the creative process is limited within ourselves, but that it is not limited in a person outside ourselves."

sense in which we may say that the giant oak of the forest lies latent in the acorn.

The true nature of prayer is then to penetrate inwards to this centre and through it to the Spirit: to discover the infinite resources which are accessible through God within.

IS THERE ANY POINT IN PUBLIC PRAYER?

In most religious services there are certain traditional elements: the singing of hymns or chants, the reading of scriptures, and joining in prayer (usually "led" by some person). It is important to enquire what purpose such activities are designed to serve.

There is an answer which can be given in psychological terms: the building up of empathy or the sense of community, so that the group feels it is together for a common purpose. This is valuable and important in itself, for some people find that the tuning of the mind to a worshipful mood is easier under the influence of a group atmosphere. A great deal depends upon the psychological type of the individual, and for some people the reverse may be true. Apart from any symbolising of higher truths which ritual may express, a good case can be made for it in psychological terms. If it is used with reverence, giving due attention to aesthetic and emotional factors, it may be the means of providing for some of the group the mood which facilitates entry upon private worship (as we outlined it in the previous section).

But to what extent can public prayer be regarded as true prayer at all? I have expressed the view that prayer is a method or technique by which consciousness is directed inwards to try to gain increasing awareness of the spiritual levels of Reality. From this standpoint is not *public* prayer a misnomer? At its worst it is a distracting noise; at its best it will contribute with other elements to the induction of a mood or mental state in the worshipper in which his sensitivity is heightened. It will then facilitate the opening of a door for the worshipper's own interior journey. Those readers who do not share this view will, I hope, make an honest attempt to discover the values which they believe exist in public prayer (other than these psychological ones).

Some comment is perhaps appropriate on the two outwardly contrasting modes of public prayer. One of these is spontaneous and unpremeditated as to its substance, as is frequently the case in nonconformist services. The other is the use of set prayers as is the case in the Church of England and the Roman and Eastern Churches. In Quaker worship the emphasis is upon silence, and this is perhaps the most logically defensible entry upon prayer, as I have defined it. Both types of prayer, if used with sensitivity and sincerity, can do much to build an atmosphere in which some of the worshippers can subsequently enter upon silence and prayer. Unfortunately public prayer is usually regarded as complete in itself, and "Amen" shuts the door just as it may have started to open. If, as I have suggested, public prayers are best regarded as specialised parts of a ritual used to induce a mood, there is probably more to be said for set prayers. Familiarity with them probably blunts the impact of their intellectual content, and this is to the good, for the entry on true prayer is not facilitated by an over-active conscious mind. I suggest that the best set prayers thus become mantramistic — a series of sounds which induce a certain mental state favourable to worship. They become the psychological equivalent of "Om, mane padme Om", the sacred and oft-repeated formula of Eastern devotion.

CAN PRAYER INFLUENCE OTHER PEOPLE?

If prayer is a technique for attaining increasing communion with a spiritual level, leading in the rarer types of mystical prayer to a communion through the centre of the soul with God, it may well be asked, "Is intercession for others properly described as prayer?" If we pray earnestly for the protection, guidance, or help of another soul, what are we doing in terms of the nature of prayer as we have described it?

Here it may be helpful to refer again to the complex structure of the self as presented in Chapter 11. The nature of prayer leads to a gradual lifting of consciousness, which is normally focused on the physical level, up to higher levels. On the way, some of the powers of the unconscious mind may be stirred up and awakened. The simplest view of intercessory prayer would indeed be to regard this as its aim. It is an early stage on the journey to true prayer: preoccupation is still with levels of the mind, not with what lies beyond them.

The question as to whether prayer can influence other people may be answered at this point by saying that there is very good evidence that it can. Books have been written presenting cases where the part played by prayer seems indubitable. One example of this must suffice here.* (The account is abbreviated.)

   Case of David Hughes. This was a little boy of 4½ who lived in a Welsh village and was seriously ill with nephritis. On January 25th his mother asked the minister of the City Temple, London, if the congregation would pray for him, and this was done corporately each Sunday evening until mid-March, and also by many individuals privately. On February 11th his mother wrote to the Minister, "All the doctors agree that permanent damage has been done to the kidneys and that David will never be the same again." The child was subsequently sent home from hospital and on February 19th the mother wrote: "Just a few lines from David's bedside. He is still with us but desperately ill. The poor little chap can keep nothing down and we expect the end at any moment. The doctor says he will get sleepier and sleepier until he sinks into a coma and then dies."
   On February 24th a letter came to say that he had amazingly enough taken a turn for the better. Since his life had been given up no more drugs had been administered. On March 6th came news that he was quite better, and that tests of the urine now showed that there was no damage to the kidneys and full recovery was assured.
   The importance of this case is that four doctors had all agreed previously upon the diagnosis. He had been given up as hopeless. His case was fully documented by hospital records and tests, and by letters of the doctors afterwards. None of them could account for the unexpected cure. From two of the letters the following extracts are made:
   "I have often thought about him (David) and his dramatic recovery. You may tell Dr. Weatherhead that personally I am *quite sure* prayer played the biggest part in his cure. He was suffering from a severe sub-acute nephritis, and in the opinion of all the hospital physicians his prognosis was of the very poorest."
   "I am enclosing the hospital report which embodies that of a very excellent specialist, Dr. X. In this report you will observe the very serious nature of the case and the unfavourable prognosis. The boy was suffering from a very serious form of nephritis. After his return home from hospital he did not make any progress at all in spite of careful treatment. I have attended a number of similar cases and never saw one recover, and owing to this and the absence of any sign of improvement, I could not give any favourable prognosis to the parents which would allay their deep anxiety. One day, which I shall always remember, the father asked me if there was any hope at all

* *Psychology, Religion and Healing*, Leslie D. Weatherhead, p. 511 (Hodder & Stoughton Ltd.).

for his recovery, and I had to reply that, as far as I could see, there was definitely no hope whatever. Within about a week after this David's condition had completely and suddenly changed for the better, and in a very short time he was practically normal, which was most extraordinary to me."

Dr. Weatherhead (at that time Minister of the City Temple) makes two interesting points in giving a detailed account of this case. (i) "One of the conditions which makes intercessory prayer powerful is that those who pray should *love* the patient. The better they know him, therefore, the more they can be made to visualise the situation, and *feel* towards the patient." (ii) "Prayers for a child seem to avail more powerfully than prayers for an adult. . . . The psyche of a child . . . is less walled in by doubt and fear and disappointment and cynicism, prejudices, and fixed beliefs."

Those who look critically at the hundreds of cases on record may find much to dismiss, but will face a solid core of facts which are inexplicable on the basis of our scientific and medical knowledge. In such cases prayer seems frequently to have been a potent agent in the cure. It has to be freely admitted that cures in such cases are very much "hit or miss". The conditions which make prayer effective in some cases and not in others are not known, although some clues appear to arise from the field of psychical research and are given below.

The fact of telepathy is one to be reckoned with. At levels below the conscious threshold it has been shown that thoughts and emotions — more especially strong emotionally toned ideas — can sometimes be communicated from one mind to another. Distance apparently does not influence this possibility. Between *A* and *B* the rapport may be considerable, while between *A* and *C* the rapport may be negligible, and it is not known what quality is responsible for this. Where strong thoughts of health and healing, associated with the emotion of love, are directed towards another mind, it is clear that in some cases they can be picked up subconsciously, and provide the necessary stimulus to recovery. If among those praying there is no one with the necessary rapport with the patient's mind, such prayers may be ineffective.

If we accept, as does the author, the survival by human souls of death, and the possibility under certain conditions of communication between the discarnate and the incarnate, we have another possibility to face. The help of discarnate beings cannot be ruled out. It is possible that intercessory prayer may be picked up by them and that they in their turn may be able to direct and use their mental powers more effectively than we, to stimulate the mind of a patient towards health.

In rarer cases, where a person is able to tread the path of advanced prayer, beyond the levels of mind altogether, something may happen which is different altogether from the above. For the mystic there is a close relationship between souls on a deeper level, which is a reflection of the ultimate unity of the One Self in all. The praying mystic and the soul prayed for may become so closely related that the latter may receive guidance, healing, inspiration or whatever be the urgent need. One would suppose that while in healing through prayer, energies of the mind are directed specifically to the end of healing, there is such a thing as spiritual healing where the healing of the body is a by-product of experience on a higher level.

IS IT REASONABLE TO PRAY FOR RAIN?

I have framed the question in this specific form to focus discussion. This is obviously a particular instance of a more general question, "Can prayer influence physical events?" If we put the question in the form, "Can the mind influence physical events?" the data of psychical research provide an affirmative answer. There is a phenomenon called psycho-kinesis which is the ability of the mind to move physical objects without any intermediate physical agency. Using statistical methods it has been shown that some persons can influence the fall of dice or spinning coins. More dramatic forms of psycho-kinesis have been reported in connection with physical mediums in whose presence heavy objects have been observed to move under conditions precluding any mechanical explanation.

Recognising these facts, it is not possible to say that the conditions in the atmosphere involved in the precipitation of rain are incapable of being created by mind. Personally, I should not describe "praying" for rain as prayer at all, but I would not rule out the possibility that the mind could be so used that this physical phenomenon might be created. At the same time the ordinary person who thinks that he is likely to cause rain by praying for it is expecting something as improbable as that he might win a football pool. It may be possible by various mental disciplines to bring into the region of conscious control some of the powers which the mind possesses, but I doubt if one man in ten million in our Western civilisation has undertaken the necessary training. There is some evidence that among what we should call uncivilised peoples some of the links between natural processes and the primitive mind still remain accessible. The following account of such an episode was given to me by Mr. Kenneth Henderson, C.M.G., of Oxford.*

The Chief of Jebel Tuleshi, an extremely primitive Nuba community in Southern Kordofan, sent word to the District Commissioner that there was going to be trouble unless the family whose business it was to provide a sacrificial bull in time of drought produced one quickly. The District Commissioner, on arrival at the foot of the hill, was given to understand that the family concerned were protesting because the family of the rain-maker owed them a cow. The Chief refused to admit this argument on the grounds that civil debts must not be allowed to interfere with religious obligations. The District Commissioner then heard the complaint about the cow and gave judgment for the complainant. The cow was handed over, and after an interval for lunch, the question of the sacrificial bull was brought up. The objection being now removed, the bull was duly produced and slaughtered on a sacrificial rock on the top of the hill. The District Commissioner started down the hill under a cloudless sky and had to run for his tent half an hour later to avoid being soaked to the skin. The season of the year was, of course, the rainy season, but this hill had been, up to that point rainless, although the neighbouring mountain group had received their normal rainfall.

It might be possible for some persons in our civilisation to learn how to do such things, but what measure of affiliation with our Western outlook would be retained at the end of the long and arduous system of discipline is another matter. It is probable that the personality-cult (with its intellectual development) of our civilised life is inimical to the necessary close relationship with the Collective Unconscious.

So-called "prayer" for rain, in so far as it may be successful, had better be called magic, for all that it has in common with prayer is that both are steps away from the outer world into the interior world of the self. Magic is playing about on the beach and High Prayer is a journey of exploration into a vast continent.†

* Mr. Henderson has given an account of the episode on p. 489 of his book *Making of the Modern Sudan* (Faber & Faber Ltd., 1953).
† See *Nurslings of Immortality*, Chapters 4 and 5, R. C. Johnson.

There are many examples of this kind of magical activity in the Book of Acts,* where it is not surprising to find that most of it is ascribed to "the hand of the Lord" or the appearance of an angel, in accordance with the ethos of the early Church. The reader of the Book of Acts will have remarked upon the extraordinary psychological atmosphere generated in those early Christian communities, which made paranormal phenomena almost commonplace. They were groups of people who felt an unusual sense of unity. Such comments as these are frequent. "They were all together with one accord in one place"; "All that believed were together and had all things common", etc. They were groups of people living through a phase of fervour and ecstasy as is indicated in many passages: "And day by day, continuing steadfastly with one accord in the temple, and breaking bread at home, they did take their food with gladness and singleness of heart, praising God, and having favour with all the people" (Acts ii. 46).

Extraordinary psychic energies were clearly being generated in the Collective Unconscious of the early Church under these conditions. Magic and miracle were the natural result. Take the records of Chapters iv and v as an illustration. The leaders Peter and John had just been released by the chief priests and elders, and had returned to their community which was engaged in fervent prayer. "And when they had prayed, the place was shaken wherein they were gathered together." This was a poltergeist activity providing a safety-valve for the unusual psychic energy they were generating. The unhappy incident of Ananias and Sapphira illustrates the dangerous character of these energies. The record says:

"The multitude of them that believed were of one heart and soul; and not one of them said that aught of the things which he possessed was his own, but they had all things common . . . great grace was upon them all . . . distribution was made to each according as anyone had need."

The offence of Ananias and Sapphira was that they sold their possessions and gave only part of the proceeds to the community, conveying the impression, however, that like the others, they were giving all. Peter was an impulsive and highly emotional man through whom these turbulent psychic energies found a ready channel, and

* E.g. Acts v, viii, xii, xiii, etc., etc.

when he confronted Ananias (and a little later Sapphira) with their deception, each of them fell dead. The narrative, naturally enough, interprets this venial offence in the most heinous manner, as "lying unto God" (an obviously impossible thing to do), for it was faced with the shock of their sudden deaths and could only suppose that they were a mark of God's judgment. It is rather shocking to discover how quickly the early Church had forgotten the spirit of its Master. In an incident during the lifetime of Jesus, these same men had wanted Him to call down "fire from heaven" on those who didn't see eye to eye with them, and He had rebuked them. Now the fire was theirs to call down. It is sad also to notice how quickly his position of leadership in the Church could lead Peter to describe what was, at its worse, an offence against the community spirit, as an offence against God.

It is interesting to observe that the outer act of Ananias and Sapphira in selling their possessions, pretending to give the whole of the proceeds to the community, and keeping back part of them, symbolised their mental state. Their individual minds were related in a loose way to the Collective Unconscious of the community, but they were not wholly in it. In other words they were keeping a mental reserve about the movement, even though to do so, they had to deceive the others. They did not realise that they were walking on the edge of a psychic volcano constantly threatening to erupt. The energy, which a short time before had found release in a poltergeist activity, was now channelled through Peter upon them. A coroner's inquest would have pronounced the cause of death as heart failure in both cases, but it would not have disclosed that it was caused by a violent psychic impact upon the heart chakram.* It is not surprising that "great fear came upon all the church" — a strangely alien note ringing for the first time its prophetic knell in the infant community. Nor is it surprising that a plethora of miracles followed as the psychic energy found a more useful outlet.

We appear to have left behind our original question about the possibility of influencing the fall of rain by using the mind, and we have found ourselves journeying into the strange hinterland of the

---

* There are certain psychic centres in the higher vehicles of man which are related on the physical level to the autonomic nervous system. They have been observed and described by clairvoyants, and because of their apparent whirling motion the Sanskrit term *chakram* = a wheel has been used for them (vide *The Psychic Sense* by Payne & Bendit, Faber & Faber Ltd.).

occult. Such powers, little-known and little-used, are seldom controlled by the Western mind. They are energies which are an aspect of mind and neither moral nor immoral except in so far as the ends which they serve are good or ill.

SUMMING-UP

We suggest that public prayer (apart from the possible exercise of psychical energies in intercession) is not really prayer; but it may, if used well, create a mood facilitating worship. If the confessions of most people are any guide, much private prayer does not go beyond the surface levels of mind. A few find the path which leads higher. It is a path which demands at least as much devotion and time as we give to the daily newspaper or television. It seems to the writer that a person can have almost anything he wants if he is prepared to sacrifice enough for it. P. D. Ouspensky once wisely observed, "A man can be given only what he can use; and he can use only that for which he has sacrificed something. . . . By your sacrifice you create causes."

The desire for wisdom is the only completely safe desire, and the wisest prayer of all is "Thy will be done."

Chapter

I I

WHAT AM I ?

... Thanks to Him
Who never is dishonoured in the spark
He gave us from His fire of fires, and bade
Remember whence it sprang, nor be afraid
While that burns on, though all the rest grow dark.
Robert Browning

IT used to be a rather proud claim of science in the nineteenth and
early twentieth centuries that its investigations had led to objective
truth — something that was true independently of the observing
mind. The deeper the probe of physics went into matter the more
clear it became that the concepts which physicists had formed,
especially their ideas of mechanism (such as orbits, and spins and
vibrations), were failing to explain things. Sir James Jeans* was
able to write in 1930:

"Today there is a wide measure of agreement, which on the
physical side of science approaches almost to unanimity, that the
stream of knowledge is heading towards a non-mechanical reality;
the universe begins to look more like a great thought than like a
great machine. Mind no longer appears as an accidental intruder
into the realm of matter. . . ."

Of course, outside those sciences which study the quantitative
aspects of the world, the world has never looked like an exclusively
mechanical reality. It has been full of colour, sound, scent, touch,
emotions, ideas, hopes, dreams, loves, etc., etc., in which the human
observer has been intimately involved. If the mechanical side did
exist, it was the invisible skeleton only which supported the beauty
of the form in which we were really interested. In all these other
humanistic fields of man's endeavour, the mind with its intellect,
its feelings, and its aesthetic sensitivity has been an unquestioned
assumption.

It is clear to some of us that those who seek to know Reality on its

* *The Mysterious Universe*, p. 148 (C.U.P., 1930).

138

deeper levels will have to go farther and emancipate themselves from the tyranny of mind. Belief, and the ideals which go with it, which constitute religion for most people, will never meet the deepest need of the human spirit. Krishnamurti has pointed this out:*

"Thought can never be free, because all thinking is the response of memory; without memory there is no thinking. Memory or knowledge is mechanical; being rooted in yesterday, it's always of the past. All inquiry, reasoning or unreasoning, starts from knowledge, *the what has been*. As thought is not free it cannot go far: it moves within the limits of its own conditioning. . . . So thought is not the way to the understanding of Reality."

It must be clear that whatever field of human endeavour interests us, we come back to the puzzle of our own selves. Who are we? What are we? What is the structure of this strange creature Man, who stands in such apparent loneliness looking at a world without him and conscious of a world within? In trying to understand him we find many words are used, such as soul, self, mind, personality, consciousness, spirit, etc. If we are going to use these we must have as clear an idea as possible what they mean to us. This chapter is an attempt to present an outline of orderly thinking about these terms.

There has been a widely held view, not confined to any race or period or tradition, that man is some entity or principle other than his physical body: this has often been termed a "soul". There is no intention here of surveying the ideas and speculations about the soul. At one extreme it has been regarded as a "shade", a "phantom", a sort of pitiable remnant left behind after the death of the body. On the other hand Socrates (described as the wisest of the Greeks), on at least two occasions, and with considerable emphasis, said that his mission was to get men to care for their immortal souls.

With the help of a parable and simple diagram, I shall attempt to present some clues to the complex structure of man which have been gathered largely by study in the fields of psychical research and mysticism. As the reader knows, psychical research is concerned chiefly with some of the lesser-known, but important faculties which the mind possesses, which are often labelled telepathy, clairvoyance, etc. Mysticism, however, is concerned with far higher experiences which have been occasionally granted to people here and there as a

* *Commentaries on Living, Third Series*, p. 234 (V. Gollancz Ltd., 1961).

result of which they have come to a conscious awareness and complete certainty of a spiritual order, in which man finds his complete fulfilment.

A PARABLE: THE HOUSE OF MAN

For the simplest purposes it is useful to picture Man as a house with three rooms, on ground floor, first floor, and second floor, and occupied by Body, Soul, and Spirit respectively. The first-floor room is the intelligence headquarters and control room. The person who uses the pronoun "I", the Ego, occupies the only chair in this room. He is the commander and yet the prisoner of this room. With the apparatus called Mind installed there, he can communicate freely with his servant the Body on the ground floor, and his servant can communicate with him. There are windows in this first-floor room but normally the curtains are drawn, and all that the Ego knows of the outside world, and all that he can do in that world, is known and done through his servant the Body. Occasionally, but rarely, the curtains are drawn or blown aside, giving the Ego a direct glimpse of other souls or of the physical world, phenomena called telepathy and clairvoyance. Sometimes the Ego keeps in close touch with his servant and enters fully into the affairs of the outer world through his servant's life: and we call such a person an extravert. Sometimes an Ego virtually says to his servant, "You keep an eye on practical matters and don't disturb me unless it is absolutely necessary: I prefer to be left alone." We call this type an introvert. The second-floor room inhabited by Spirit is the most mysterious of the three. It has no direct line of communication with the imprisoned commander on the first floor. Perhaps we may suggest that it broadcasts its wisdom as a radio station might do, and the Ego can pick this up if it will tune-in and desires to do so. Some people are inclined to dismiss the second floor as a figment of the imagination and claim that the house has but two stories; but to those who have tuned in to it, or to those few who have been invited up the secret staircase to visit it (as in mystical experience), nothing is more certain than its reality.

This parable of Man must not be pressed too far, and for many purposes it is not detailed enough. Let us look at Man in more detail.

LEVELS OF REALITY

None of us doubts the physical world, for we say that we "know" about it through our senses. It is when we ask *how* they inform us about the world that the process starts to look mysterious. The light from a tree enters our eyes, and, as in a camera, an image of the tree is formed on the retina of the eye. The cells under the image are stimulated by the light, and as a result, thousands of electrical impulses are passed along the optic nerve to the brain. Something which we call Mind interprets this electrical storm and says "I see a tree". It is not material in its nature, but it possesses an amazing knowledge of the brain-machinery, and it also has access to all the memories of past electrical storms of every kind. It is able to say immediately, for example, *that* storm is the face of Tom Jones, this is of Bill Smith, and that other is of an ink-stain on the carpet. There are many theories of perception, and none are completely satisfactory, but here, all we need say is that the existence of Mind cannot be doubted since without it we should know nothing of the world. We must therefore rank Mind as higher on the levels of Reality than Matter.

When we think about the strange connection between the non-material mind and the physical brain, we recognise a gap that we do not understand. What connection can there be between the mental impression of a graceful willow tree and a storm of electrical impulses in a part of the brain? Like oil and water, how can the non-material and the material mix? This issue is so fundamental that some of us are inclined to take the view that there are not two contrasting entities Mind and Matter, but only one. Tested in certain ways it has mind-like qualities such as memory, purpose, intelligence, etc., and tested in other ways it has qualities such as hardness, resistance to touch, shape, mass, etc. If the reader will look at the diagram on page 142 he will see that we have solved this problem by the inter-position of a bridge substance (labelled etheric), and to this "substance" we attribute both these sets of properties so that it is capable of closing the gap. If the reader asks, "Is there any evidence for such a medium?" we can reply that there are many strange phenomena in the field of psychic research in which mental and physical characteristics cannot be separated. Take apparitions, for example. Some apparitions appear to be wholly subjective (or mental) and are a projection of the perceiving mind, others may be seen by more than one person simultaneously, and may scatter enough light to be photographed. In all of them mental and physical qualities seem to be blended. Take as another example object-reading, where it would appear that if a

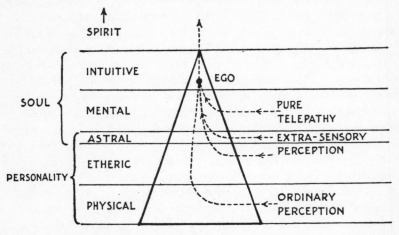

physical object such as a fountain-pen is presented to a good sensitive person, the latter can identify in that object certain mento-emotional qualities which enable him to get into telepathic rapport with the mind of the person whose object it is. The object appears to have much more than merely physical characteristics associated with it. They are almost the psychic equivalent of a fingerprint! In terms of our hypothesis of a psychic ether we might say that the etheric duplicate of the fountain-pen retains these mento-emotional characteristics.

In the diagram, the level labelled Mental is doubtless capable of sub-division into a complex group of sub-levels, some of which are normally accessible to us, and some are not. Everyone is familiar with the fact that when we dream, some mental stratum has a surprising dramatic and creative ability, while other levels accept the role of an interested observer or participant. We may label the functions of Mind, but as to the nature and structure of this instrument we are abysmally ignorant. Above the level Mental I place another one labelled Intuitive, and regard this as the storehouse of such wisdom as the soul has gathered on its journeying through time, as the source of creative imagination and of insights and inspirations. The relation between this level and the Mental ones is perhaps similar to that between the architect and the builder of a structure, or between the author and the producer of a play. A competent artist, be he a painter, poet, sculptor, or musician, has given years of discipline and devotion to his craft and thereby made his mind (and body-brain) a trained and skilled instrument to express inspirations when they come. But great art is not within his power to command and produce when he wants. The wind of inspiration blows when and where it will, and descends from this Intuitive level to be captured by the artist's trained mind. Matthew Arnold realised this when he wrote:

> *We cannot kindle when we will*
> *The fire that in the heart resides,*
> *The spirit bloweth and is still,*
> *In mystery our soul abides:*
> > *But tasks in hours of insight will'd*
> > *Can be through hours of gloom fulfill'd.*

I am disposed to locate the sense of the "I", the soul's centre, on this level.

Above the Intuitive level I have placed the label Spiritual to stand for what is ultimately Real — those divine levels of being which are unbounded, in which some day our own destiny will be realised. The human being does not participate in them normally: but they are glimpsed by the mystics in their moments of exaltation. Even if we knew much about them, language would fail us as an instrument of communicating that knowledge. The Ego which is the centre of each unique soul, has been well called the divine spark in man. Its native air is the Spiritual level, but it is a spark, or better, a seed exiled from its proper environment and sown in the level below, where it constitutes the centre of the soul. By the term "soul" I mean this Ego together with as much of the Intuitive level as it participates in (according to its development), and so much of the mental level as it has appropriated to be its own instrument, together with a vehicle closely related to the emotional levels of Mind, which is sometimes called an "astral body". This astral body is used by the soul in the after-death state. When a new physical body is started there is also an astral counterpart which grows *pari passu* with the physical. The latter is basically the pattern of which the physical body may be regarded as a somewhat inferior replica. The astral body has its own senses of greater power and range than those of the physical body. Normally we do not use them because of the closer interlocking of the astral and physical which tunes them down to the limits of the physical. After the death of the physical body when the astral body becomes the vehicle of the soul and has separated from the physical body, it gradually takes up its own natural rhythm which brings it into relationship with, and awareness of, the astral levels of life. These are the "heaven" of Christian belief. There is sometimes in ordinary physical life a residual fringe of astral sense faculty, often referred to as extra-sensory perception, or more popularly as a sixth sense or second-sight.

The soul is generally understood to be that part of the whole self which survives death of the physical body. At a much higher stage of development the astral body may itself be discarded in favour of a still more subtle vehicle. The term "personality" as I use it, refers to the outward expression of the soul. "Persona" comes from a Latin word meaning "mask", so that the significance of the term is that it is the man as he is seen and known to others.

ASTRAL PROJECTION

The reader may wonder what evidence there is for what we have called an astral body, the vehicle which we shall use after the physical one is discarded at death. There is a phenomenon, not perhaps commonplace, but certainly not rare, which deserves to be more widely known. It offers evidence which bears strongly on the subject of human survival. There are many recorded instances of people who have had the experience of being fully conscious outside their physical body, and seeing the latter apparently asleep on a bed. Some observers have reported a silvery-looking cord which appeared to link them with the physical body. Spontaneous projections of this kind are often associated with times of illness or extreme weakness, sometimes with the taking of certain drugs or anaesthetics, and sometimes with sudden shock where death might have been anticipated as imminent. There are also methods which some persons have developed for getting outside the body at will and functioning for a time in this astral body. (A friend of mine who died some years ago did this deliberately on many occasions during his lifetime, when he wanted to gather knowledge or help someone in need.) Those who are interested will find a good deal of literature now available.* So that the reader may have

* *vide* Appendix.

an idea of this kind of experience I will record one or two examples. A person functioning in his astral body is usually invisible to others, but there are a few cases on record of the projector becoming visible to someone else. The possibility of the latter would obviously depend on the psychic state of the percipient.

Case 1 (*Journal S.P.R.*, Vol. 34, p. 210, 1948)

"I was stationed in Aden in 1913 and was seriously ill with dysentery. I got to the stage of having to be lifted from side to side as I was too weak to move myself in bed. From the instructions I heard the M.O. give the orderlies (we had no nurses in Aden then), I gathered that a collapse was expected, and that in the event of this occurrence I was to be given a saline injection via the rectum. Shortly afterwards I found myself lying parallel to the bed, about three or four feet above it, and face downwards. Below me I saw my body and witnessed the giving of the rectal injection. I listened to all the conversation of the two orderlies and of a strange medical officer who was directing affairs, and was indeed a very interested spectator of the whole business. I remember well that the saline came from an enamel kind of vessel which was connected to a rubber tube, the vessel being held up at arm's length by an orderly. I found myself next back in bed feeling much better. I told my story to the orderlies who were quite sceptical. I particularly enquired about the strange M.O. I found there had been one; he was en route for Bombay, I think, and had called at the hospital in time to help. I never saw him again. . . . I find I have omitted to mention that the orderlies said I couldn't possibly have any knowledge of the matter, as I was quite unconscious before and after the operation."

It may be mentioned that many accounts of the process of exteriorisation of the astral body record that it is rigid or cataleptic in the process, until a certain minimum distance of about eight to twelve feet from the physical body is attained. After this it is released and capable of free movement.

Case 2

"The person involved in this case was a trusted citizen in a small American township. He had hitched his team one day in winter and gone into the country to get a load of firewood. On his return he was sitting on top of a loaded sleigh. Light snow was falling. Without warning, a hunter who happened to be near the road, discharged his gun at a rabbit. The horses were startled and jerked the sleigh so that the driver fell to the ground head first. No sooner had he landed on the ground than he was conscious of standing up, and of seeing another 'himself' lying motionless near the road, face down in the snow. He saw the steam rising from the horses and saw the hunter running towards him. All this was very clear, but his conclusion was that there were two of him, for at the time he believed that he was observing everything from another physical body. As the hunter drew near and tried to revive him, his outer consciousness grew dim, and he found himself coming-to in his body on the ground. He could not believe that there were not two physical bodies involved, and he even went to look for tracks in the snow where he knew he had been standing."

Case 3 (from Rev. George Hepworth's book *Brown Studies*)

"While sitting with my right arm resting on the arm of the chair, I seemed to step out of my body, and stand beside it, looking upon it with mingled curiosity and astonishment. I felt as light as air and said to myself, 'This must be what St. Paul called the spiritual body.' It is true that I looked upon what sat in the chair with a kind of tenderness, but the sense of freedom that I soon became conscious of was almost ecstatic, and it seemed as though I would not go back into those narrow quarters again for worlds. The body was so clumsy, so heavy, so uncomely, so uncouth and ungraceful, while this other body, on the contrary was a delight, a dream, a poem.

"Then something happened which perhaps you may explain; but I confess it puzzled me at the time and has continued to puzzle me ever since. I moved away from my body towards the door, thinking to open it and go out into the starlight; but to my surprise I found that the door was no obstruction whatever. I simply passed through it as the sun's rays pass through a pane of glass. When I stood in front of the camp I knew that a cold wind was blowing and that it came from the snow banks far away to the north of us; but I was not chilled. I could feel its impact and hear it whistling through the forest, but was not affected by it in the least degree. I shall never be able to tell you how the stars looked that night. The heavens were an astonishing revelation to me. Not only did I see with perfectly clear vision, but there seemed to be a penetrating, far-reaching quality to my sight which doubled the number of glistening lights above me, and the spectacle was so marvellous, so beautiful, that I stood entranced. . . .

"Then I stepped back into the room to get another glimpse of the body. It was still in the chair, and I noticed that the breast rose and fell at regular intervals. It is not dead, I said to myself, only in some mysterious way, I have stepped out of it. I shall have to return to it by and by, and at that thought, I shuddered. . . .

"While I stood there my dog Leo awoke from a long nap, stretched, yawned, and then looked about the room. He approached my body in the usual way with a wag of the tail, snuffed at my legs, and then appeared to be confused and disappointed. Something was not as he expected to find it, and I wondered at the time what it could be. He then deliberately, but it seemed to me rather disconsolately, walked around the chair to the point from which he started, and snuffed at my legs a second time. Not satisfied, he sat on his haunches a full minute gazing into the face, and I thought perhaps his confusion arose from the fact that the eyes were closed and the body appeared to be asleep. On ordinary occasions when he wished to awaken me from a doze, he put his paws on my knees and gave a quick sharp bark, as though to say, 'Come Master, rouse yourself.' But this time he must have concluded that a serious mishap had occurred, for he exhibited signs of terror, his tongue hung out of his mouth, his eyes had an expression of agony in them, and he uttered a prolonged but low and mournful howl. Scarcely had it ended, however, when he caught sight of me apparently, standing near the door. With a single leap he reached my side, but turned instantly, took his place between me and the body, looked first at one and then at the other, and trembled in evident agony. . . . I am sure that Leo saw what was in the chair and also what stood by the door."

Testimony of this kind could be multiplied, but it must suffice to say that there is a considerable and growing amount of evidence supporting the existence of an astral body which is the outer vehicle of the soul on the next level of existence.

SOUL AND SPIRIT

I hope the diagram earlier in this chapter will convey to the reader the idea that the "soul" is the real person, the individual who says "I". He remains fundamentally unchanged by the death of the physical body. We shall have more to say about the astral body in Chapter 13.

Nothing so far has been said about the highest of the levels which has been described by the term "Spirit". It may be asked whether man does not participate in this level also? The level of Spirit (which may be infinite) is one of which we know little: we believe that it is ultimately Real and that it is the source and primary origin of all the levels which lie below it in the scale of reality. The Ego is a spark of this spiritual level, but it is a spark in exile from its true environment. It has drawn around itself in the long process of its evolution the instruments and vehicles which the diagram shows. It has built up walls of selfhood. All the sages and teachers of mankind say in their own way that man's future destiny is to make, through his divine spark, a fully conscious union or contact with his divine parent, the Spirit. Of this supremely satisfying possibility most people have no knowledge, and only a few people whom we call mystics have had any experience. In the very advanced man, his Ego has this constant conscious awareness of illumination by the Spirit. This is the goal of man's life as man, in which his Ego is surrendered to the Spirit and becomes its perfect vehicle and servant.

Immersed in the flesh and limited by the five senses to the physical view of the universe, not many people are aware of their true nature or the infinite possibilities which lie before them. Yet in man's heart there is a restlessness — for what he does not know — but it is for something that will bring him complete satisfaction. He searches for it in the world around, and he never finds it there. It is rooted in a spiritual homesickness of the soul. I think the poet George Herbert may have known this when he wrote:

> *When God at first made man,*
> *Having a glass of blessings standing by,*
> *"Let us," said He, "pour on him all we can;*
> *Let the world's riches, which dispersèd lie,*
> *Contract into a span."*
>
> *So strength first made a way;*
> *Then beauty flow'd, then wisdom, honour, pleasure;*
> *When almost all was out, God made a stay,*
> *Perceiving that, alone of all His treasure,*
> *Rest in the bottom lay.*
>
> *"For if I should," said He,*
> *"Bestow this jewel also on my creature,*
> *He would adore my gifts instead of Me,*
> *And rest in Nature, not the God of Nature:*
> *So both should losers be.*
>
> *"Yet let him keep the rest,*
> *But keep them with repining restlessness;*
> *Let him be rich and weary, that at least,*
> *If goodness lead him not, yet weariness*
> *May toss him to my breast."*

Chapter

12

DO I SURVIVE DEATH?

Love runs into the arms of death and finds not destruction, but the beauty
and the mercy of life.

Hugh I'A Fausset

THERE are moments in the lives of all men when this question seems
one of the most urgent and important that they can ask.

Think of the world's long story, of all the civilisations which have
risen to their zenith and decayed; of the teeming millions of human
beings, each of whom had feelings very like our own, who lived their
little lives and passed away. They had their fears and hopes, they
loved and suffered, they knew courage and despair, they dreamed
their dreams and are gone. Are they, in a phrase of Whittier's, just
dead facts:

stranded on the shore
Of the oblivious years.

Men generally only face this question when they are called upon to
meet great danger or serious illness. Millions in our day have faced
it amid all the tragedies of war. The question comes to haunt us
when someone we dearly love has passed away. The voice, the lips,
the hands, and eyes — all the precious emblems of personality have
vanished and only memories remain. Our own turn will come. Perhaps
a few friends will cherish our memory for a little while, but they too
will pass, and we shall join the uncounted multitudes who are as
though they had never been.

Is this true? If a man really believes this he may well despair of
the world. He may sympathise with the melancholy notes of A. E.
Housman, or he may resign himself to the despairing agnosticism of
Thomas Hardy. Towards the end of his great novel *Tess of the
D'Urbervilles*, Tess is talking to her husband Angel Clare in the last
few minutes of her freedom before she is caught and hanged.

"Tell me now, Angel, do you think we shall meet again after we are
dead? I want to now."

He kissed her to avoid a reply at such a time.

"O Angel — I fear that means no," said she, with a repressed sob. "And I wanted so to see you again — so much, so much! What — not even you and I, Angel, who love each other so well?"

Hardy could offer no hope, and as his great story closes he can only say that, "the President of the Immortals . . . had ended his sport with Tess".

Lord Russell is perhaps the best-known representative of those intellectuals who believe that death ends all. He once indicated that he was building his house "on the firm foundations of unyielding despair". He has said comparatively recently, "I can see no reason whatever to suppose that the universe takes any interest in our hopes and desires." While one must admire the Stoic honesty of Russell, he unfortunately gives no indication that he has studied carefully the kind of evidence which would offer him solid ground for optimism.

If it is true that man perishes with the death of his body, let us admit frankly that we live in a world which is deplorably and fundamentally unjust to many people, and which is tragically disturbing to all who think about the issues. Some human beings have started life with major handicaps: they have had to contend with frustration and suffering, poverty, cruelty, and discouragement. Some of these have made a marvellous fight. Others, through no merit or effort of their own, seem in contrast to be favoured and fortunate. The observer of human life to whom moral justice means a great deal must find the problem insoluble if his horizon is bounded by this life. Neither reason, morality, or justice are clearly pervasive in this spectacle, and if a man believed in God under such circumstances it would naturally be with fear or antagonism.

If this life is all, then it is a tragedy for human beings, born without choice and perishing without hope, especially where the years between are spent in a loaded struggle against circumstance. If the truth is that we perish when the body dies, then the things which we have most valued while alive, the love we have known, the beauty we have seen, the sacrifices which others have made for us — these things bring to us our saddest thoughts.

There is no more urgent question we can ask than this: "Do we survive death in the fullness of our powers?" We have a right to expect an answer, satisfying alike to our thinking and feeling, both in its nature and reliability. May I say frankly that unless I believed I had such an answer, equally available to others who desired enough to have it, I should not be writing this book.

In a moving passage in his poem *Good Friday* John Masefield says through one of his characters:

> *Friend, it is over now,*
> *The passion, the sweat, the pains,*
> *Only the truth remains.*

What is this truth? Everything that is worth being and knowing is involved in the answer we give.

IS THERE A SATISFACTORY ANSWER?

There are some people who are in a fortunate position. They can say with complete sincerity and conviction, "I *know* I shall survive death. I need no evidence to support this. It is for me an intuitive certainty." I do not think such persons are more than a small minority of the community, and those of us who do not belong to this select number have to go out seeking for an answer.

The convinced Christian tells us that he derives his confidence in survival from two sources. (1) He believes in a God Whose nature is disclosed in the life and teaching of Jesus Christ. "If ye, being evil, know how to give good gifts unto your children, how much more shall your Heavenly Father ... Are not two sparrows sold for a farthing, and not one of them shall fall on the ground without your Father ... Fear not therefore ..." This teaching of a loving God Who cares for all His children is completely satisfying *to those who can accept things on authority.* (2) It is pointed out that Jesus rose from his tomb on the third day, that He made many appearances to his disciples and friends in the weeks that followed, that He convinced them that death had no power over Him, and sent them out to preach what He had taught them. In this event the Christian finds strong support for belief in his own survival of death. He can point to such sayings of Jesus as, "Because I live, ye shall live also," and "God is not the God of the dead but of the living."

There are many people who are able and satisfied to accept such authority, and they do not feel it necessary to make any distinction between belief and knowledge. They do not usually feel any sympathy for people who either cannot or are unwilling to do this: they look at them a little reproachfully as people who "lack faith". This will not do. There are a great many people today (and the number is perhaps increasing in this scientific age) whose attitude might be put into such words as these: "Faith is not natural to us. We can't 'adopt' it. We first require that our minds shall form a judgment on such evidence as is available. We realise that feelings, hopes, and desires can easily lead people astray, and we do not want to be led up the garden path. If our minds can be satisfied of the reasonableness of a position, then, although conclusive proof may be unobtainable, we may come to accept it as a probability." I have great sympathy with this attitude, and I hope to indicate in this chapter a few of the lines of evidence which converge on the issue of survival.

WHAT WOULD BE PROOF OF SURVIVAL?

If you started to receive communications allegedly from a friend of yours in a different country, could you satisfy yourself of his identification? I think most people would reply "Yes". I suggest you could form a sound opinion based upon such things as (i) memories shared in common but not shared with anyone else who might possibly impersonate the friend, and (ii) personal characteristics such as moral sensibility, sensitivity to beauty, views and ideals upon a variety of themes, peculiarities of phrasing, sense of humour, type of reaction, etc.

Each of our friends has a different sum of personality traits which, given a sufficient opportunity for expression of them, would enable one to say with conviction, "This is my friend." It is this kind of material which forms the most satisfying evidence of a friend's survival of death, in those cases where it can be obtained freely. The problem of communication is in this case, not one of distance, but of consciousness being focused on two different levels of existence. In my experience the gulf between the incarnate and the discarnate mind can be bridged, and this brings us to the question of mediumship.

There are here and there persons who can apparently withdraw their consciousness from the physical level at will or, as we simply say, go into a trance. We call them sensitives or mediums. It appears that under favourable circumstances a discarnate being may use a trance medium to write or speak through. There seem to be two different methods of communication used. In one of these the discarnate communicator makes a telepathic link with the medium and plants thoughts in the subconscious mind of the latter. The medium then has to find words to express the ideas through speaking or hand-writing and so becomes an interpreter. In the second method the discarnate communicator may control the medium in a more immediate and quasi-physical manner, as by some control of the hand or voice. Some of the handwriting or speaking characteristics of the communicator may then become evident. Sometimes a combination of these methods may be used.

PERSONAL EXPERIENCE

It may interest the reader to know that my own convictions are based upon communications in writing from a medium in London whom I met for the first (and only) time in October 1953. The occasion was a social one. I asked this lady if, some time when she felt so disposed, she would attempt to make a contact with "the other side" which might be of some interest to myself. No persons or names were suggested, but I provided some of my handwriting to be a possible psychic link. In March 1954 I received a script, which the medium told me, she had written slowly and with difficulty while in a withdrawn semi-trance state holding the sample of my handwriting in her other hand. This communication claimed to be from "Astor", a control of the medium, and gave me a description of a friend of mine who died in Melbourne in April 1944. The name of this friend Ambrose Pratt, was worked out by Astor from symbols which he said were shown to him. All the facts given about my friend were correct: no mistake was made. I thanked the medium, said the data presented were correct, and encouraged her to try again. I enclosed a letter which I wrote to my friend A. P. as though he had been alive in the flesh. I asked him several questions and suggested to the medium that she should read this letter before attempting another contact. A few weeks later I received another script containing answers to my questions which I felt were satisfactory. The most remarkable feature of this second script however was that Astor, after writing two or three lines said he would relinquish the pen to my friend, and from this point onwards a different handwriting to that which Astor had used was maintained. In my opinion it was not the same as A. P.'s earthly handwriting, nor was it quite the same as the medium's normal handwriting, although it was much closer to the latter than to the former. From this feature I concluded that the communicator was using substantially a telepathic link with the medium.

It must suffice to say here that this was the first of a series of communications (which covered a period of about five years) in which my friend wrote with an intimacy and an authority characteristic of the man, whom I had known well, and who possessed a distinctive and distinguished personality. The primary reason which led him to search for this contact with me, so he said, was to make a request to me on behalf of a group of scholars on his side (naming them) with whom he had certain links. The request was that I would study the philosophy of Douglas Fawcett and write an exposition of it for the thoughtful man of today. This task I did in fact undertake, and I discharged it by writing *Nurslings of Immortality* which was published in 1957. I may later publish more detail of these communications: for the present I shall merely say that they convinced me of the survival of my friend Ambrose Pratt.

To those who may wonder whether the correct description of my friend and his interests was not a brilliant piece of thought-reading — the medium being in Britain, and I in Australia — I can only say that in the light of the nature of the communications and several subtle features they contain, this hypothesis is not satisfactory to me. I knew nothing at that time of Douglas Fawcett's thought (with one minor exception), and the idea of writing a book expounding his ideas could never have had a place in my mind. If it is suggested that (i) this plan was formulated in the medium's own mind (for she had met Fawcett on a few occasions), and (ii) the dramatic form in which the request was made to me per my friend A. P. was wholly derived by her thought-reading of my mind, such a possibility cannot be completely ruled out. I consider, however, that it leaves unaccounted for other material in the scripts which is characteristic of my friend. Although there were some scripts in which I judged the subconscious mind of the medium had been markedly active and contributory, I have retained my conviction that my old friend A. P. was undoubtedly there in the background as the originator and principal factor in the scripts.

PROBLEMS OF COMMUNICATION

Let us consider now, some of the problems of communication. In the first method, which is likely to be used where the communicator has advanced a long way from physical conditions, there is a risk of misinterpretation by the medium whose knowledge of the subject or whose vocabulary may be limited. There is also a real possibility that ideas in the medium's own subconscious mind may be intermingled with the communicator's implanted ideas. The second method, of near-physical control (probably at the etheric level of the medium), is less likely to be interwoven with the medium's subconscious material, but is more likely to be used by those discarnate beings who are still not far from physical conditions. Many of these have probably little which is significant to communicate. The fundamental problem of communication by either method is this, however, that the medium's own psychic faculty may be exercised in the trance state. The mind of the entranced medium may frequently be in telepathic rapport with the mind of one or other of the sitters present, and by a process commonly called thought-reading such a medium may speak (or write) of things which are believed to be known only to such a sitter — or at least to the communicator and the sitter. The question now arises: what really is their origin? Is a deceased communicator conveying the data through the medium, or is the medium drawing the material from the subconscious mind of the sitter? This is the most fundamental problem involved in assessing the origin of supposed communications from a deceased person.

Someone will suggest, "Couldn't a communicator disclose something significant which *he* knew, but which no living person knows, something which could afterwards be verified by the research of the sitter?" For example, the communicator might disclose the exact place of a buried treasure or a hidden object. Such experiments have been carried out. The position of the lost "Edgar" chapel at Glastonbury was communicated in this way.* In another instance, a person before his death took a brick, made certain marks across it, broke it into two, and gave one half to his sister saying that he proposed to hide the other half-brick and would disclose where he had hidden it after his death, if that were possible. This was done successfully.† But is this kind of evidence an absolute proof of survival of a person with the knowledge? It might be claimed that the medium in trance had used clairvoyant power to discover the whereabouts of these

---

* *The Gate of Remembrance*, F. B. Bond (Oxford, Basil Blackwell, 1921).

† *Human Personality* Vol. II, pp. 183–5, F. W. H. Myers (Longmans Green & Co. Ltd.).

things. A trance medium is not usually able to distinguish material from different sources in this way: at any rate the issue is not one of conscious fraudulence.

Someone may suggest, "If X wants to get in touch with his deceased friend Y, then instead of X going to sit with the medium, why should not X send a friend of his as a proxy?" This would establish that anything which the medium disclosed about Y was not due to tapping the mind of X for memories of Y. Such proxy-sittings have been carried out scores of times, sometimes with quite remarkable results, where the friend of X knew nothing about Y except his name. If we are determined to be sceptical, however, it could be claimed that the medium discovers from the sitter's mind that the sitter is there as a proxy for X, and could then telepathically draw the information from X's mind.

A remarkable experiment was carried out some years ago by Dr. Richard Hodgson, a very competent investigator with a sceptical turn of mind. He had a friend whom he had known well, called George Pelham, and after the latter's death, he communicated with Hodgson over a period of several years through the mediumship of Mrs. Piper. Dr. Hodgson declared in the end that he was convinced beyond any reasonable doubt of the survival of his friend George Pelham. Among many tests which Dr. Hodgson made, one of the most impressive was that over a considerable period of time he introduced more than one hundred and fifty persons to sittings with Mrs. Piper. Thirty of these had been personal friends of the communicator when alive on earth, and he recognised them all. He made no false recognitions or mistakes and he conversed with those he knew on matters of mutual interest, showing the appropriate emotional reactions and degree of intimacy in each case. This sort of test is impressive because it is subtle, as we should admit when we recall the different degrees of friendship and varying mutual interests which we share with our own friends.

EVIDENCE OF PURPOSE

There is another type of communication which is impressive as a pointer to the survival of personality with its wishes, loves, concerns, memories, etc. Sometimes there suddenly breaks into a sitting a discarnate person not known to the medium or sitters, who makes use of the medium to communicate something for which there would seem to be a compelling motive. The motive might be to warn someone in great danger, to make amends for a wrong done, to help a person in great distress through a crisis, etc. The intrusion might not be into a seance, it might be into a dream, or as an apparition in a waking state. Here is an example of the last kind.

A minister was sitting alone in his study one night when he heard the bell ring. Going to the door he found standing there a young woman whom he knew fairly well. She was from a village some five miles away. The village was in an adjoining circuit from which the minister had moved some sixteen months before.

"Good evening," she cried, "I expect you have forgotten me, but I have come on a very urgent errand. My father is dying. He never attended church much, but once or twice when you were in the circuit we persuaded him to hear you preach. I do wish you would come and pray with him before he passes away."

"I will come at once," replied the minister. Putting on his hat and coat and taking an umbrella from the stand, he set off in the pouring rain on a five-mile walk, accompanied by the young woman.

On his arrival at the house, the wife welcomed him warmly. "Oh, how good of you to come," she said, "but how did you know that my husband was passing away?"

"Your daughter came for me," he replied, with some surprise at the question. It was the woman's turn to be surprised now.

"Come upstairs at once," she said, "and we will talk afterwards."

The minister went to the bedside of the dying man, spoke to him and prayed with him, and shortly afterwards, the end came. Turning to the woman, who was now a widow, he asked where the daughter was, for he had not seen her again since they entered the house. The woman replied, "I was surprised when you came to the door this evening, and I asked you who told you that my husband was dying. You said that my daughter called, and that you had come out together. You have not heard then, that my daughter died a year ago?"

Now the minister was astonished indeed. "Dead!" he exclaimed, "she came to my door, rang the bell, and walked out here with me.

"But there," he said, "I think I can prove that. As we came along together, the road was up in one place, and a watchman and another man were sitting in a hut in front of a fire. They saw us go by. I'll speak to them on my way home."

He set off on his return journey, and found the two men still sitting in front of the fire. "You saw me go by an hour or so ago, didn't you?"

he said to the men. "Was I alone?" "Yes sir," one of them replied, "and you were talking away to yourself as fast as you could go."*

The next case is of interest (although an old one), because it became the basis of a lawsuit, and the facts were therefore subjected to careful investigation.

The Chaffin Will Case †

A farmer, James L. Chaffin, who lived in North Carolina, made a will on November 16th 1905 in which he gave the farm to his third son Marshall, leaving his widow and three other sons unprovided for. On January 16th 1919 he apparently repented of this unfairness and made a second will which was unwitnessed, but which would, according to the State law be valid, providing it could be proved that it was in the testator's own handwriting. No one knew of the existence of this second will, which the farmer placed between two pages of an old family Bible. The eccentric old farmer told no one that it was there prior to his death, but apparently stitched up the inner pocket of his overcoat with a roll of paper inside it. This paper bore the words, "Read the 27th chapter of Genesis in my daddy's old Bible." The farmer died on September 7th 1921, and soon afterwards the third son Marshall, obtained probate of the only known will.

About June 1925 the second son, James, started to have a number of vivid dreams in which his deceased father stood at his bedside wearing his black overcoat, and said to him, "You will find my will in my overcoat pocket." James was sufficiently impressed to do something about it, and with others as witnesses he found the overcoat and the roll of paper, and finally the old Bible containing the second will. It became the basis of a lawsuit in December 1925 and was finally admitted as valid.

The most plausible explanation is that the eccentric old farmer survived death, and with a troubled conscience took the initiative which caused the dream appearances to his son James. If it is suggested that it might have been clairvoyant activity on the part of James, the information disclosing itself in dream form, two difficulties arise. Why did the clairvoyance take about four years to become active? Why did it not disclose the second will's location directly, instead of via the roll of paper in the old overcoat?

I will present a third example‡ very briefly, because it discloses

---

* Rev. Dr. Leslie Weatherhead vouches for the authenticity of this case, which is quoted from his book *The Resurrection and the Life* (Epworth Press, 1948).

† Full detail is in *Proc. S.P.R.*, Vol. XXXVI, p. 517.

‡ I am indebted to Mr. Norman Hunt for allowing me to use this account.

a strong motive for intervention. In a circle of friends in England there was a Czech lady (who will be called Edith) in the account below.

On one occasion Edith was unexpectedly controlled in trance by a person who gave his name as C——. C—— implored us to try to help his wife who, he said, had been arrested and was then in prison in Prague, the name of which he gave us. If, he said, she would get into touch with a certain Dr. K. — giving us his address — this person had access to documents which would secure his wife's release from prison.

On returning to normal consciousness Edith was told of this, but beyond knowing of C——'s death, she was quite unaware of the other circumstances and the fate of C——'s wife, as indeed unaware of the existence of any person called Dr. K. She wrote guardedly, owing to the political situation, and received a letter in reply, which angrily told her not to meddle in such dangerous business. There the matter rested for eighteen months, when a former acquaintance of Edith's, a connection of C——, escaped from Czechoslovakia and made his way to England. He sought out Edith and related to her the following story.

C—— had three daughters. At his death the youngest was only eleven months old. When she was only three or four years old she was found to be writing little messages which she said came from her daddy. He was, she insisted, constantly present in the house. Soon afterwards, she began to hold conversations with him, and to see him so plainly that she was able to describe his appearance in detail. Her family rejected the whole thing as fantastic, and the child's supposed mental state was the subject of grave anxiety.

A little later, this family had a visit from a gentleman who was a complete stranger to them, who explained that he was a member of a spiritualistic circle in Prague (to which the narrator belonged). He said that a person who called himself C—— had spoken through their medium and had asked that someone should visit the address — which he was now doing in fulfilment of this request. C—— had particularly requested that his youngest daughter should be allowed to visit their circle. This was granted, and a photograph of a group of people which included C—— was produced there. The child picked out C—— from this photograph ˙and said, "That's my papa who comes and talks with me."

C—— had also begged that someone in their circle should contact a certain Dr. K., giving his address, and this was done. It was found that he had, as Edith had been informed in England, access to certain papers. Apparently his mood was more propitious and these papers were sent on to the Public Prosecutor in whose hands the case of

C——'s wife rested. Shortly afterwards she was released from prison.

This kind of evidence where a number of separate events took place, all converging on an event which the communicator had every reason to be profoundly interested in, points with the greatest cogency to the survival of C——.

THE CROSS-CORRESPONDENCE EXPERIMENTS

These "experiments" took place on many occasions between 1907 and 1916 and the material occupies many volumes of the Proceedings of the Society for Psychical Research. Its importance can only be assessed properly by a person prepared to make a detailed study of it. All that will be done here is to indicate the nature of this work and its important bearing on the survival issue.

F. W. H. Myers, a distinguished classical scholar and Fellow of Trinity, Cambridge, died in 1901. He was one of the founders of the Society above referred to, and had been as active as anyone in assessing evidence bearing on the question of survival. Associated with the Society about this period, there were a number of ladies who had some mediumistic capacity which took the form of automatic writing. The facts point to the deceased Myers as author of the type of experiment which I shall describe. He composed an erudite classical essay, and proceeded to communicate some parts of it through the automatic handwriting of one of these ladies, other parts through a second lady and the remainder through a third lady. He introduced a number of allusions and cross-references in each of the scripts, but all this made very little sense to the automatists. When these scripts were brought together and examined at the Headquarters of the Society, they were found by eminent classical scholars to be interlocked in a way which could not possibly be conceived as due to chance. Perhaps an analogy will make the matter clearer.

Suppose a large jigsaw puzzle was shuffled and divided into three portions: one pile of pieces is given to each of three persons who are kept apart. Each is told to make what they can of the puzzle. It is clear that each of them would only be able to make very limited sense of the picture, since considerable portions would be missing. But if the three attempts were brought together in one place, then the relationship would become apparent to study, and it would be inconceivable that the three piles of pieces had any other origin than one complete jigsaw puzzle.

A classical essay was transmitted again and again over a period of years. Its nature was frequently such that it required the skill of classical scholars to show they were inter-related. Those best qualified to judge were driven to the conclusion that Myers was indeed the author of them, and was attempting from the other side of death to present the strongest possible evidence of his own survival.

COMMUNICATION WITH THE DISCARNATE

Assuming then the possibility of communication with those who have passed on, a number of questions arise. People ask: is it a good thing? Does it in any way hamper or hold back those with whom we get in touch? Is there any danger involved in mediumistic communication? What do you think of spiritualism?

Is it a good thing? We use such means as are at our disposal to keep in touch with those we love when they are on earth, but separated from us by distance. No one, so far as I know, has ever suggested that this was undesirable. The fact that one of the parties is discarnate does not seem to me to change the naturalness or rightness of this desire at all. Different techniques are necessary, of course. Whereas physical means were formerly sufficient, psycho-physical means are now necessary.

Does it hamper those with whom we get in touch? Surely communication is a two-sided affair. It is as absurd to suppose one can compel communication as it is to suppose you can compel a correspondent to reply to a letter. Those who do so do it voluntarily, and probably are free to use different methods (discussed earlier in this chapter). The evidence suggests that those who have passed on like to feel that they are remembered with affection. What tends to hold back and hamper the progress of those who have passed over is inconsolable grief by those on earth — the mood of the perpetual mourner.

Is there any danger involved in mediumistic communication? There is probably some danger involved in every enquiry of mind or of body. We accept danger when we board a bus by crossing the street, but we do not stay at home for this reason. The person who goes into a mediumistic trance clearly exposes himself to some measure of control from without. This kind of work is not usually undertaken without some knowledge. Frequently it is done under the protection of the higher self, or under the direction of discarnate beings who co-operate from the other side. There are, of course, mischievous and evil discarnate beings just as there are on the incarnate level. This is to be expected: but it need not determine the issue of communication or not.

What do you think of spiritualism? I am not favourably impressed. The great majority of those who attend spiritualistic meetings and seances have no clear appreciation of the mind's extra-sensory powers. They naïvely assume that all the phenomena are what they purport to be or what they wish them to be. This is far from being the case, and great critical discrimination is called for in the field of psychical phenomena. The possibilities of self-delusion and suggestion are almost limitless, and while I do not doubt that there are often genuine data, the sifting of them from the false, the classification of them and the interpretation of them is something which cannot be undertaken on a public platform or under conditions of a demonstration at a fixed time.

To the bereaved person who has a strong urge to explore this field in order to contact a loved one, I should say: make your journey of enquiry with carefully chosen mediums in private. Before you do so, learn all you can of the pitfalls. Keep your critical faculty alive and sensitive, and do not expect to get startling results immediately. It is no easy road upon which you are proposing to set out: you will probably have to find your way through a jungle of trivialities and nonsense, but if you persist, you will probably acquire in the end the conviction which you desire.

The orthodox religious-minded person who dislikes to face the facts of psychical research frequently says, when discussing communication, "Why are all these so-called communications so trivial, so ordinary and platitudinous, when there is so much of value that could be passed on to us?" Surely this question is based on the assumption that the change called death gives the soul an outlook and a wisdom which it did not possess prior to the change? Obviously death can add nothing to the quality of the mind and character. Ninety-nine per cent of the communications which people have with each other when alive are banal, ordinary, and platitudinous: why should we expect it to be different for those same people after death? It is indeed probable that those who remain close to earth-conditions and therefore find communication most easy, would have nothing of importance to say. There is no reason why the more advanced souls, who probably do not remain for long close to near-physical conditions, should communicate with us unless for some very good reason. This sometimes happens: and their communications do not consist of trivialities.

CONCLUSIONS

The case for survival does not rest upon a few examples and others like them, such as we have used in this chapter, but upon many lines of converging evidence. Some of these we have not been able to mention in the limited space. It is rather a paradox that it is our knowledge of the extra-sensory powers of Mind which make it so difficult to devise a conclusive test of survival, while at the same time these powers make it seem less and less likely that Mind has any essential dependence on Matter.

Perhaps conclusive proof may be impossible: but how rarely is such proof available in any field of enquiry! My own judgment is, however, perfectly clear: there is a vast amount of well-attested data which make man's survival of death seem highly probable. It is immensely satisfactory that this should be so, for in the light of a destiny which we conceive of as extending far beyond death, we can begin to make some sense of the world we know. We need not be unduly depressed by events which appear to be meaningless, or fears that perhaps the world is fundamentally unjust, when we can see this earthly experience as part of a greater whole which stretches out beyond the portals of birth and death. A man who entered a theatre on one side and walked across to the exit on the other side might draw some strange and wrong conclusions from the glimpse which he got of events on the stage. He might impulsively suppose that the author of the play was callous, cruel, or unjust, until he remembered that he had seen but a glimpse of the whole. If he had knowledge of what had gone before and what would follow, he might completely alter his attitude. He would certainly be able to make a sounder judgment.

The acceptance of survival does not solve our many problems, but it does make a solution a possibility. In later chapters we shall look at some of the indications that the solution will ultimately be satisfying to man's dearest dreams and hopes.

Chapter

13

WHAT IS IT LIKE AFTER DEATH?

If it were possible for the soul to die back into earth again, I should die from sheer yearning to reach you, to tell you that all we imagined is not half wonderful enough for the truth.

F. W. H. Myers
(communicated through Mrs. Holland)

I was called from fairer realms than you can ever possibly imagine or even faintly conceive so long as you are in the flesh.

A .P. to the author
(communicated through Miss Cummins)

THE majority of people who accept the Christian teaching of a life after death appear to have few ideas about its nature or characteristics. The subject has been clothed in vague symbolical language, and by and large, the Churches have made very little effort to enlighten people. All too often, when bereavement comes, people are assured that their loved ones are "with Christ — which is far better" or are "serving God with fuller powers". These things may be true, but those who wish to bring their minds to bear upon the problem of human destiny must feel profoundly dissatisfied with such answers. It is easy for the Church to say, "We know very little, and must be content to have faith in God until He chooses to unveil these mysteries to us." This attitude of making a virtue out of pious ignorance is so out of tune with today's scientific spirit that it does not commend itself to men. Man's mind has been applied to resolve many "mysteries" of the world around him, and his success has aroused wonder and admiration. With death a certainty for everyone, men rightly wish to know all they can about their future journey. If someone says "How *can* we know?" the only answer is that we ought to apply our minds as systematically to this problem as we have done to our other problems. The Society for Psychical Research has been doing this for almost eighty years, and it looks probable that the mind of man has powers which should· enable it to gather the kind of knowledge it desires to have.

The fact of telepathy, that one mind can communicate directly with another without the use of the senses, has been established beyond all doubt. When one of the minds becomes discarnate, this possibility is still there, and thus we have the possibility of acquiring knowledge of life after death. The practical problem is one of sifting the genuine knowledge from the subconscious imaginings or acquisitions of the receiving mind. With great care and skill, this can be done.

WHERE IS THE "NEXT WORLD"?

This is one of the obvious puzzles to anyone who thinks around the subject. Consider first a slightly different question. When we dream, where is the space in which we see things happening? Perhaps we say that in the dream we saw a tree on the left, a stream on the right, and a hill in the background: but it is clear that it is our own mind which has created this awareness of space, and while we are dreaming we do not doubt that it is real space. May it not be true that *all* space is mind-created? I am not suggesting that our three-dimensional physical space is created by *our* minds, but rather that it may be the product of a powerful Mind or Minds to which our own are in some way related. The phenomenon of dreaming shows that the human mind is, in its own small way, a creator, and may be active for a time in a space which is not identical with that of the waking world. One of the differences between our dream space and physical space is that it is not generally shared with other people. But there is no reason why it should not be so shared if a number of minds were in an appropriate relationship with each other. (I have come across rare cases in which dreamers shared a common space.)

Consider another familiar fact. The room in which you are reading is occupied by many different kinds of invisible waves — light waves, heat waves, radio waves, etc. They are filling the room with changing patterns and are not interfering with each other. We happen to have senses which make us aware of the first two, but mercifully, not of the third type. Radio waves require a special instrument to transform them into sound before we can become aware of them. This is only an analogy, but it may assist us to appreciate that different worlds of experience may exist together and occupy the same space, and yet we may be aware of only one such world. Another being in the same space might be aware of a different world. Some few beings might be aware of two different but co-existing worlds if they tuned their minds appropriately. The Austrian scientist and philosopher Rudolf Steiner* possessed this faculty from his earliest years.

The point we are making is that it is the state and nature of the mind which determines what we have the ability to discern. The "next world" of discarnate beings could be all around us, yet without our having any knowledge of this fact, or their having any knowledge of it, except in rare cases. A sufficient answer to the question "Where is the next world?" is surely this, it is wherever there are minds capable of tuning-in to it. If the blood contains sufficient ether or pentothal, traces of drugs such as mescalin, or even enough of the toxins of fatigue, then the associated mind becomes no longer aware of the physical world, or that alone. It is the state of mind which determines what we are aware of. Presumably when the mind is released permanently from its close linkage with the physical brain, then it will become permanently attuned to a higher order of perception — or a higher "vibratory rate". It is then able to perceive and act in a world of new experiences. The name we give to this state, whether the "astral world" or "heaven", does not matter.

DESCRIPTION OF THE NEXT WORLD

The next world apparently offers an enormous variety of experiences because souls are themselves so different in interests and capacities. If half a dozen persons went on the same journey through another country, and we asked each of them what they had seen, we should have some common elements, but on the whole, six different answers. One person was impressed by the magnificent scenery, another by the wild flowers, another by its economic possibilities, another by its political stability. They notice what they have trained themselves to notice: their impressions reflect their interests and capacities. This should be borne in mind when we compare the account of different communicators purporting to describe the next world. Accounts which differ may not necessarily be contradictory or untrue.

In the description which follows I have presented for the reader's consideration a composite picture of life after death, which I believe is reliable in its main outline. The factual didactic presentation is adopted for the sake of brevity. The reader has every right to ask on what sort of evidence it is built. The reply is that it is built upon

* *A Scientist of the Invisible*, A. P. Shepherd (Hodder & Stoughton Ltd.).

descriptions found in communications which are thought to be reliable and trustworthy. When from different sources we find obviously intelligent communicators presenting similar information, which is, moreover, consistent with what we might anticipate from our knowledge of the mind's powers, such a picture should be looked upon as at least a reasonable hypothesis. In the Appendix I have named a few books from which I think a sound description may be gathered. Many people have been profoundly dissatisfied with the symbolism and vagueness which characterise the references of orthodox religion to life after death.

THE IMMEDIATE AFTER-DEATH STATE

In Chapter 11 we described an experience which quite a few people have had, called astral projection. They were frequently aware of themselves in another vehicle or body outside their physical one. In these cases the "etheric" structure to which we referred remained closely associated with the physical body, which it does not normally leave during the life of the latter. When physical death takes place this is an astral projection in which the cord is finally severed, and in which the etheric material withdraws from the physical and surrounds the astral body like an overcoat. The livingness of the physical tissues then departs and they begin to decay. What an individual now experiences depends upon whether death has been sudden and unexpected, perhaps as in war or in an accident, or whether it has come gradually, as at the end of a long illness.

In the first case the soul is suddenly projected in his astral body, and for quite a time may have no clear awareness that anything unusual has happened. The astral body will retain for a period its rhythm or attunement to physical conditions, only slowly acquiring a higher "vibratory rate". The person's environment therefore continues to be the physical one. A soldier on a battle-field may go on fighting or wandering about as he was doing a few minutes before, and he may require some convincing that he is "dead". It may finally be made clear to him through seeing his own dead physical body, or by his inability to make his friends take any notice of him, or by the fact that he cannot lift or move a physical object. During the war, many who passed over suddenly and acquired familiarity with their new world, undertook the task of helping others who were often rather bewildered on this borderland.

Where, on the other hand, the approach to death has been more gradual, the links which bind the etheric to the physical are progressively severed, and the etheric overcoat or husk withdraws rapidly and usually places the astral body fairly quickly in a drowsy state of rest or sleep. In very old age we can almost see that these links are being severed, and we sometimes gain the impression that the soul has half-departed from its physical tenement. In sudden death, the etheric withdrawal is slower, but as it proceeds the soul in its astral body loses slowly its clarity of physical vision, and in the end rests or sleeps. In this time on the borderland, when we are told that friends of the person often gather to welcome and greet him, the restful phase is associated with the dissolution or evaporation of the etheric overcoat for which there is now no further use. The process may take from a few hours to a few days, and for the soul it is a period of dreamy sleep at the end of which it arrives at a clear awareness of the astral world which is its future environment. In this borderland location sometimes called "Hades", the astral body slowly acquires its own natural rhythm. It may possibly be some awareness of this intermediate phase which has given rise to the teaching of the Roman Catholic Church of a state of Purgatory interposed between earth and heaven. This is not, in our view, a stage of moral significance, but one rendered necessary by the changes just described.

It might interest the reader to read some sentences of F. W. H. Myers describing his own experience.*

"Pray do not conjure up unpleasant associations with Hades. I died in Italy, a land I loved, and I was very weary at the time of my passing. For me, Hades was a place of rest, a place of half-lights and drowsy peace. As a man wins strength from a long deep sleep, so did I gather that spiritual and intellectual force I needed, during the time I abode in Hades. According to his nature and make-up every traveller from the earth is affected in a different or varying manner by this place or state on the frontier of two lives, on the border of two worlds."

Another communicator describes a very different experience of an unpleasant nightmarish quality.†

"I think I really had the maximum difficulties: an attitude of blank unbelief in any future life, a repressed and powerful emotional make-up, the shock of a violent death. So this was not the normal

---

* *The Road to Immortality*, Geraldine Cummins (Aquarian Press).
† *The Country Beyond*, Jane Sherwood (Rider & Co. Ltd.).

passing, but just a difficult and painful personal experience. . . . When I tried to think, a swiftly racing flood of images and impressions tore through my mind, but they were incoherent and unmanageable. I could not learn how to control my emotions, which were like an unruly army suddenly released from all discipline. But gradually this delirious confusion passed. . . . Help was offered me, remember; but that my pride and prejudices made me such a difficult person to help, I should not have slipped back so often into confusion."

AN OBJECTIVE WORLD

When the ordinary person thinks about the world which he perceives with his senses, he does not doubt for a moment that it is "real". It can be seen and touched, and to him this is proof enough. As we have remarked, that which a mind calls real, depends entirely on the state of that mind. We must therefore emphasise that the next world, or astral world, which the mind discerns after death, is quite as real to souls using astral senses, as the physical world is to souls using physical senses. We must dismiss the idea that the after-death state is something vague and formless. Why should it be? In the diagram on page 142 we placed the mental level above the physical, on the basis of the evidence before us. The astral level being closely related to the lower levels of mind, is a step nearer to the absolutely Real. All the expectations which we may form on this ground are supported by the most reliable communicators.

The physical body appears to be a somewhat inferior replica of the astral body. The latter has its own senses which it at first uses freely in relation to the new world. But the soul finds increasingly that he need depend less and less on these senses, wide though their range is, since the powers of mind are more accessible to him. We are told that speech and hearing which are at first adopted as the natural means of communication, come increasingly to be replaced by the interchange of thought — a direct mind to mind communication. It is interesting to recall that J. Stuart Mill the philosopher once said, "That the eye is essential to sight seems to me the notion of one immersed in matter." The poet Rupert Brooke foresaw a day when we should "see no longer blinded by our eyes".

In view of the relationship of the two worlds, it is not surprising to be told that the astral world embodies to a considerable extent the best natural features of our physical world, its countryside, trees and flowers, fields and houses. The things which we have appreciated and desired on earth, to which we have made a response of value, we find again in a more satisfactory form on the astral level. Within limits this level might be described as the country of wishes-come-true. Things which misfortune once destroyed, dreams which we would wish to have realised, hopes which we cherished but could not bring to fruition — these are possibilities which, if we desire, we can resume on the astral level. Because of this, it has been described by most communicators as a pleasant idyllic kind of existence which may be prolonged as long as the soul desires it. Apparently the basis of this level of existence is sustained and created by powerful Beings who, however, look upon it largely as a world of illusion. It is not illusory to those who inhabit it, any more than the physical world is illusory to its inhabitants. More advanced beings may well look upon this immature outlook, as we in our turn look back with some tenderness to the immaturity of our own childhood's outlook. The astral world provides a setting for all newly arrived souls, which is not too different in its nature from that with which they have been familiar, so that they can feel "at home". The minds of dwellers on the astral plane have a modifying effect both upon the appearance of their astral body and upon their immediate environment. This is an aspect of the greater degree of inter-penetration or relationship which exists as we move upwards in the scale of Reality (see diagram p. 142). It is on earth that separateness is most marked. Here, if we want to change our environment, e.g. by constructing a garden or a piece of furniture, we form the mental pattern first and then have to carry it out by using our muscles aided perhaps by suitable tools. In the astral world the mind begins to exert a direct creative and modifying effect on its environment.

This bears upon the question of the outward appearance of souls in the astral world. Do old people look old, and young people look young? The astral body being a specially appropriated part of the environment would be expected to be very subject to the mind's own determination. Old people may therefore modify their appearance to look younger, and young people can change it to look older if they wish to do so. Clothing, which is obviously an appropriated part of the near environment is presumably modified to suit the mind's desires.

What is it Like After Death?

It is not to be supposed that there is one vast astral world equally accessible in all its parts to all souls passing over at death. As on earth there are many countries with many different cultures and modes of life, and within each country there are groups and societies with special interests in common, so in the astral world. Perhaps the right impression can be conveyed by saying that souls who are approximately on the same level of development live in a great variety of communities, small and large, serving common interests, having a common outlook, and often a particular historical period of culture. There is freedom to move on this level between all such groups, just as there is freedom to move on earth from one country to another. But there is another kind of separation, perhaps best described as though there were different levels of the astral world corresponding to markedly different spiritual development. By a principle of psychic gravitation souls are drawn after death to the particular sub-level which is most appropriate to their nature, so that there they feel most "at home". There is therefore some kind of separation based upon the inherent soul-development of people. Apparently it is possible for souls on higher levels to "tune down" and visit those on the lower levels, but it is not easy for those on the lower levels to visit those on the higher.

The prospect before souls in the after-life is not, as orthodoxy would seem to suggest, a state of perpetual undiluted bliss in a static heaven; it is rather of an infinite ascending scale of being which beckons to the souls of men if they have the vision to discern it. Where souls live on different levels it is no arbitrary external judge who decrees it. Since souls modify the environment by what they are and desire, there are natural laws which draw souls to the levels for which they are most suited. The attraction of like to like in this sense, produces an aspect of harmony in which the tensions and clashes characteristic of earth-life are largely eliminated. On earth these tensions are very much present with us, and although we may not like it, it is because of such tensions and struggle that our souls develop. Most of this is absent on the astral plane and there is therefore a general sense of peacefulness and happiness. Communicators have variously described the atmosphere as a lotus-paradise, a summer-land, a heaven, in which communities maintain the kind of life they desire. Groups may preserve the patterns of life of different historic periods, sometimes for centuries, but in the end they start to disintegrate, since satiety itself leads to discontent. Moreover these patterns are simply idealised human patterns, frameworks of past human achievement, and such cannot indefinitely satisfy the souls of men. When a soul reaches this point it has to make a choice, but of this we shall write later.

The ancient traditions of various religions speak of a hell as well as a heaven: is there any truth in this? In terms of the ideas presented, viz., of the attraction of like to like, and the inevitable influence of minds upon their environment, it would be expected that certain sub-levels of the astral world would become as unpleasant as higher levels are attractive. These former regions are probably the foundation for the ancient idea of hell. Their nature is determined by the souls of those who inhabit them: it is not a region prepared by a wrathful Deity to accommodate those worthy of punishment. Communicators say that there are many souls on higher levels who give devoted service to try to help those who live in these regions, but that help cannot be given except where a soul's own aspiration is awakened and directed towards the light.

SOCIAL RELATIONSHIPS

The nature of the astral body makes it a very sensitive creator and register of emotions. Emotions in fact play a similar intimate part in their relation to the astral body as physical sensations do for the physical body. On earth, our emotional life is subjective, and in any case it is considerably damped down by the presence of the physical body. In the astral world our emotional life is to a considerable extent objective. Thus, the astral body expresses by its aura and radiations the emotional moods and tones of the soul, so that these are felt and perceived by other souls in the neighbourhood. On earth we may entertain negative emotions such as jealousy, hate, cruelty, lust, and envy, and manage to some extent to keep them to ourselves. As long as outer conduct does not express them we may manage to deceive others. But in the astral world emotional states are apparent to those in our vicinity and no pretence is possible. This makes a great difference to the nature of social relationships. Those who have frequently indulged in negative emotions during their earthly life arrive in the next world with a diseased astral body. As one communicator expressed it, "The moral law, as you would describe it on earth, is expressed for us in physical terms." Diseases of the astral body are not merely unpleasant to perceive, they also create a radiation of an unpleasant and even painful kind to which those around are subjected. Treatment is therefore essential if the society of such persons is to be acceptable to others. The physician's work on the astral level calls for great devotion and self-sacrifice, for he must subject himself to the unpleasant symptoms from which his patients are suffering. Where treatment is ineffective and a cure not possible, such persons prefer to seek a lower level where their condition is more easily tolerated. The positive emotions of love, kindness, goodwill, and compassion are said to be beautiful and radiant in the astral body, and properly directed and used can be powerful instruments of healing.

If these things are realised it will be clear that all earthly relationships which are hypocritical or based upon pretence are seen in the astral world for what they really are. Likewise, those based upon real love and affection are clearly recognised to be such. In these facts there is inevitably a resolution of many of the tangled problems of human relationship. Insincerity which is possible on earth can no longer be masked, and with such cleansing knowledge social relationships rest upon a different basis.

We are told that the differences which characterise men and women are still present in the astral world, and provide for souls who love each other experiences of a far richer kind than earth has to offer. The emotional heights are higher and the depths lower. The saying attributed to Jesus, "Those who are counted worthy to attain that world, neither marry nor are given in marriage" is said to apply to higher levels than those of the astral world. Childbirth is unknown.

There are some sincere people who will be a little shocked by these ideas: that sex differences persist, that people enjoy their homes and gardens, that they live in cities or in the country, that they enjoy work, play, and travel. Such ideas, they will say, are materialistic. When they are asked for their own ideas of heaven, in which they claim to believe, they either remain silent or repeat some of the traditional notions which have from time to time had a religious currency. There have been periods when religious people imagined that after death persons slept in their graves (whatever this means!)

until some distant day of judgment, when presumably their re-
assembled bodies were in some miraculous way restored to them. At
other periods it has been supposed that the faithful would spend their
everlasting future singing praises or playing harps. It is indeed
lamentable that modern orthodoxy has nothing more satisfactory to
offer men and women of an enquiring mind than vague generalisations
and symbolic imagery. They have rightly wondered whether these
do not obscure complete ignorance.

The picture which we have presented in very brief outline is based
upon communications which are believed to be reliable. It is one in
which human interests are still very clearly expressed; and this is
very much so in the astral world. It is an objective world of existence
in form, offering to souls experiences not too different from those they
have known. We have stated that souls discover a limited power to
modify their appearance and environment. On higher levels these
powers are greater and more fully used. Experiments are made with
types of form and formlessness, with vehicles more akin to light and
flame than to what we call substance. We are told that the avenues of
service are many, and that souls may choose to do what they desire,
there being no compulsion or necessity other than that which they
lay upon themselves.

That the mind controls the astral body is evident from the accounts
of those who have experienced astral projection. They state that the
formulation of a clear wish to be in another place is itself sufficient
to move the astral body with great rapidity. Presumably this applies
equally to the after-death state. On the other hand souls may choose
to travel how they wish. We have already indicated that there is
something akin to space which separates communities approximately
at the same stage of development, although this space is no barrier.
We have indicated, however, that there is another kind of separation
based upon different degrees of soul-development: this we described
in terms of different sub-levels of the astral plane. Those on any
such level do not find it easy to enter a higher one, in the same way
that plain-dwellers on earth would not find themselves acclimatised
to high mountains. From higher levels souls can apparently "tune
down" to visit the lower ones. The same process is involved when
dwellers on the astral plane desire to see those incarnate on the
physical plane. After the etheric vehicle has been discarded, the astral
body acquires its natural higher "vibratory rate" which brings it into

relationship with the astral world. There is therefore no constant awareness of earthly life. Thought, however, has the freedom of all levels, so that there may remain a constant awareness of the ideas and doings of souls in the flesh with whom one has some real affinity. Dwellers in the astral world who desire to "see" the near-physical world again have to make a special effort in the way of "tuning-down". A friend of mine whose normal habitat on the other side is on a level beyond the astral one, told me that in a search which he made to find a medium he "felt like a worm grubbing in the clay of earth".

THE PRESENCE OF CHRIST

Those who accept in general terms the Christian outlook will certainly raise the question, "Is Jesus Christ visible to us after we pass over?" It is an impossible question to answer, for no one can presume to say under what circumstances the Christ may appear, or to whom. It can, however, be said that the records of communicators in contact with higher worlds than the astral ones make no mention of the "visible" presence of Christ there. All make it clear that as they go higher there comes to them an increasing awareness of spiritual values and an increasing sensitivity to the Divine presence, also that communion is possible with souls who have advanced far beyond the levels of which we have been writing. It is quite naïve to suppose that the Christ-spirit limits Himself by an astral body and moves about among souls on this level as He did once in a physical body during His years in Palestine. Freed from the limitations of a human form one can only speculate that the Christ-spirit may have resumed His own formless state and power. The increasingly clear recognition of a Presence is one thing: the assumption of an immediate contact is quite another — and I venture to suggest it is a childish assumption. Men can have a real awareness of the unclouded radiance of the sun as they go about their tasks, but they seek to gaze into the sun at their peril.

JUDGMENT

One of the beliefs which orthodoxy hands on from generation to generation is that after death the soul of man passes under judgment and receives either the commendation, "Well done, good and faithful

M

servant," or the command, "Depart from me." The assumption is made that the thoughts and deeds of the immediately preceding life on earth have determined the soul's eternal destiny. In other forms of the myth there is a "Last Judgment" or a "Grand Assize" which is envisaged at some indefinite future time described as a "Last Day". Such ideas display clearly the prevalent human weakness of thinking of God in human terms. The language of the law courts is quite out of place, and it is the language of love to which we should pay attention. When we recall that the teaching of Jesus about the Heavenly Father was, "If ye, being evil, know how to give good gifts unto your children, how much more shall your Heavenly Father . . ." we can dismiss crude conceptions of judgment as the notions of those who have never understood His life, His spirit, or His teaching. They savour too much of the use of fear as a weapon to inculcate a morality, which so based, is no morality at all.

Let no one doubt that there is a principle of justice which undergirds the world (see Chapter 6). The fact is that all our moral choices and our attitudes, our kindness and our cruelty, our love and our hatred, have not only affected others deeply, they have affected ourselves most of all. They have made us what we are — and such we are after death. The casting off of the body makes not the slightest difference to character. We are neither more angel nor more fiend after this transition; we are the same human being. We have already pointed out that the soul's own development determines in a broad sense the sub-level of the astral world on which we shall feel most "at home". Has a conception of judgment any relevance to the soul's progress or to its destiny? I think it has, but in a very different sense to the traditional one.

All judgment is self-judgment. There is a centre in the soul of every man which is the divine spark, and this judges him. It is said by many communicators that at a certain point after death there is presented to the soul something that might be described as a moving picture of its past life. It is an experience in which the truth is made clear, and the soul can assess its own success or failure. But this is not necessarily a spur to progress. So long as a soul is content to live without spiritual aspiration in an environment of his own choosing, he can doubtless do so. Millions do this on earth: they have freedom of choice and there is no compulsion. But if a soul aspires to progress to higher levels, he can only do so by being worthy of it, and the key to the beginning of this journey is self-knowledge. We are told that those who seek to advance must undertake a prolonged process of self-examination in the course of which the soul reviews in a special way the life he has lived on earth. It is not a superficial process of remembering, but one of detailed recollection in which the soul has the necessity laid upon it of entering into the feelings of all those persons whose lives were affected by its words and actions. This is a very humbling experience in which there may be much cause for remorse when the full consequences of one's own behaviour are realised. There is every opportunity to learn humility, to see one's faults, to make new resolves, to root out weaknesses, and to strengthen goodness. In this sense self-judgment is the condition of progress, and such judgment may be fraught with suffering as a soul realises how far short he has fallen from what he might have been.

There are some people who imagine that the next world will be a state of untroubled bliss where no sorrow or suffering can exist. This may be so on higher levels, but it is not true of the astral world, where some degree of suffering is still, as ever, an opportunity given to a soul to progress. How could there be a heaven-world entirely free from suffering for those whose dearly loved kindred are passing through sad and tragic events on earth? If the price of happiness there is indifference, then many would doubtless prefer to carry a burden of suffering, although it may safely be assumed that with a wider understanding, events will be viewed in a truer perspective.

CONCLUSION

We may safely claim that life after death is nothing to be feared by the ordinary person who has some love in him. Death is the door to a country with no frontiers except those which the soul erects for itself. When it passes through this door the soul finds itself with a wider range of sensibility and power which imprisonment within the physical body had restricted. The soul will be drawn towards those with whom it has bonds of real affection, and the way is open for it to tread with new joy that infinite road which leads to the mountains of God.

Chapter

14

SHOULD THE IDEA OF REBIRTH
BE TAKEN SERIOUSLY?

After all, it is not to be twice-born, but to be once born, that is wonderful.
Voltaire

MOST people in our Western tradition are unlikely to have given any thought to this question, nor is there any particular reason why they should, unless they want to probe into the mystery which is interwoven with our human life. On the other hand, in the East the idea is much less strange. Buddhists and Hindus take for granted that life after life on earth is the normal occurrence. They suppose that the human soul is committed to an indefinite round of births and deaths until in the end it discovers its true nature as divine, recognises the physical world as a state of illusion, and finally attains through this understanding its freedom. There are, of course, corrupt forms of the doctrine, such as, that the soul evolves through vegetable and animal forms and may indeed slip back again. The only form of the idea which we shall consider is that the soul which has incarnated in a physical body once, may do so more than once, expressing a part of itself in a new personality with the aim of fuller experience and in the interests of its own progress. The soul is considered to be something enduring, and greater than its manifestation in a particular earthly personality. By "budding forth" a part of itself, perhaps in various periods of history and in a variety of settings, it may gather experience and wisdom into itself. The idea itself is not intrinsically unreasonable, for what the soul has done once, it presumably could do again for a good reason. We should therefore try to set aside any emotional reactions we may have to the idea of reincarnation, and consider whether there is any evidence to support it, and whether there are problems of human life which seem soluble if we accept it.

SOME PROBLEMS

(1) We have probably all puzzled over the gross inequalities of the conditions into which children are born. Some children are born to

parents who love them and surround them with affection and security, giving them every opportunity to develop as persons. Other children are either dominated and warped or treated with indifference and neglect. Life seems to be loaded against them and opportunity never seems to come their way. Some are born with sound minds in sound bodies; others seem to be handicapped from the start by ill-health or abnormality. This situation raises in our minds the question of moral justice in the world. If these babies are the vehicles of newly created human souls, we want to ask what sort of a Creator is this who shows such marked favouritism? If the soul is fresh from the hand of God, and the body fresh from Mother Nature, the imperfections of the latter may be excusable, but the indifference of the former is shocking. If a human being had power to introduce souls into the world and placed some of them at a wholly defenceless stage into situations where cruelty, disease, neglect, or discouragement would be their daily lot and might warp their nature, his callousness would call forth our fervent denunciation. We should accept no excuse of the type, "When the race of life has been run, ample allowance will be made for the handicap." This completely evades the moral issue. If there is only one life to be lived on earth, what are these handicaps doing there at all? What allowance shall be made to the congenital idiot? The problem has only to be stated clearly, for us to realise that God (because of His nature) cannot act in this way. We must therefore abandon the naïve idea that each child born into the world is a soul fresh from the Divine hand.

If we postulate that souls have pre-existed their present incarnation, and that a soul undertaking this task afresh, brings with it the stains and weaknesses, the strengths and wisdom which it has gathered in the course of its long journey through prior lives in time, we have the possiblity of another outlook. We can then suppose that inequalities and *apparent* injustices arise from that soul's past. What people commonly do is to make moral judgments without any knowledge of what has gone before. This is like condemning a play on the strength of a brief glimpse of it. This new outlook permits us to believe in a principle of justice and love running through the whole created world. It is at least possible that the things which stagger us may be the outworking of just and kindly laws which we should clearly recognise if we could adopt a wider viewpoint.

(2) A particular case of the problem of inequality is that which is

disclosed by the appearance of the child-genius or prodigy. Such cases are not common, but they should not be ignored. In scientific work it is often the exceptional happening which offers us clues to wider understanding. We think of the musical genius of a Chopin or a Mozart who, at the tender age of five to ten years, showed musical maturity which could produce compositions and execute them in a manner completely inexplicable at their age. From time to time there are mathematical prodigies whose knowledge and skill cannot be explained by anything they have learned or been taught. We are told that Sir William Hamilton at the age of five, could answer a difficult mathematical question and would then "run off cheerfully to play with his little toy cart". If we are prepared to recognise the possibility of previous lives, then we might have a basis for explaining these things as a rare example of overflow of previously attained ability into a succeeding life. The permanent soul which stores the wisdom, goodness, artistic sensitivity, interest, and skills of the past, surely influences in some degree the new personality which it is sending forth into the world. Normally, we should expect some of these interests or capacities to awaken as the child develops. Some may remain wholly latent, for a soul may desire to broaden its experience rather than to intensify certain aspects of it. Plato had a theory that the kind of knowledge which comes easily is "old" knowledge, in the sense that we have laid foundations for it in prior lives, while the learning in which at first we find little interest or which presents difficulty, is probably being met for the first time.

On this view, the child prodigy would be the reincarnation of a soul of very specialised development. It is sometimes found that the genius fades out at an early age, as though the soul, as soon as it was able to do so, threw up other fields of interest and withdrew the exceptional one, for the sake of a wider and more balanced development.

(3) Most people have commented upon the striking contrasts in temperament and disposition, interests, sensitivity, intellect, and spiritual outlook of members of one and the same family. All its members may have been subjected to approximately the same external influences. The differences in physical appearance and build can be accounted for by the crossing-over process which takes place in the germ-plasm when the ovum is fertilised. It is surely of equal importance to account for the many differences found on other levels of the

personality. Some of these are disclosed at quite an early age, and it is unconvincing to talk vaguely of psychological factors. If we take the view that each human being born into the world is a soul which has acquired a new body, and that each soul has characteristics which are accounted for by its past history, we have a reasonable viewpoint. The body may be quite fully accounted for in terms of heredity and genetics, but the soul, too, may have its history which has made it what it is.

(4) Although the theme of love at first sight (and hate at first sight) has been exploited by romantic novelists, there is nevertheless a puzzling element in it which requires explanation. Occasionally psychological factors explain this satisfactorily, as where there is an unconscious association with another person who is loved or hated: but this is not always the case. We are sometimes offered a plausible viewpoint in the idea that we may be dealing with relationships which pre-existed the present lives. None of us live our lives in isolation. We manifest in a web of relationships with other people's lives. Some of these may have no deep significance, but of others this is not true. Love and hate are energies which draw souls again and again into inter-acting orbits.

Among my friends are an elderly couple of considerable culture and intelligence. They first met in middle life, and at the first meeting recognised the occasion as significant. The lady *knew* that the man she was meeting was the same one who had been her husband in a former life in a very different setting. Some years before the meeting she had a poignant vision which came to her with all the force and characteristics of a memory (supposedly of a former life). In this vision she had given birth to a child, and her husband was setting out on a mission from which he did not expect to return alive, and was saying goodbye. The lady affirms that she knows beyond any doubt that these two men are one and the same.

I have a letter from a friend whose work lies in the Far East, in which he refers to a person with whose views and policies he was in constant conflict. "Beyond any doubt," he said, "we are *old* antagonists." By "old" he meant that each of them knew that this was not the only life in which they had opposed one another.

(5) The claim is often made for the soul that it has the quality of immortality: its nature is eternal. By saying this it is meant that while the soul may manifest in time, its real existence is rooted in a level

outside time. Those who hold such a view must inevitably find it difficult to suppose that a soul is newly created when a child is born on earth. To put it simply; if the soul has a far-reaching future ahead of it, is it not reasonable to suppose that it has a far-reaching past behind it?

These are some of the puzzles of human life. If we accept as plausible the soul's pre-existence in earlier lives, then we have a new viewpoint from which the puzzles may perhaps be resolved.

AN ANCIENT IDEA

The idea of reincarnation has had a long history. It belongs to a long and ancient tradition in Indian thought. It was part of the mystery teachings of Ancient Greece, and it appeared to be current among the Jewish people at the time when Jesus was teaching in Palestine. It will be recalled that after Jesus had healed a man blind from birth He was asked the question, "Lord, who did sin, this man or his parents, that he should be born blind?" Obviously, if he was *born* blind, the circumstances of his sinning must have been in a prior life. On another occasion Jesus asked His disciples, "Whom do men say that I am?" He received the answer, "Some say John the Baptist, and others Elijah, but others one of the prophets." Jesus neither confirmed nor denied the validity of the popular notion that a person alive in the flesh could be the reincarnation of a past figure. It is interesting to note, however, that such ideas must have persisted in the times of the early Church, since they were declared a heresy at a Church Council held in the sixth century.

It would be easy to name many poets and philosophers to whom the idea of rebirth has made an appeal, so that if we feel it has a place in our philosophy of life, we need not regard ourselves as in unrespectable company.

EVIDENCE IN SUPPORT

We now come to the important question, "Is there evidence to support the idea?" It is not scientific to propound a theory which becomes a happy dumping ground for all our unsolved problems, unless it can be supported by evidence or tested by experiment. What sort of evidence is there?

Rebirth

There are memories which some people have which they believe to be memories of former lives. The cautious reader will comment rightly that a person's claim might be a piece of fantasy. This is possible, and the weight one is disposed to attach to such testimony must depend a good deal upon the standing and reliability of the witness. In the case of the couple I mentioned previously, the lady and her husband have been personal friends for many years and I could not doubt there integrity. The vision which the lady had was very poignant and she could not account for it other than as a previous-life memory. She has no doubt whatever that her husband in that life is her husband in this, and her husband — a critically minded man — accepts her testimony.

A short time ago there came to see me a lady who had held a very responsible position in a large organisation, and had retired therefrom, believing that this course was indicated. The standards which she believed should be maintained were falling badly, and her efforts to maintain them were being frustrated by another. She found herself getting increasingly depressed and starting to think in terms of hanging herself. At this juncture a friend of many years previously, came over from the U.S.A. and renewed the old link. She had psychic faculty remarkably developed and was able to make contact with the deeper soul of her friend and describe what appeared to be a number of her past lives. The most recent one prior to the present life held the clues to the present one. She had in that life suffered a great disappointment and hung herself at a comparatively early age. She had been permitted to come back to Earth after some ten years in order to expiate her fault: this she had done by her devoted and self-sacrificial work, and could now with a clear conscience retire from the position she had held. There was much more detail into which it is unnecessary to enter. It must suffice to say that this disclosure of the soul's past which placed the events of the present in a new light carried inner conviction to this lady. Her depression lifted, confidence and serenity returned, and with it a quiet conviction that she had done what she had come again to Earth to do.

Krishnamurti, one of the greatest living teachers, said on one occasion, many years ago, that he had experienced certain things which made reincarnation for him, not a theory but a fact. Immediately, and characteristically, he stressed that our concern, however, should be with the present, not with either past or future. Eternity is here and now, and the present moment is our only road of access to it. There are a number of recorded cases of Indian children apparently having memories of former lives and their setting, where the rebirth was so short a time after the previous decease that the memory data could be checked. In two recent papers* Dr. Ian Stevenson of the Department of Psychiatry in the University of Virginia lists forty-four cases which he has analysed. In most of these cases the person whose life was ostensibly remembered had lived in a different town or village, and the evidence seemed strong that the child recalling these memories had no possible means of access to the locality. The detail remembered correctly was sometimes very remarkable. It was interesting that of the forty-four persons, thirty-eight remembered a life of the same sex and six of the opposite sex. In reviewing the data Dr. Stevenson cautiously concludes that, "The evidence I have assembled and reviewed here, does not warrant any firm conclusion about reincarnation. But it does justify, I believe, a much more extensive and sympathetic study of the hypothesis than it has hitherto received in the West. Further investigation of apparent memories of former incarnations may well establish reincarnation as the most probable explanation of these experiences."

I present below two records which have not been published before. The standing of the lady who sent them to me and kindly allows me to use them leaves no doubt whatever in my mind that their accuracy can be relied upon.

"To what extent dreams are true could be endlessly disputed; but when I was about eleven years old I had a series of dreams concerning which I kept silence, as I had been told that it was very wrong to boast. As in the dream I had manifestly been of some consequence, I thought it would be wrong to claim this, as I was of no account today.

"The dream was of being a prisoner in a place that I knew to be the Tower of London. I had not seen it in real life, but I had no doubt where I was. It was very cold weather (in waking life, a hot summer). I was aware that I had been condemned to death, and I hoped that the execution would not be on so cold a day, because to shiver would look like fear, which would be most undignified! I was not at all apologetic or inclined to admit I had been in the wrong; nor was I tired of life. I felt sorry to have my activities cut short; but consoled myself with

* *Journ. American Soc. for Psychical Research*, Vol. LIV (1960).

184

the assumption of a clear conscience. This, I used to dream over and over again, and after being in the dream a vigorous man, to wake up and be a little girl felt rather strange.

"At last the dream changed, and I was standing on a scaffold which must have been newly erected as it smelt of sawdust. Everything was decorous and decent. The executioner knelt and apologised for what he was about to do. I took the axe from his hand and felt it, and handed it back, bidding him do his duty.

"Someone (George Trevelyan, I think), alleges that beheading was painless. How can he know? On the contrary, it was excruciating. But now comes the part of the dream which most impressed me. The executioner was holding up my head, and pronouncing some usual formula but I, my real self, was looking on, feeling extraordinarily free from all my woes, and much more vigorous than previously. I must have believed firmly in the immortality of the soul, and yet, I was utterly astonished to find myself in the dream so much more vividly alive than previously.

"When I woke up I made a drawing of the axe, which was of a peculiar shape. Some time after this I asked to be taken to the Tower of London, and I explained to a friendly gunsmith that I wanted to write history but could not understand the battles perfectly until I understood the weapons.

" 'Right you are, Missy,' he said, and demonstrated to me the various uses of pike, lance, crossbow, etc. I then asked had he an axe that beheaded people? He said, 'Yes, this certainly beheaded the Jacobite Lords, but it is supposed to be very much older.' Somehow, I was not surprised that it proved to be the exact shape of the axe in my dream. I said 'May I hold it in my hand a moment, please?' for I felt that if I *touched* it, I would never have the execution dream again. I took off my glove, felt the edge, and then handed it back again.

"My aunt who was with me made no comment, but long afterwards when reading the typescript of my book, especially of the treason trials, she said, 'I did not make any remark at the time, but do you remember asking to see the axe in the Tower? It seemed odd for a very gentle little girl to be interested in the method of execution but you looked almost exultant when you handed it back to the gunsmith, and he gave me such a look as much as to say "How incongruous"!'

"I have resolutely *not* tried to imagine who I might have been in the past—but long before I heard the word 'reincarnation', I felt convinced that I had lived in some of the periods I wanted to write about; also that I had come back for a purpose.

"An old peasant woman (a seventh child of a seventh child) said to me (and she did not know who I was), 'You *do* need rest; but yer wont never 'ev it; and if yer died termorrer, yer'd come 'urrying

A Religious Outlook for Modern Man

back because yer work ain't finished yet.' She was a fisherman's wife, old and frail and quite illiterate. But she apparently 'saw' various people out of the past. 'One of the gentlemen was you, me dear,' she said 'and couldn't you 'andle a sword in those days'!"

"In about 1913 my cousin and I had occasion to examine some illustrated Persian manuscripts. A few days later, a neighbour asked if she could bring to tea a French friend, who would be interested to see an old English country house. To our surprise, Mlle. de H. did not *look* French, but she reminded us both of one of the Persian mediaeval paintings. She had none of the vivacity of a Frenchwoman, but a courteous aloofness. When we got to know her better she told us something about herself.

"She had been an only child, and very lonely; so she had, as her parents supposed, *invented* a baby language in which she sang little songs to herself, and recited what she called poems, which they regarded as sheer gibberish.

"Her father had a cousin, a Jesuit priest, whom he had not seen since before this child was born. The priest's career had been set in the East, but on his return to France he came to visit his kinsfolk and spent some days with them. The child, then about five, grew weary of listening to grown-up conversations, and sitting in a corner began to murmur to herself her usual recitations. The priest stopped talking and listened, and then asked, 'Where did Laurence learn Persian?'

"'Persian!' said her father, 'it's nonsense, sound without sense.' The priest then asked her to speak to him in her own language—which she did, and he said to her father, 'This is Persian, not Persian of today, but of the epic era.'

"The parents were amazed: they said nobody who knew Persian had been near the child or near them. They could not account for her conduct. They had none but European heredity, etc. After he left, they forbade her to talk her gibberish any more.

"She told us later that she had never felt as if she really 'belonged' to France, but she had deliberately not pursued the Persian line of enquiry, as she had come to the conclusion that for some reason unknown she was meant to be taken away from it. She had, however, no doubt that France was not her *real* country. Nor was she attracted to modern Persia. Her Persian recitations (the meaning of which she had not known) were of the days of 'ride and shoot and speak the truth' of Persian epic poetry."

Such experiences as these, and others of which it would have been possible to write, point to the likelihood that as personalities, we are

186

each expressions of a deeper underlying self or soul, and that these souls are engaged on an enterprise of development which involves long stretches of time.

SOME OBJECTIONS RAISED TO REBIRTH

Undoubtedly the idea of rebirth or reincarnation on earth raises in the minds of many Western people emotionally based objections. Where the current life has been unhappy or full of suffering, there is a natural reluctance to contemplate another life in which similar ordeals might have to be confronted. This assumption is, however, unlikely to be sound. If the soul decides once more to put forth a personality into physical existence it is quite improbable that in the process of widening experience anything repetitive will be involved. Certainly the soul may again be faced with moral choices in which it failed before, but these may occur in a completely different setting. It may be assumed that breadth and variety of experience are part of the soul's purpose. We must endeavour to look at the hypothesis of reincarnation on its merits. As we have said already, what the soul has done once, it may, for good reasons, decide to do again.

A commonly raised objection to the idea is expressed in the question, "Why do we not remember our past lives?" We have already seen that occasionally persons do apparently remember parts of them, but this is admittedly unusual. Why should we normally expect to re-member them? We are all aware that our memory becomes poorer as we approach our earliest years. It must be rare for events of the second year of life to be recalled, and extremely rare for events of the first year. Why then should it be expected that events of a still more remote past should be accessible? Although no memories may ever be wholly lost, the accessibility of remoter memories would be expected to be less.

I think we should also appreciate that forgetting is a function which can serve our interests as much as remembering. It may be fortunate that our minds are not cluttered up with masses of detail among which we have to delve to find significant things. A learned or skilled person does not need to remember all the detail of the way he has come in acquiring his knowledge or facility. All the efforts he made as a schoolboy, the mistakes he made, and the problems he tried to solve are mercifully forgotten, but he retains something which is far more important. This is the distilled essence of experience, and it is in virtue of this that he can tackle any problem of a new kind which is presented to him. It is so with ourselves. We are faced in life with moral choices, with situations requiring decisions, and with fresh opportunities. What is available to us in making these choices is the prompting of the soul through the wisdom or insight it has acquired because of its journey in the past. This distilled wisdom is available to the new personality, and this is the important thing.

Another objection raised to the idea of reincarnation is on the grounds of justice. Many of the events and relationships which form the substance of the present life are rooted in trains of thought and action set going in a previous life, so that a person may be reaping the fruits of both happiness and sorrow which had their origin in an earlier life. Is this just, says the critic? If Jones of the twentieth century has no memories of Smith of the sixteenth century is it right that he should reap what the latter has sowed? Are they not from every viewpoint separate individuals? Our viewpoint is that both Jones and Smith are manifestations of one and the same soul, which is bigger and more fundamental than either personality. The consciousness of this soul will include the memories of both these personalities and any others put forth for the sake of experience. It is the growth of the soul which is enduring and important, and questions of justice must be in reference to this soul which is gathering a breadth of experience and distilling wisdom from it.

Sometimes the critic of reincarnation says, "But why here again? Is not the universe wide?" Certainly it is, but we suggest that the soul is drawn back to earth as the country of a man's childhood draws him back to see it again, however far afield he may have travelled. It is the place where friends and spiritual kindred may still be struggling, helping each other, and perhaps needing help. Earth is a magnet until a soul has progressed to the stage of no return, and its progress can take place better on higher levels.

The logic of rebirth is perhaps somewhat like that of education. It is no good attempting tertiary education until a sufficient standard has been attained on the secondary level. To attempt it would be a waste of time. It seems that certain important and necessary qualities can only be acquired within the restrictions and limitations which a physical body provides. We can only learn fortitude and courage where the issue of events is uncertain. Kindness and compassion grow amid suffering when we share the common lot. It is here that comrade souls learn to bear one another's burdens and so fulfil the law of Christ. Here within the darkness of Earth's soil is sown the immortal seed. Here it must grow its roots, before it can expand and flourish in the light.

Chapter

15

WHAT IS THE MEANING AND PURPOSE OF HUMAN LIFE?

Within us we have a hope which always walks in front of our present narrow experience; it is the undying faith in the infinite in us; it will never accept any of our disabilities as a permanent fact; it sets no limit to its own scope; it dares to assert that man has oneness with God; and its wild dreams become true every day. (p. 51.)

Every morning the day is reborn among the newly blossomed flowers with the same message retold and the same assurance renewed that death eternally dies, that the waves of turmoil are on the surface, and that the sea of tranquillity is fathomless. . . .
    It is for our self to know that it must be born anew every moment of its life. It must break through all illusions that encase it in their crust to make it appear old, burdening it with death. (p. 89.)

Our life, like a river, strikes its banks not to find itself closed in by them, but to realise anew every moment that it has its unending opening towards the sea. (p. 90.)

Sadhana
Rabindranath Tagore

THE great majority of people are for most of their time too pre-occupied even to ask this question. They are living, but they don't ask why they are living. They are doing, but they don't know why they are doing — except in so far as "common-sense" provides the answer through some immediate end which is being served.

If we try to stand aside and survey the whole spectacle of humanity, living, doing, and dying, it arouses strange and melancholy thoughts. An endless stream of human beings seems to come out of the mysterious portals of birth, devotes a few years to crossing the lighted stage of human life, and then disappears through the mysterious exit door of death. The stream has been moving for hundreds of thousands of years. Has it any meaning? All of these tens of thousands of millions were people basically similar to ourselves. They dreamed their dreams, they loved and hated, they suffered and hoped, they sorrowed and rejoiced; but in the great drama of the human story what did these lives mean? To whom or to what were they of any value? A well-known hymn says:

190

Meaning and Purpose of Human Life

Time, like an ever-rolling stream,
Bears all its sons away;
They fly forgotten, as a dream
Dies at the opening day.

This may possibly be true, but it offers no understanding of what the process is all about. Almost every verse of the Persian poet's famous Rubaiyat expresses the same melancholy thoughts.

The worldly Hope men set their hearts upon
Turns ashes — or it prospers; and anon,
Like snow upon the desert's dusty face
Lighting a little hour or two — is gone.

'Tis all a chequer board of nights and days
Where Destiny with men for pieces plays
Hither and thither moves and mates and slays
And one by one back in the closet lays.

We all appreciate the poignancy of this spectacle without necessarily sharing with Omar Khayyam a fatalistic standpoint. This is indeed the world's story as it *must* appear to the sense-centred outlook. If we want meanings we must seek for them on those higher levels of Reality which interpenetrate and account for the physical world. Some of these are represented on the diagram in Chapter 11.

THE MEANING OF EXISTENCE

In discussing the ultimate questions it will be realised that we are necessarily moving in a rarified air of speculation, and dealing with things which the human mind has not the capacity to grasp in any adequate sense. The views put forward are therefore presented in a tentative way: those who desire to know further what has led to them should study an earlier book.* Our view has been that there are numerous levels in the structure of the world, and to these we ascribe different degrees of reality. The physical level is the lowest of these. Now the evidence of modern astronomy has disclosed billions of

* *Nurslings of Immortality*, R. C. Johnson (Hodder & Stoughton Ltd.).

physical worlds, and we may therefore infer that myriads of experiments concerned with the evolution of *consciousness* are taking place in the universe. We can only speak with any knowledge of our planet the Earth, which is one of nine circling around the sun. Our sun is one star in about one hundred thousand million which constitute our galaxy. Moreover this galaxy of ours is only one of at least one thousand million galaxies which have been observed in the remote depths of space. We cannot say how the germinal Egos which constitute the central points of human souls were first created. They may be regarded as seeds of the level of spirit which have a potentiality of development within them. As the seed has within it the power to reproduce its parent, but in order to do so must be sown in the soil and subject to the influences of a lower order, so the germinal centres of human souls needed to descend from their ancestral estate in order to unfold their potentialities. This process of descent is linked up with the establishment of a "self" which will be distinguishable from all other selves. In the early stage of descent these germinal centres each appropriated for themselves a portion of the various levels of reality they descended through. Thus, each of them appropriated a portion of the collective or undifferentiated Mind to become its own personal instrument of memory, perception, and action.

Meanwhile, for hundreds of millions of years, as we measure time, other powers (which I have called elsewhere Imaginals) had been actively promoting what the biologist calls evolution on the physical level of Earth. Somewhere about a million years ago there had evolved an advanced type of ape-like being with a sufficiently good brain and foundation for mind, to offer to souls which had descended to the penultimate stage, this last and most restricted type of experience. Waiting souls entered into these hominid-apes and thus there appeared on the physical scene — Man. He proved an adaptable creature, able to meet successfully both dramatic changes in his environment and attacks from other forms of life. The better quality of his mind-brain gave him enormous advantages which he used to survive with increasing facility. He invented the wheel, he discovered fire and the possibilities of agriculture. He invented language and he assisted action with tools. If, as we believe, the whole process subserves the end of the evolution of consciousness, one may surmise that three purposes are served by the experience of physical life.

(i) Individuation: the process of building up a permanent centre of selfhood, distinct from other selves, and distinguishing itself from its environment, also, particularly developing the conscious part of mind as an instrument of soul.

(ii) Building up a healthy astral body, which is needed in the first stage of the process of ascent

(iii) Learning certain truths of a moral kind, and appreciating certain values.

INDIVIDUATION

The levels of reality have been labelled from above downwards, spiritual, intuitive, mental, astral, etheric, and physical. Before the process of man's descent took place these regions of diminishing reality were themselves created, each one being precipitated from the one above it. This creative process, which was the fundamental one, gave rise to states of increasing restriction and increasing separateness. Conversely we may say that in passing from lower to higher levels there is increasing freedom and increasing inter-penetration. On the lowest physical level, the process of communication between selves is very indirect, and they have to make use of elaborate physical devices in the process. Sound and light are the chief agents of communication, supplemented by many ingenious physical inventions. When we ascend to the level of mind, the fact of telepathy is a reminder to us that one mind can be in direct communication with another mind, even though the physical brains with which they are associated are thousands of miles apart. Moreover, one of the unanimous affirmations of those who have had experiences on higher levels still, is the extraordinary sense they have of belonging to a great Unity.

One may envisage the stages of descent as follows. After creation the egos appropriate their first vehicle or sheath on the level labelled Intuitive. We know little about this level except that it is essentially creative, and the fountain of imaginative activity. Descending into the region of mind, each ego appropriates a portion which becomes its own particular instrument. One might picture as a parable, a number of men going out into virgin country, each enclosing a portion and building walls around it before they start to cultivate it. The walls mark off his territory and give him a chance to cultivate it without the encroachment of the environment. In the process of descent these walls are built by the egos and the instrument of mind is cultivated.

In the diagram below, we have changed the simile and represented islands of mind rising up from the submarine continent, and apparently separated from each other by the sea of matter. Each island stands for an individual whose mind has emerged from the more primitive strata which we have labelled. The animal mind was itself a

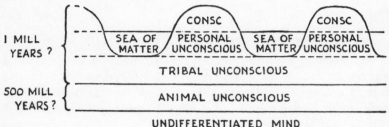

product of the long evolutionary process which Darwin described. The tribal stratum is a higher degree of organisation built by earlier types of man which have long since disappeared. Homo Sapiens is represented by the individualised growth of each island peak. Such a diagram should not be pressed too far, but it helps to convey a little of a process which language is inadequate to describe. The growth of the conscious mind with its intellectual power was a development of enormous importance. In more primitive man there is less marked individuality and a closer relationship with the tribal mind. The final stage of descent into matter has particularly favoured the development of self-consciousness and the critical intellect. Animals have a simple type of consciousness: they *know*, but do not know that they *know*. The latter implies self-consciousness.

The necessity of the last stage is perhaps this. We know that mind has a very wide power of gathering knowledge in space and time. We do not know whether there are any spatial limits to such powers as telepathy and clairvoyance, nor to what extent the mind can roam in time. But if we can imagine such powers being exercised by an ego which has never been incarnate, it seems probable that it would have no sense of individuality. To feel an individual and be self-conscious must surely depend upon these powers being referred to a centre located at some point of space, and some moment of time, and this is presumably what incarnation in a physical body is designed to achieve.

We can understand why some of the mystery-religions thought of the human body as a tomb or prison, and described incarnate existence as a death from which men afterwards escaped to life. Nevertheless we can see that limitation and restriction have played an important part in the ego realising itself as separate from others and from the not-self. When first created, egos may have had infinite knowledge at their disposal, but not self-knowledge. They may not have been aware that they existed. Descent into matter and subsequent incarnations may be necessary in order to build a sufficiently permanent foundation of individuality to sustain future expansion and development on higher levels.

Another simile may help us. If the walls of a river bank are not clearly defined, the water may spread widely and become a scarcely moving and ineffective pool. But if the river is given definition by confining it between narrow banks, it will acquire energy and power to do work. In the case of some souls on the astral level who have lingered too long in pleasant stagnation, reincarnation may be the means of providing this revitalising energy and drive.

BUILDING THE ASTRAL BODY

It is common knowledge that through some nine months of intra-uterine life and twenty years of development in the outer world, the mature human body is built. Although we know extremely little about the process of incarnation it seems probable that something of a similar character is taking place at the same time on those levels of mind which we call "astral". In other words we might conceive that a germinal seed of the astral body is sown in close relationship to the conception of the physical body, and that it grows concurrently with it. We have already seen that the health of this body is considerably affected by the emotional attitudes which we cultivate in this life (see Chapter 13). I shall quote from a communication believed to be from a physician "on the other side".*

"It is possible for you on earth to ignore the state of your feelings, as being relatively unimportant: you think that only the state of your body really matters. But when the state of your feelings *is* the state of your body, and when, moreover, those feelings being no longer dulled by the physical, are ten times more acute, it becomes a matter of the

* *The Country Beyond*, pp. 48–50, Jane Sherwood (Rider & Co. Ltd.).

first importance that the state of your feelings should be healthy and happy.

"If you were suffering from an unsightly disease that made you objectionable to your friends and abhorrent to yourself, you would take any possible means to cure it. That is literally the case with people who come here suffering from faults of disposition and temper, from fears and anxieties, from old angers and envies. For their own sake as well as for the sake of others they must be cured, or they cannot bear to live among us, where their disease must be seen in ugly and disagreeable auras, in harmful emanations, or in noxious odours. . . .

"I myself think that the discipline of earth is specially important for the following reasons: the actual emotional processes are masked by the physical, and the strength of the sensations are dulled by it; hence, although fear of injury to the physical body is added to the dangers to be faced, yet the conditions do make it possible for each to fight his own fight while maintaining a bold face to the world. Here no concealment is possible. . . .

"I think the task of building up a healthy and happy emotional body is peculiarly the mission of one's earth experience."

These views I believe to be quite sound. In the business of living with our fellows there are far more important things than merely correct outward conduct. If we persistently maintain moods of jealousy, envy, anger, hatred, suspicion, and fear (even though we manage in some degree to conceal these from others), we ought to realise that they are far more lasting in their effects than what are sometimes called "sins of the flesh", for they are stored in, and affect the health of the astral body.

LESSONS OF EARTH LIFE

We have suggested that experience on the physical level represents not only the most restricted type, but also provides conditions in which the tensions of conflict and opposition are a maximum. The long process of descent of the egos (of which we know practically nothing) has been associated with the establishment of a self, and in this process what we describe as selfishness and egotism have arisen. After this age-long phase, souls are faced with the great ascending arc, and the process of return involves their free choice and adoption of a completely contrasting principle — that of Love. The walls of egotism built up in the process of descent have to be pulled down in the process of ascent. This is not a meaningless process like that of the famous Duke of York

> *who had ten thousand men,*
> *He marched them up to the top of the hill*
> *And he marched them down again.*

Souls who reach again high levels of the ascending arc, reach them no longer *as* they left them. They are now fully self-conscious beings with many of the god-like potentialities which were formerly latent and embryonic, now unfolded and available for use. Self-consciousness is not lost again, but as souls approach this stage of perfection, they come to know themselves as essentially one with the Whole, though not lost in it. On these high levels, our attempts to use descriptive language break down: there is infinite variety within unity, there is differentiation without separation.

It is on the level of earth that the first upward steps have to be chosen in freedom and the principle of unselfishness voluntarily adopted as the only means of ascent. Whether to cling to the old principles of the descent or to venture on the new principles of the ascent was referred to by Jesus when He said, "Whosoever would save his life shall lose it, and whosoever will lose his life for my sake, shall find it." In old-fashioned language, this new orientation used to be called conversion.

This situation of conflict between good and evil, love and hate, kindness and cruelty, which is characteristic of the earth level, is one which few of us like, either within ourselves or around us. We are happier when things go smoothly: but we should face the fact that growth of character depends upon how we meet adversity and how we react to difficulty. How could we learn courage unless we were placed in positions where events look menacing and fearful? How could we learn fortitude unless we had to take the blows of circumstance? How could we know of space and time unless we had known what it was to be bound and limited by them? What could we know of the valley of the shadow if we had only surveyed it from Olympian heights? What could we know of others' suffering unless we too have suffered? It is certain that these considerations must have been present to Christ when He undertook incarnation here. It is clear that this battle-field of earth gives us an opportunity to grow morally in a way which no lotus-paradise could possibly provide for.

It may well be that having once lived on earth, further lives are desirable, if not essential, for all but a few rare souls. The reasons for this are associated with the idea of "karma" which we have dealt with earlier. This principle is a statement of the law of cause and effect as it concerns the moral order, so that thoughts and actions set going trains of consequences which affect others for good or ill and ultimately react on the originator. Since none of us live in isolation, more lives than one in a physical body may be rendered necessary by these consequences. The same souls, expressed in different personalities, may be drawn into our orbit of life again and again. A new personality is called upon to meet some of the fruition of seeds of latent karma which the soul has sown with it. I have no doubt that many of the events and persons whose lives interact significantly with our own are also involved in this karmic process. Some of the situations we have to meet are essentially those in which we have failed to take a right course in the past, and new opportunity is given to us. Both joy and suffering, help given, and help received, sometimes have their roots in a far past. A new personality has available to it throughout life, the prompting of the soul's intuitive wisdom, but it is a free agent with power to reject or accept it. When a personality chooses rightly because it desires no other way, that soul has reached a level of development where a new personality in the flesh can no longer serve its interests.

There is a passage in the Gita* which recognises that there are men on earth who are living quite free from further karmic entanglements. Perhaps they are incarnate to help mankind in its evolution, or perhaps to help some particular struggling soul whom they love.

"The wise call him a Sage: for whatever he undertakes is free from motives of desire; his deeds are purified by the Fire of Wisdom. Having surrendered all claim to the results of his actions, always contented and independent, in reality he does nothing, even though he is apparently acting.

"Expecting nothing, his mind and personality controlled, without greed, doing bodily actions only; though he acts, yet he remains untainted.

"Content with what comes to him without effort of his own, mounting above the pairs of opposites, free from envy, his mind balanced both in success and failure, though he act, yet the consequences do not bind him."

* *The Geeta*, Shree Purohit Swami (Faber & Faber Ltd.), IV, 19–22.

SOME ATTITUDES TO LIFE

In the light of the purposes which lie behind the experience of earthly life, it is of interest to look at some of the ways of living that men choose to follow. Is there a best kind of life? By "best" I mean, not that which is necessarily the pleasantest, or which outwardly offers the most satisfactory results, but that which ministers most effectively to the soul's development. Is the life of a monk or a recluse better than that of a business-man? Is the life of a scientist better than that of a fisherman, or of a career-woman better than that of mother of a family? Is poverty or wealth a handicap? A hundred such questions might be asked, yet the only answers of any value must be given in terms of general principles. One soul may require a very different opportunity to that of another.

In a broad sense we can observe men reacting to the experience of life in either a positive and world-affirming way, or in a negative and world-denying way. The first group enter into life and taste its experiences as fully as they can: the second group shrink from life and seek for interest and security within themselves. They correspond to the two types of mind which Jung called extravert and introvert respectively. The great majority of people are neither at one extreme nor the other, but have different proportions of these two attitudes in their make-up. I have selected five types of attitude which are by no means mutually exclusive, on which to comment. They are not comprehensive, but are selected to illustrate the range of world-affirming and world-denying attitudes, and to show their strengths and weaknesses.

(1) THE WAY OF ACTION

This way of life includes many different temperaments ranging from the "gallant blade" to the moral reformer. Here is one of the former type:

Here we are in the world, let us enter into it and make the most of it. It may not be a perfect world but it has its attractive features. It is a challenge to those with courageous hearts. Let us therefore drink the wine of life and give thanks. It was the spirit of Hotspur and Falstaff, of Henry V at Agincourt, and of the seamen of Elizabethan England. Professor Macneile Dixon described the type when he wrote:*

* *The Human Situation* (Edward Arnold & Co. Ltd.), 1937.

"He thinks seldom and little about learning, the problems or the prizes of the world. Light-hearted, unaffected, this Mercutio-like person is without aggravated solemnity or portentous gloom. He has his faults. His days and nights are not devoted to meditations upon virtue, to theories either of living or of art. He is destitute of metaphysical gifts. He has no talent for reforming his neighbours, rather, he rejoices in their society, and himself radiates good humour and cheerfulness, making his contribution, and no negligible one, to the welfare of society. He carries with him a gusto for the present hour, which even moralists might envy and saints forbear to chide. And when adventure offers, he tosses his sword in the air to catch it to the hilt. He is hope incarnate."

By no means all outward-turned men find variety and stimulus in action itself, sufficient satisfaction. Some are very much concerned with rewards, power, fame, and ruling over their fellows. Some are concerned with industry and business and strive hard for the prizes of success. Others are concerned with the senses, seeking luxuries, pleasures, and comforts. Still others are filled with moral purpose. They are conscious that the world is a battle-ground of good and evil, where justice and injustice are constantly in conflict. They desire to serve the good, to right the wrong, and help the needy. They are "doers of the word, not hearers only", and in this group are some of the greatest servants of mankind. Here are social workers, teachers, philanthropists, reformers, and many who have helped social progress and given to us the best things in our civilisation.

The biggest group who follow the way of action are millions of ordinary people who have little choice in the matter. Caught in the inexorable demands of an unexciting routine, they must work to live, and much of this work is dull, repetitive, and uninspiring. It calls for no comment, it earns no praise, but it allows bills to be met. Can it be claimed that the mere routine of a commonplace life — work in a factory, or housekeeping — are means of the soul's progress? Before we answer, let us consider whether any action, however spectacular, can be a means of the soul's progress. Browning was surely right when he said, "All service ranks the same with God," for it cannot be supposed that God is more concerned with a man underwriting a loan than with a woman dusting a room. If the way of action could not be a means of the soul's progress, then for many people much of life would be a round of futility, our Western civilisation would be a great mistake, and the first thirty years of the life of Jesus could be without much meaning. In considering the way of action as a means of the soul's progress, we must look not at the outward impressiveness of the action, but at the motives which lie behind it, and indeed at the whole spirit which pervades the living and the doing. The great teachers of mankind have all made it clear that Action, *when offered as a sacrifice to God* (because it is the fulfilment of one's duty), not for the sake of results which may accrue, is well-pleasing to Him. Thus in the Gita we read:

"Whatever a man offers to Me, whether it be a leaf, or a flower, or fruit, or water, I accept it, for it is offered with devotion and purity of mind. Whatever thou doest . . . do all as an offering to Me."

And in the New Testament Jesus states the same truth:

"Inasmuch as ye did it unto one of these my brethren, even these least, ye did it unto Me."

We are told that "the cup of cold water given in my Name" will not lose its reward. The phrase "in my Name" is important, and conveys the idea that even a simple and uncostly action done out of love for God or for one of His creatures, is a significant one. Indeed, the perfection of the life of action is found in the doing of all things as an offering to God, where the offering has become second nature, and is no longer a consciously directed one.

(2) THE WAY OF THE ARTIST

Artistry is grace in living, and need not be confined to those few who pursue Art as a vocation. These latter, however, through their art may be doing something which permanently enriches the life of mankind. At their best, they are making man's distinctive contribution to creation. This path has primarily an inward-turned aspect, and subsequently an outward-turned aspect. The good artist observes more carefully and feels more deeply than most of us, and he has applied himself to the discipline of a craft which will allow him to express these sensibilities in a form which others can appreciate. If he is a painter pigments will be his medium, if he is a sculptor clay or marble, if a poet language, if a dancer the movement of the human form. Whatever craft is used, the artist is giving expression to transient insights, feelings, and perceptions, and in this way is doing something

for us which *may* be, according to our ability to share it, an enlarge-
ment of our own insight, feeling or perception. Perhaps an artist is
chiefly externalising emotion, but the greatest art encompasses all
three. Listening to great music, a person may say, "This is telling me
something about Reality: it is helping me to know more of the truth
and beauty of life." The same words may be used of great painting,
great poetry, or sublime architecture, and this I think is the best test
of its greatness.

It is said that spectators see more of a game than the players. In
this sense an artist is perhaps a spectator of life, and to this extent
apart from it. If what he offers to us is so expressed that we the players
can see more than we saw before, he enriches by his art the heritage
of mankind.

(3) THE WAY OF LOVE TO GOD AND MAN

This is perhaps a middle path between the inward-looking and the
outward-looking life. Here are the real saints, often uncloistered and
unrecognised, who would be surprised and even troubled to know
that they were so described. They reach out with one hand to the
world of spirit, and with the other to those who need them. Some of
these such as Schweitzer, Grenfell, and Damien, are well known to
history, but there are thousands, whose names are unknown, who are
the salt of the earth. They have little or no concern for self; they are
generous without measure and always ready to help another. They go
the second mile but are unaware of having done so. Frequently, though
not always, their faith is quite simple. They are content to leave the
mysteries in the quiet confidence that when they need to know the
clues will be forthcoming. When they pass on, they leave behind
memories of kindly acts and unfailing cheerfulness for which others
give grateful thanks. It is possibly true to say that it is with this group
that many of us would like to feel worthy to be associated. It happens
also to be a group from which none of us are excluded by lack of
talents, intellect, or skill. We exclude ourselves by our thoughtless-
ness and self-centredness.

(4) THE WAY OF KNOWLEDGE

This is rather a specialised way. There are persons who are tem-
peramentally more interested in ideas than in people. Since their

concern is to understand the world, they tend to be more inward-looking. In this group are most of the intellectuals, philosophers, readers, thinkers, pure scientists, etc. They are manipulators of symbols and users of logic. If the symbols can be shown to correspond with physical things, then applied science and technology may owe great inspiration to the theorists. The symbols are often ideas and concepts with no such certain application, and the shelves of libraries bend under the weight of these systems of conceptual thought to which men have devoted their lives. Some have been an inspiration to mankind; the great majority are mercifully forgotten. The sincere search for knowledge, of the world around, of the nature of man himself, and of all those levels of reality which we have seen to be of significance in understanding him, can never be other than important. It is a noble pursuit as long as we remind ourselves of the undoubted limitations of the intellect.

(5) THE WAY OF THE ASCETIC

The extreme inward-looking view of the ascetics or world-deniers is a remarkable and interesting one. It has been traditionally associated with the East, and in particular with Hinduism and Buddhism, but it is present as an underground current which occasionally comes to the surface in Christianity. There was a period in the history of early Christianity, in the second, third, and fourth centuries when tens of thousands of people forsook the pagan world to live frugal and ascetic lives in the deserts. The age of the monasteries, and in some degree Puritanism, were forms of it. Bunyan's great classic *Pilgrim's Progress* is permeated by the spirit of it. It will be recalled that the hero of the narrative, Christian, seeks to escape from the City of Destruction, and the author says:

"So I saw in my dream that the man began to run; now he had not run far from his own door, but his wife and children perceiving it, began to cry after him to return; but the man put his fingers in his ears and ran on, crying 'Life, Life, Eternal Life'."

"Fools" cry the ascetics to us. "What is all your trouble about? You are caught in a round of futile activity, and what does it yield you? Only more futility and dissatisfaction. What becomes of all the things you value and create? They pass away and become another's.

You will never find satisfaction in the flux of things: it will yield you nothing that you can truly keep. Nature is indifferent to your welfare, tyranny is everywhere, injustice is widespread in the world, wars breed wars, and life with all its effort and struggle is unrewarding. It passes away with the lusts thereof. Start the search within where alone true joys are to be found. Here you will find the pearl of great price: why bother to search for lesser pearls? 'Men who desire nothing in the world are rich in joy and free from pain' said the Buddha. Therefore renounce: detach yourself from things and events and then you will be able to rise above the world, to a serenity which the world cannot take away. It cannot take from you things which you don't possess. It cannot deprive you of things which you don't value."

This may seem strange talk to Western ears, but it must be remembered that millions of people have subscribed to this viewpoint. Because of it, men have lived without ambition, they have eschewed civilisation, they have taken vows of silence, they have worn hairshirts in deserts and caves, they have sometimes beaten themselves, they have sometimes not even washed themselves, they have fasted and gone without sleep, they have turned away from human society and human love to pursue the lonely quest of spiritual things. "Kill out desire"; "It is desire which leads you to constant suffering," says the Buddha. "Love not the world, neither the things of the world," says the Christian apostle. It is all a protest against incarnate life. What are we to make of it?

I find the world-negating attitude a very strange one. It is a curious compliment to the Creator, as someone has said, to fly to God from the works of God. Surely something of great importance is to be learned from the experience of earth-life however frustrating and difficult it may appear to be? We did not ourselves create the basic situation, although we may have made a contribution towards it. Surely the physical world is a phase with something of value to teach us, which perhaps we could learn in no other way? If, for example, it is thought of as a school for character-building, then there is no solution in running away from school. Furthermore, we must remember that it is the will-to-live in relation to our fellows, which has given rise to human love and compassion, which has nourished art and such precious virtues as kindness and generosity. If therefore we are going to despise and reject life, we shall set aside these things, and the possibility of practising those virtues which cannot be practised in isolation.

To turn away from life here, as though it were either a super-tempta-
tion which the saint should avoid, or as though it were a mistake which
the Creator could not really have meant, is a strange reaction. It cannot
draw much support from the example of Jesus, who voluntarily
entered upon human life to help mankind in its need, and who
clearly was no stranger to the problems of ordinary people.

If earth-life is something to be escaped from, the will to live must
be regarded as evil. Such escape contrasts markedly with the courage
and self-sacrifice of many ordinary people who devote themselves
to uplifting the world.

I confess my sympathies are more with the world-affirmers than
with the world-deniers, but I cannot help feeling that for the great
majority of people there is a middle path which it would be wisest
to tread. This middle path involves entering fully into life, while not
allowing the world to be too much with us. It means balancing service
with meditation, love of people with love of the world within, keeping
a balance between the outer and inner worlds which allows us to bring
through the fruits of the spirit into the common ways of men.

I have a friend (referred to in Chapter 12) who, for a period of a
few years, communicated with me through the automatic writing of
a sensitive. He was a very interesting and remarkable man while on
earth, and it may be of value to quote here from one of his letters
where he deals with the subject we are discussing.

"On earth during my lifetime, I had certain mystical experiences,
and I lived and worked as an ordinary man. That, I am now of opinion,
is the better way, save in the most exceptional cases, for mystics. We
are born into the world, not to fly from life, but to experience it for at
least a fair span of the years allotted to us. I have never, since my
passing, regretted the fact that I did not become a contemplative,
retiring into a hermitage or monastery and staying there. . . .

"I do not approve of the Buddha's saying, 'Men who desire nothing
from the world are rich in joy and free from pain.' If not in their
present earthly life, then in another future life, they have to experience
joy and pain. . . . Admittedly there is more than one way for the seeker
of Pure Light to choose from at the outset of his earthly pilgrimage.
But the mystic who lives *in* the world, radiating the joy of his mystical
experiences as Christ did, chooses the better part — better than the
Indian mystic who sits under a tree, remaining in complete withdrawal from the spurned world. . . . He has his reward, but he has only
developed one half as it were, of his soul, at the expense of the other

half. So following promotion to this other life, he has not achieved wholeness.

"Western mystics should not be fugitives from Time, seeking only their personal salvation. By all means it is well that they meditate and retreat into the solitude, and through development obtain mystical experience. But they should mix with the world of men for the sake of their future wholeness, and seek in action to serve them in continual perfection of love — letting their light shine before human beings. Gandhi did more for the people of India than all the yogis of his period put together. Yet Gandhi was a practising mystic and derived his great spiritual strength from times of union with the Divine Spirit. He lived two lives, one on the plane of men, and one on the plane of mystical experience. Thus he was a practitioner of the higher mysticism.

"A. E. was another of such children of the Kingdom of God. So, in the after-death, these two men's selves have a wholeness lacking in those mystics who devote their lives to the development of their own souls, and do not serve humanity; world-forsakers only — ignoring the reminder of selfless love, 'We are members one of another.'

"One of my previous lives was spent in India. Hence my remarks may seem in this letter rather over-critical of Indian philosophy. But in that previous life I saw too much of tragedy, partly because the finest men retreated from life instead of endeavouring to serve the people in the awful conditions prevalent there (during that incarnation of mine). Seeking in the contemplative life their personal salvation, they displayed a neglect of the primary and fundamental virtue of loving one's neighbour."

These are interesting views to have from one who has had the opportunity to survey his past lives and distil wisdom from them.

In summing up, I should judge that there is no one kind of life which one could designate as "best". One soul may need for its further growth a particular kind of testing. The ascetic who sits under a tree, *may* have been a busy merchant with no time to think of higher things, in a former life. Perhaps a certain measure of withdrawal from life is essential to him. Likewise, how do we know that the busy extravert is not being called to redress the disbalance arising from former lives of withdrawnness? We must be content to direct our own lives and recognise that the best kind of life is relative to each soul at its own stage of the journey.

"By whatsoever path you come to Me, I shall welcome you, for the paths men take from every side are Mine."

Chapter

16

FINAL REFLECTIONS

I cannot feel myself as one apart,
Eternal man is dreaming dreams in me,
Deep in my breast I hear him ceaselessly
Treading the lonely roadway of my heart.
His goal I know not, save that it exist
High in the distant peaks of destiny,
Beckoning him from out Infinity,
Shrouded in still impenetrable mist.

I cannot feel myself as merely naught,
Eternity is dreaming dreams in me,
Dreams of some wondrous final unity
Beyond the gold horizon of my thought.
There shall I learn how wakes to life the seed,
Towards what ecstasy the stars are rushing,
What saith the lark, and why the rose is blushing,
And why night weeps upon the slumbering mead.

Cyril Upton
(from *Musings in Provence*)

MOST of us are immersed in a routine: we are caught in a round of daily events of a prosaic and uninspiring kind. Very few people feel their ordinary work offers them the chance to live creatively or in freedom. We are caught in nets of circumstance or necessity with things we are obliged to do and others for whom we are responsible. We have no likelihood of changing the situation.

Occasionally the routine is broken. It may be that a holiday has allowed us to get out of the groove and see life as a whole. It may be that our emotions have been deeply stirred. Perhaps we have been jolted out of the rut of monotony by a tragedy which has shocked us and changed the face of life. Then we start to think about what we call "the deeper things of life". We ask ourselves about death, and the possibility that human beings survive death, about what we are here for at all: what the purpose of living is, and how we can fulfil it. We know we have need of some soundly based philosophy of life and of contact with some Power in which we could rest.

Some people apparently find all that they need in orthodox religious teaching and worship. They are not troubled as Job was when he cried out:

> *But where shall wisdom be found?*
> *And where is the place of understanding?*

If however, you are among those who are still seeking and have as yet found no solid ground on which to rest, I would like to make a few suggestions.

In the end, it is impossible to rest satisfied in second-hand truth. All the most important truth has to be discovered for one's self. There is an Eastern saying: "All the Buddhas point the way, but because it is the Way, everyone must tread every step of it himself alone." Here, I should put the emphasis on "himself" rather than "alone", for contrary to popular ideas, it is on the lower (physical) levels of the world of Reality that loneliness is most marked, and on the higher levels that communion becomes most real. The text is a useful reminder that the insights, teachings, and experiences of others are useful as guides, as maps and guide books are useful to the person who wishes to go travelling. They may save one from many false starts and difficult explorations which will lead nowhere. However much we study them, however, they can never be a satisfactory substitute for one's own journeying and direct experience. The Truth in which we can expect to find that our problems have disappeared, wherein we can rest with serenity and joy, and through which we can face with confidence the changes and chances of this mortal life, must be our own discovery. If we are colour-blind no one can convey the sensation of a new colour to us; if we are deaf no one can tell us what music really is; and if we have not opened and used the eyes of the soul no one can convey to us any truth beyond the bounds of sensory experience. All books and lectures, creeds and philosophies are indications of directions in which others may have found something worthwhile, but this second-hand search may help some and lead to utter confusion for others. The testimony of the world's great souls is that by love, sincerity, and perseverance, they found in the end what they sought — and none of these qualities, be it noted, is a mark of intellect. *What* they found can never be expressed in words. They may call it God, the Divine Self, the Atman, the Spirit, Enlightenment — these are names for a Reality which can never be grasped or understood by the mind, because it lies beyond Mind, just as Mind lies beyond Body (though it is not unrelated to it).

Throughout this book we have from time to time made reference to mystical experience in which for a moment the centre of the soul contacts a reality higher than itself — the Spirit. It is a state in which this union is permanent, a state of Illumination, which we are all seeking for, whether we know it or not. Everything that we can desire in our highest moments is satisfied in this union. It places the soul above the ebb and flow of change, serene and satisfied, the willing and fully conscious instrument of the Spirit. Every dissatisfaction we have with life is a reflection of our failure to discover this experience.

What prevents the earnest seeker from finding this union with the Divine Spirit, which is his true Self? Wise men have always told us that it is the mind which intervenes and by its uncontrolled restlessness prevents us finding — or rather being found by the Spirit. Between the Reality which we call Spirit and the centre of the soul which says "I" (and is a spark of Spirit in exile), intervenes this useful but restless instrument which we call mind, and until we can control and still it, the light of Spirit cannot break through into union. Krishnamurti, for example, is constantly teaching, "It is only when the totality of the mind is still, that the creative, the nameless, comes into being."

Our minds are like the restless surface of a lake, with ripples of thought constantly moving on the surface. Anyone who has ever tried to pray with sincerity knows how difficult it is to keep the mind from wandering. By prayer here, I do not mean asking for anything, or holding a devout soliloquy, but silent adoration. This is why we are told that the mind can be our enemy on the spiritual search, for it resents any attempt to bring it under control of the will, and it will fight hard for a long time to do what it likes. The goal of mind-control is important: the particular method used to reach the goal is not. It can be undertaken as one might undertake a mental gymnastic discipline in concentration; or by sitting in silence and turning intruding thoughts away from the mind as they come. We can practise concentration in the prayer of adoration. When the restless mind is finally controlled and held still, the higher levels of our being have a chance to reveal themselves. Those who have trodden this path and finally come to glimpse the Reality which lies behind mind, tell us that it is unforgettable, peaceful, satisfying, and blissful beyond the power of words to describe. But it should not be thought that this is an easy task and quickly to be accomplished. It would, however, be a very good thing if people in our Western culture, so deeply immersed in doing, would give more attention to being, and they could do something towards it by setting aside even twenty minutes a day to undertake the task of discovering that true Self from which the uncontrolled mind separates us.

Of course whatever inner discipline is undertaken, the outer life has concurrently to be lived in the right way. All great teachers have stressed this. What does it mean for ordinary people? We started this chapter by remarking that much of the daily round for many people intrinsically offers little creative opportunity or satisfaction. It may indeed seem to the doer little more than a repetitive round of futility and worthlessness. If this is done as a duty and as an offering of service to God, as distinct from performance in a mood of grumbling, grousing, and fault-finding, this is spiritual achievement of no mean order. If in contrast with this, the occupation is itself interesting, but the attitude is possessive and acquisitive at the expense of others, then there can be no progress. The desire to possess for one's own benefit, wealth, power, or fame, is only building higher the walls of the ego — which have to be levelled before the Divine Self can be found.

If a person's daily round is dull and uninspiring, let him say, "I do it gladly because it is my duty: I do it because it is *my* offering of service to God." If a person's daily round is interesting let him in gratitude offer his work also as a service to God, not concerned with benefits to himself but with help to others.

The highest attitude is one of positive Love. We have all known souls from whom there has come a radiation of active goodwill or positive love. In their presence we have seemed to be our best selves. Many of these were persons of no outward distinction or importance, but they spread around them unknowingly a radiation of goodness and kindliness. Because of this, life seems less drab for others, problems seem no longer insuperable, tragedy seems no longer just tragedy, but a part of the mystery of life which is a shadow of the greater good to be. These make happier all around them, not so much by what they say, but by what they do so unselfishly, and most of all by what they are. In the maelstrom of life where good and ill jostle each other continually and suffering is so much the common lot, they bring with them encouragement and peace. This is redemptive work: the good taking up into itself the sadness of life and transforming it into joy.

I have one last thing to say. The world appears to be taking a path which is slowly leading it nearer to catastrophe. You and I know this with our minds although we dare not let ourselves *feel* it too much. I send this little book out into the world at such a time as this, in the hope that it will bear with it some encouragement to meet these days with serenity. In spite of many prophets of doom, I do not believe there is anything determined or inevitable in the world situation which justifies despair. The forces of evil working on both sides, have always used fear as one of their most effective weapons, and they are at work visibly and audibly at the present time. Let us not forget that there are also spiritual powers at work in the world for good, and that they work for the large part silently and without ostentation. We can offer our greatest help to them by our state of mind. We can refuse to be afraid. We can refuse to be caught up in any collective emotion of hate or antagonism for those who are regarded as potential enemies. We can constantly pray for those in the world who are disinterestedly working for peace. We can practise in our personal life those attitudes of goodwill to difficult neighbours which are so much needed on the national level. Life and Death are not issues which are wholly within our power to determine either as to time or circumstance. It is only asked of us that both on familiar paths and in the crises of change, we are worthy habitations of an immortal spirit.

> *You that have faith to look with fearless eyes*
> *Beyond the tragedy of a world at strife,*
> *And trust that out of night and death shall rise*
> *The dawn of ampler life:*
>
> *Rejoice, whatever anguish rend your heart*
> *That God has given you, for a priceless dower,*
> *To live in these great times and have your part*
> *In Freedom's crowning hour.*
>
> *That you may tell your sons who see the light*
> *High in the heavens their heritage to take:*
> *"I saw the powers of darkness put to flight!*
> *I saw the morning break!"**

* *War-Time Verses* by Sir Owen Seaman (Constable & Co. Ltd., 1915).

APPENDIX
SUGGESTED BOOKS FOR FURTHER STUDY

PSYCHICAL RESEARCH

Science and Psychical Phenomena, G. N. M. Tyrrell (Methuen & Co. Ltd.).
The Personality of Man, G. N. M. Tyrrell (Pelican Books).
The Nature of Human Personality, G. N. M. Tyrrell (George Allen & Unwin, Ltd.).
The Psychic Sense, Payne & Bendit (Faber & Faber Ltd.).
Psychical Research, R. C. Johnson ("Teach Yourself" Books).
Psychical Research Today, D. J. West (Gerald Duckworth, Ltd.).
Zoar, W. H. Salter.
There is a Psychic World, Horace Westwood (Crown Publishers, N.Y.).

MYSTICISM

Mysticism, Evelyn Underhill (Methuen & Co. Ltd.).
Watcher on the Hills, R. C. Johnson (Hodder & Stoughton Ltd.).
Philosophy of Plotinus (2 vols.), W. R. Inge (Longmans Green & Co. Ltd.).
The Teachings of the Mystics, Walter T. Stace (Mentor Books).
How to Know God, Prabhavananda & Isherwood (George Allen & Unwin Ltd.).

TIME AND FOREKNOWLEDGE

An Experiment with Time, J. W. Dunne (Pelican Books).
Foreknowledge, H. F. Saltmarsh (G. Bell & Sons Ltd.).
Supernormal Faculties in Man, Eugene Osty (Methuen & Co. Ltd.).
The Future is Now, Arthur Osborn (University Books Inc., N.Y.).
The Imprisoned Splendour (Chapter VII), R. C. Johnson (Hodder & Stoughton Ltd.).

RELIGION AND RELIGIONS

The Religions of Man, Huston Smith (Mentor Books).
Religion and the Cure of Souls in Jung's Psychology, Hans Schaer (Routledge & Kegan Paul).

Towards Fidelity, Hugh I'A Fausset (Gollancz & Co. Ltd.).
So Great a Mystery, Kenneth Walker (Gollancz & Co. Ltd.).

ASTRAL PROJECTION

The Imprisoned Splendour (Chapter X), R. C. Johnson (Hodder & Stoughton Ltd.).
The Study and Practice of Astral Projection, Robert Crookall (Aquarian Press Ltd.).
The Mystical Life, J. H. Whiteman (Faber & Faber Ltd.).
The Projection of the Astral Body, S. Muldoon (Rider & Co. Ltd.).
The Case for Astral Projection, S. Muldoon (Rider & Co. Ltd.).
The Phenomena of Astral Projection, S. Muldoon (Rider & Co. Ltd.).

SURVIVAL OF DEATH

This World and That, Payne & Bendit (Faber & Faber Ltd.).
The Imprisoned Splendour, R. C. Johnson (Hodder & Stoughton Ltd.).
A Life after Death, S. Ralph Harlow (Gollancz & Co. Ltd.).
They Survive, Geraldine Cummins (Rider & Co. Ltd.).
The Betty Book, Stewart Edward White (E. P. Dutton & Co. Inc.).
The Supreme Adventure, Robert Crookall (James Clarke & Co. Ltd.).

NATURE OF LIFE AFTER DEATH

The Road to Immortality, Geraldine Cummins (Aquarian Press Ltd.).
Beyond Human Personality, Geraldine Cummins (Psychic Press Ltd.).
The Country Beyond, Jane Sherwood (Rider & Co. Ltd.).
The Unobstructed Universe, Stewart Edward White (E. P. Dutton & Co. Inc.).

MEANING AND PURPOSE OF LIFE

The Human Situation, W. Macneile Dixon (Pelican Books Ltd.).
Nurslings of Immortality, R. C. Johnson (Hodder & Stoughton Ltd.).
The Expansion of Awareness, Arthur Osborn (Omega Press Ltd.) and (T. P. H. Adyar).
Commentaries on Living (Third Series), Krishnamurti (Gollancz & Co. Ltd.).

A Scientist of the Invisible, A. P. Shepherd (Hodder & Stoughton Ltd.).

Venture with Ideas, Kenneth Walker (Jonathan Cape Ltd.).

The Axis and the Rim, A. W. Osborn (Vincent Stuart Ltd).

And without apology my favourite book — out of print but occasionally to be found second-hand:

The Corner of Harley Street, H. H. Bashford (Constable's Miscellany).

INDEX